Strategic Business Communication

An Integrated, Ethical Approach

Strategic Business Communication

An Integrated, Ethical Approach

Robyn C. Walker, Ph.D.

Center for Management Communication

Marshall School of Business

University of Southern California

THOMSON

SOUTH-WESTERN

Australia · Brazil · Canada · Mexico · Singapore · Spain · United Kingdom · United States

THOMSON
SOUTH-WESTERN

Strategic Business Communication: An Integrated, Ethical Approach
Robyn Walker

VP/Editorial Director:
Jack W. Calhoun

VP/Editor-in-Chief:
Dave Shaut

Executive Editor:
Neil Marquardt

Senior Developmental Editor:
Taney H. Wilkins

Senior Marketing Manager:
Larry Qualls

Production Project Manager:
Heather Mann

Manager of Technology, Editorial:
Vicky True

Technology Project Editor:
Kelly Reid

Web Coordinator:
Scott Cook

Manufacturing Coordinator:
Diane Lohman

Production House:
Interactive Composition Corporation

Printer:
Transcontinental Louiseville, QC

Art Director:
Stacy Jenkins Shirley

Internal Designer:
Kim Torbeck, Imbue Design

Cover Designer:
Kim Torbeck, Imbue Design

Library of Congress Control Number: 2005929569

For more information about our products, contact us at:

Thomson Learning Academic Resource Center

1-800-423-0563

Thomson Higher Education
5191 Natorp Boulevard
Mason, OH 45040
USA

Table of Contents

Preface

Strategic Business Communication: An Integrated, Ethical Approach provides a unique methodology to the coverage of all the critical aspects of business communication. Unlike other textbooks, it integrates the discussion of all channels of business communication—written, oral presentations, interpersonal and small group, visual, ethical, and technological—into each of its chapters. This approach is taken for two reasons: to better illustrate and support the strategic nature of business communication and to show the interconnections among these channels to improve student understanding, retention, and transfer of this knowledge. The result is this textbook, which provides comprehensive coverage of the critical elements of business communication in a compact, highly readable form. The features of *Strategic Business Communication: An Integrated, Ethical Approach* are discussed below.

Comprehensive, yet compact. The text covers all the communication topics that are relevant and critical for successful business communication—written, oral presentation, interpersonal and small group, visual, ethical, and technological—in eight highly readable chapters.

Systematic approach to strategic message formulation. The text discusses the elements of business communication in a systematic way, exploring seven essentials, or steps, that should be considered in strategic message formulation. These seven steps of strategic message formulation are covered in the eight chapters of the text:

- Chapter 1: Communication Strategy

- Chapter 2: Purposes of Business Communication

- Chapter 3: Audience Analysis

- Chapter 4: Channels of Communication

- Chapter 5: Organization

- Chapter 6: Content

- Chapter 7: Verbal, Vocal, and Nonverbal Expression

- Chapter 8: Visual Impression

Categorizing the material into seven simple steps makes it easier for students to retain the strategic approach presented in the text and thus enhances long-term retention. Each chapter also provides a foundation of knowledge that subsequent chapters build upon and reinforce; this systematic, cumulative approach to strategic message formulation further enhances student understanding, retention, and transfer of knowledge.

Integrated coverage of business communication topics. The text covers the critical elements of business communication—written, oral presentation, interpersonal and small group, visual, ethical, and technological communication—in an integrated manner. That is, each chapter discusses each step in the strategic message formulation process in such a way as to cover its application in all the relevant channels of business communication. This integration gives a clear, comprehensive demonstration of the interconnections and similarities among these topics, and increases students' understanding and retention of the topics, as well as effective transfer of information.

Boxed features. Each chapter includes two boxed features, **"Responsible Communication"** and **"Communication in Your World,"** as well as **Critical Thinking Questions.** The Responsible Communication boxed features present an ethical situation or issue that is related to each of the seven steps of strategic message formulation and include questions to encourage discussion and analysis of each of those issues. The Communication in Your World boxed features are intended to show the applicability of each of the seven steps and thus to support knowledge transfer, by discussing an issue that is pertinent to the lives of today's students. Critical Thinking questions can be found throughout each chapter and are intended to encourage more in-depth thought, analysis, and application of the materials presented in each chapter.

End-of-chapter exercises. To further support understanding and information transfer through the application of relevant concepts and principles, the following exercises are included at the end of each chapter: key terms with page number references, discussion questions, applications (or assignments), InfoTrac exercises designed to encourage use of the Internet, and a case analysis that further explores issues presented in each chapter. InfoTrac® College Edition is included with each new textbook.

Supplementary materials. *Strategic Business Communication: An Integrated, Ethical Approach* provides supplementary materials to aid instructors in the optimal use of the text. These materials include PowerPoint slides to accompany each chapter and an Instructor's Manual and Test Bank. These supplements are available on the Instructor's Resource CD (0-324-37432-1) and can also be accessed at the text support Web site: http://walker.swlearning.com.

I would like to thank all my colleagues who helped me in the writing of this textbook. First, I thank all those who reviewed a draft of the textbook and who provided me encouragement and support, as well as many valuable suggestions for improvement. Specifically, I would like to thank

Peggy Beck
Kent State University

Lynnea Brumbaugh
Washington University

Merry Buchanan
University of Central Oklahoma

Kathryn A. Cañas
University of Utah

Sandra Chrystal
University of Southern California

Molly Epstein
Emory University

David G. Mosby
University of Texas, Arlington

Sandra S. Rothschild
University of Arizona

Diza Sauers
University of Arizona

Heidi Schultz
University of North Carolina, Chapel Hill

Marsha Tomlin
Sam Houston State University

Elizabeth A. Tuleja
University of Pennsylvania

Christine Uber Gross
Thunderbird

I would also like to thank Diza Sauers, my former colleague at the University of Arizona, for preparing the PowerPoint® slides that accompany the textbook.

Robyn C. Walker

ABOUT THE AUTHOR

Dr. Robyn Walker is a professor of business communication at the Center for Management Communication at the University of Southern California's Marshall School of Business, where she teaches business writing and business communication courses. She earned a master's and a doctoral degree in communication from the University of Utah and also holds an MBA. Dr. Walker has held faculty appointments at the University of Arizona and California State University-Fullerton. While a graduate student at Utah, she taught MBA courses in business writing.

Before entering academia, Dr. Walker worked as a professional writer and editor with such organizations as United Press International, McGraw-Hill, and Novell. She also has worked as a writing consultant for companies such as Hoffman LaRoche Pharmaceuticals and Franklin-Covey, Inc. She continues to write and conduct research and has delivered dozens of conference papers on rhetoric, cultural studies, and business communication pedagogy. She is a member of the Association of Business Communication and Management Communication Association.

Communication Strategy

GLOBAL MEDIA VENTURES, INC.: A COMPETITIVE WORLD

Global Media Ventures, Inc. is a publicly owned corporation comprised of subsidiaries involved in various media-related enterprises. These subsidiaries operate television networks and stations, radio stations, film production enterprises, and magazine, newspaper, and book publishing companies.

Although all Global Media Ventures (GMV) subsidiaries are based in the United States, a significant amount of its business and profits come from international sales of its products and services.

However, GMV was not always a media conglomerate. It started out in the 1950s with a single television station in southern California and over the years has acquired businesses to grow to its current size and diversification. Like many large corporations, GMV's method of growth, as well as its involvement in the global economy, has created many communication challenges for GMV.

© RYAN McVAY/ PHOTODISC/ GETTY IMAGES

discussion...

1. What are some communication challenges that are faced by GMV because of the location of its subsidiaries and sales offices across the United States and the world?

2. What are some of the communication challenges faced by GMV because of its diversification into various types of media enterprises?

Better understand the importance of studying communication.

Explain four models of communication and distinguish among them.

Discuss the dialogic model of communication and its application in today's business environment.

Explain the basics of communication strategy.

List the elements of message formulation.

This textbook is intended to help prepare you for the communication challenges you will meet in the modern workplace. It will provide you with a comprehensive, systematic way to approach the differing communication situations you may face in the business world and to create strategies intended to ensure productive outcomes for all those involved.

WHY STUDYING COMMUNICATION IS IMPORTANT

Globalization has had a dramatic effect upon the business environment in which we now operate. While it has presented numerous opportunities to business organizations, it has also increased the potential for greater instability and greater competition. These two forces have had varied effects, including greater merger activity and the flattening of hierarchies within organizations. To remain competitive in the current business environment, organizations must be flexible; strict rules and procedures are a hindrance in organizations that must be able to move quickly to adapt to the changes in their environment.

These changes in the business world also affect employees, and the primary effect is the increasing importance of communication for the success of individuals and the companies in which they work. The flattening of hierarchies and pressure for companies to improve productivity to remain competitive have made interpersonal relationships and the ability to maintain them more crucial than ever. Rosabeth Moss Kanter (1989) claims that this change began as early as the 1980s. Kanter noted that the work of a manager was particularly affected by these changes in the business environment. Instead of an emphasis on planning, organizing, and coordinating, the focus moved to communication.

Such changes as the flattening of organizational hierarchies mean that "influence must replace the use of formal authority in relationships with subordinates, peers, outside contacts, and others on whom the job makes one dependent" (Keys and Case, 1990, p. 38). Since positional authority is no longer sufficient to get the job done, a web of influence or a balanced web of relationships must be developed. "Recently managers have begun to view leadership as the orchestration of *relationships* between several different interest groups—superiors, peers, and outsiders, as well as subordinates" (Keys & Case, 1990, p. 39).

These networks of relationships have a secondary effect: they provide employees with opportunities to influence others. It also means that the flattening of hierarchies has made us more reliant upon others to achieve the goals of the organization as well as our own career objectives.

The increased importance of communication and its changing role in the workplace is also reflected in U.S. Department of Labor statistics. In the table below, the descriptions of skills and abilities necessary to succeed in today's workplace emphasize communication: the ability to write, speak, listen, work in teams, be sociable, negotiate, provide feedback, and use new technologies.

TABLE 1-1. *Necessary workplace skills.*

NECESSARY WORKPLACE SKILLS

The Foundation

Basic:	Reading, writing, mathematics, speaking, and listening.
Thinking:	Creativity, making decisions, solving problems, seeing things in the mind's eye, knowing how to learn, reasoning.
Personal Qualities:	Responsibility, self-esteem, sociability, self-management, and integrity.

Job Skills

Resources:	Allocating time, money, materials, space, and staff.
Interpersonal:	Working on teams, teaching, serving customers, leading, negotiating, and working well with people from culturally diverse backgrounds.
Information:	Acquiring and evaluating data, organizing and maintaining files, interpreting and communicating, and using computers to process information.
Systems:	Understanding social, organizational, and technological systems; monitoring and correcting performance; and designing and improving systems.
Technology:	Selecting equipment and tools, applying technology to specific tasks, and maintaining and troubleshooting technologies.

Source: U.S. Labor Secretary's Commission on Achieving Necessary Skills, June 1991.

The changes in the workplace created by globalization and its associated pressures mean that employees must have better communication skills than ever in order to be successful and reach their career goals. And such skills shouldn't be taken for granted. In fact, a National Assessment of Adult Literacy study conducted in 1992 by the National Center for Education Statistics reported that about half of the adults in the United States lack the skills necessary to read simple directions or write a grammatically correct letter (Donovan, 2002, p. 2). A more recent study supports those findings. According to the 1993 nationwide study, "Adult Literacy in America," 90 million to 191 million adults in the U.S. (47 percent) do not have sufficient proficiency in basic skills to work effectively in today's workplace (McVey, 1997, p. 17).

The government isn't the only institutional force that recognizes the importance of communication in business. Employers also rank communication as the top skill that they are looking for in applicants. According to a poll conducted by *The Wall Street Journal* in September 2003, recruiters rank communication skills as numbers one and two in their list of the most attractive characteristics of prospective employees. The top five skills are listed below.

1. Communication and interpersonal skills.

2. Ability to work well within a team.

3. Analytical and problem-solving skills.

4. Personal ethics and integrity.

5. Leadership potential.

Models of Communication

Over time, the definition of what constitutes communication and how it occurs has evolved. This section will provide a basic overview of the development of our ways of thinking about communication, ending with the dialogic model, which is the foundation for this textbook. Four major definitions of communication that are applicable to organizations are discussed: 1) communication as information transfer; 2) communication as transactional process; 3) communication as strategic control; and 4) communication as dialogic process.

Communication as Information Transfer Model 1, communication as information transfer, assumes that one person can transmit the information in his or her head without distortion or personal interpretation to another. We now know that this approach to communication ignores the effects of distortion on information transfer or the multiple possible interpretations that a receiver might make of a message. Because of the effects of globalization in terms of the increasing diversity of the workforce and the influence of international and multinational corporations, most of us know that people of different cultures interpret the world differently. Consequently, this model of communication is no longer considered useful in thinking about how communication between two or more people occurs.

Communication as Transactional Process Model 2, communication as transactional process, acknowledges that both senders and receivers are active and simultaneous interpreters of messages. This model acknowledges the importance of feedback, particularly of the nonverbal type, in meaning making. However, this model of communication also has received criticism for its emphasis on shared meaning. Studies have shown that much organizational communication is characterized by ambiguity, deception, and diversity of viewpoints rather than shared meaning (Conrad, 1985; Eisenberg, 1984; Weick, 1979). In fact, some researchers view organizational cultures as contested political domains, in which the possibility for genuine dialog is often seriously impaired (Frost et al, 1991).

Communication as Strategic Control Model 3, communication as strategic control, assumes that communication is a tool that individuals use for controlling their environment. From this perspective, a competent communicator chooses strategies appropriate to the situation and accomplishes multiple goals. The major criticism of this approach is that it recognizes that people should not be expected to communicate in any objectively rational way. Instead, communication choices are socially, politically, and ethically motivated. In extreme cases, this model could lead to communicative practices that ignore the goals of clarity and honesty when it is in the communicator's best individual interests to do so (Conrad, 1985; Okabe, 1983).

Dialogic model of communication

The Dialogic Model of Communication takes other people's points of view into account, acknowledging that the speaker and the listener may have different perspectives.

Communication as Dialog Process Model 4, the **dialogic model,** goes beyond the information transfer model to focus on the contribution of the "receiver's" perspective to a jointly-arrived-at interpretation and course of action. The dialogic model attempts to deal with the contested nature of communication that is ignored by the transactional model, by acknowledging these differences of perspective that may exist between communicators. It also attempts to moderate the ethical problem of the strategic model by acknowledging that we are not isolated individuals but that we live in groups and communities and our actions affect others.

According to the dialogic model, the strategies that we use to communicate must take into account how our messages affect others' perception of us as well as the effect of our communication upon others. This model implicitly recognizes the growing importance of interpersonal relationships upon our own success and happiness in the workplace as well as our personal lives, although the boundaries between these two have become blurred. With the proliferation of technology—cell phones, laptops, e-mail, and so on—our work has moved into our personal spaces: our homes, our cars, and even our "vacations."

Communication as *dialog* is characterized by such attributes as trust, lack of pretense, sincerity, humility, respect, directness, open-mindedness, honesty, concern for others, empathy, nonmanipulative intent, equality, and acceptance of others as individuals with intrinsic worth, regardless of differences of opinion or belief (Larson, 2004, p. 36). This attitude contrasts with an understanding and practice of communication as *monologue,* which is characterized by such qualities as deception, superiority, exploitation, dogmatism, domination, insincerity, pretense, personal self-display, self-aggrandizement, judgmentalism that stifles free expression, coercion, possessiveness, condescension, self-defensiveness, and viewing others as objects to be manipulated (Larson, 2004, p. 36). Communication as monologue means that you are talking to yourself. You are not responding to the effects your communication has on others or their needs or concerns. Communication as monologue is an *egocentric* process, in which you do not show concern or empathy for the needs or feelings of others.

The dialogic model differs from the earlier models of communication in which other people are sometimes viewed as beings to be acted on, communicated to, ordered, and controlled (Eisenberg & Goodall, p. 35). In contrast, the dialogic model perceives others as *interdependent* partners capable and deserving of their own voice to influence the organizational dialog. The dialogic model thus is considered an index of the ethical level of communication to the degree that participants in communication display the attributes listed above (Larson, 2004, p. 36).

Ethics is an issue that is on nearly everyone's radar screen because of the numerous corporate meltdowns in the media. Enron, Arthur Andersen, Worldcom, Tyco, Martha Stewart—every day another corporation ends up on the list of organizations accused of ethical and legal digressions. And this occurrence is not a just a recent trend; "between 1975 and 1985 two-thirds of the Fortune 500 firms were convicted of misdemeanors after extensive plea bargaining, and a still larger number settled suits out of court" (Conrad, 1990, p. 15).

Ethical issues pervade organizational behavior, including communication practices. According to W. Charles Redding (1991):

> *The preponderance of everyday problems that plague all organizations are either problems that are patently ethical in nature, or they are problems in which deeply embedded ethical issues can be identified . . . if we take a close look we can discover, in almost every act of human communication, an ethical dimension. (pp. 1–2)*

The dialogic model with its inherent concern for ethics is thus a good model to use in the study of business communication.

The dialogic model of communication has some affinities with systems theory because of its focus on interrelationships. According to this theory, groups and organizations are systems. A system is a complex set of relationships among interdependent parts or components. Interdependence is the primary quality of a system and refers to the wholeness, or the total workings of the system and its environment as well as the interrelationships of individuals that fall within the system. Although there are weaknesses in the systems theory approach, it has demonstrated once and for all that individual actions can only be understood within a network of relationships. Systems theory highlights the importance of communication in maintaining the relationships within an organization or group and between it and its environment. It is this focus on relationship that corresponds with the dialogic model.

Two additional effects of globalization that reinforce the importance of adopting a dialogic model for business communication are the increased diversity of the

© RYAN McVAY/ PHOTODISC/ GETTY IMAGES

The processes of globalization have increased the diversity of the domestic workforce as well as the interdependency of inter-national and multinational cor-porations and the interactions of their employees.

Plurality

Plurality is the concept that recognizes that there are multiple different interpretations of any situation, and that no one communicator can control all these interpretations.

Intercultural communication

Intercultural communication refers to the exchange of information among people of different cultural backgrounds.

workforce as well as the interdependency of national, international, and multinational corporations and their employees. The dialogic model is useful in dealing with these changes since it includes the concept of **plurality,** which refers to the fact that people in communication mutually construct the meanings they have for situations and each other. Plurality means that there are always multiple interpretations of any situation and that no one person can control those interpretations, try as he or she might. Recognition of the reality of plurality requires that we be open or willing to listen to the voices and opinions of others if there is any hope of achieving something approaching shared understanding. In the workplace, attempting to move toward shared understanding is of course important if we are to achieve organizational and personal goals.

Therefore, the dialogic model of communication is compatible with many of the concerns and goals of intercultural communication. **Intercultural communication** is the exchange of information between individuals who are unalike culturally (Rogers & Steinfatt, 1999). The most effective way to deal with the challenges posed by conducting business across cultures is openness to what may be learned about another culture and then used to communicate more effectively with its members. In this regard, plurality and its requirement of openness to the opinions of others help us to practice more effective intercultural communication.

The Challenges of Dialogic Communication

Because of the increased interdependency of people around the world and the diversity in the workplace, successful communication requires recognition of the contested nature of reality and our interpretation of it. It thus requires openness to others' views and opinions if we are to communicate effectively. This required openness creates some challenges. It requires recognition that because of the contested nature of reality, reaching understanding may take more time and effort. It requires recognition that others' views and perceptions may be as valid as our own. Finally—and perhaps most challenging—is the need to be open to the views and perceptions of others. This situation may be challenging because in these cases our personal identities, how we believe ourselves to be, may seem threatened.

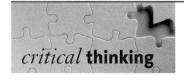

critical **thinking**

Have you experienced a situation in which people perceived a situation in different ways? What could have contributed to these differences in perception?

An overly rigid view of one's identity or self-perception may lead to unwillingness to engage in dialog with others who have differing perspectives. Becoming comfortable with the new realities of the business world brought on by globalization thus requires high levels of self-awareness and self-esteem. **Self-awareness** is defined as an understanding of the self, including your attitudes, values, beliefs, strengths, and weaknesses. Self-awareness is developed in two ways: by communicating with oneself and by communicating with others. In other words, we develop self-awareness by reflecting on our thoughts and actions to understand what motivates those thoughts and actions. We also learn about ourselves by observing how others respond to us.

For young people, much of their self-awareness may be based on the responses and expectations of others, particularly parents and later on, peers. The more you learn about yourself, the easier it will be to learn how and why you communicate with others. In other words, we need to have a realistic view of ourselves, our strengths as well as our weaknesses and in spite of that knowledge—or perhaps because of it—be able to feel good about who we are. We must also be knowledgeable about how others perceive us, since our professional success depends so much upon relationships with others and their perceptions of us.

The second part of self-concept is **self-esteem** or how you feel about yourself, how well you like and value yourself. Perception and communication are both affected by self-esteem. According to Baumgardner & Levy (1988), people with high self-esteem tend to view others who are motivated as bright people and those who are not motivated as less bright. People with low self-esteem do not make this distinction. In the contemporary business world, high levels of self-awareness and self-esteem may help us be more open to the opinions and perspectives of others—the basis of dialogic communication.

Without high levels of self-awareness and self-esteem, we may feel threatened when we meet others who are different from ourselves, and that feeling may get in the way of our ability to be open to listening to and considering their perspectives and opinions. A high level of self-esteem also is important because we must be willing to admit that perhaps we don't know everything; we always have opportunities to learn. According to Evered & Tannenbaum (1992), in order to engage in dialog, we must be able to take "the stance that there is something that I don't already know." We must be able to engage with others "with a mutual *openness* to learn" (Evered and Tannenbaum, 1992, p. 45).

In addition, a high level of self-esteem is needed so that we are not afraid to be ourselves within the constraints of the communication situation. In authentic dialog, we learn to speak from experience and to listen for experience. In authentic dialog, we treat others as persons and not as objects. This contrasts with inauthentic dialog, in which we pretend to be someone we are not. In reality, our communication is often a combination of inauthentic and authentic behavior because of the context of the interaction, or the expectations that come with certain situations.

Self-awareness

Self-awareness is an honest understanding of oneself, including strengths and weaknesses, values, attitudes, and beliefs.

Self-esteem

Self-esteem refers to how we like and value ourselves, and how we feel about ourselves.

Responsible *Communication*

One ethical problem that is exposed by the dialogic model of communication is what is termed *moral exclusion*. According to Susan Opotow (1990), moral exclusion occurs when the application of moral values, rules, and fairness is not considered necessary for particular individuals or groups. The practice of moral exclusion results in individuals being perceived as nonentities, expendable, or undeserving. The result is that harming such individuals becomes acceptable, appropriate, or just.

Persons who are morally excluded are thus denied their rights, dignity, and autonomy. In her analysis, Opotow identifies several dozen ways in which moral exclusion is manifested; of those, many involve communication and language use. For example, showing the superiority of oneself or one's group by making unflattering comparisons to other individuals or groups is one manifestation of moral exclusion. Another example of language use

to morally exclude others is by characterizing them as lower lifeforms or as inferior beings. Other examples of moral exclusion include:

☐ Placing the blame for any harm on the victim.

☐ Justifying harmful acts by claiming that the morally condemnable acts committed by "the enemy" are worse.

☐ Misrepresenting harmful behaviors by masking or conferring respectability on them through the use of neutral, positive, technical, or euphemistic terms to describe them.

☐ Justifying harmful behavior by claiming that everyone is doing it or that it is an isolated case.

Question for Thought

1. Can you think of recent examples in the news of the use of moral exclusion?

If authentic dialog is practiced, communication becomes an authentic meeting, in which we learn to interpret communicative action as a dialogic process that occurs between and among individuals, rather than as something we do *to* one another (Eisenberg & Goodall, p. 43). This perspective also has an ethical component as mentioned earlier. Rather than seeing others as something to control or manipulate, we recognize that they have opinions and values that may be as valid as our own and thus deserve our attention. The value of listening to others goes beyond respect and supportive relationships, though. In organizations that are peopled by talented, well-educated employees, listening to others provides us access to information that can improve processes, products, services, and the organization's financial bottom line as well as our own standing within the organization.

Other challenges to effective communication with others who may be of different cultures or hold differing values and beliefs include assumptions of superiority and universality and ethnocentrism.

When we are faced with persons who hold differing values or perspectives, one common reaction is to reject them because of their difference. It is more comfortable to believe that your own views are better; recognizing that other views also have validity may threaten some aspects of our identities. Consequently, it may be easier to assume that our own culture or belief system is superior to others. However, such an assumption tends to preempt our ability to be open to others' views. In the best-case scenario, an assumption of superiority may encourage us to recognize differences but treat them in a patronizing manner.

Another challenge to the practice of the dialogic model is the assumption of universality, or the belief that deep down, we are all the same. Such an assumption can lead to misunderstandings, since people can be enculturated so differently that they are in effect living in a very different world, in which almost every aspect has a different meaning from our own. For example, researcher Qi Wang (2000) has shown that American adults and preschool students recall their personal memories differently than do indigenous Chinese. "Americans often report lengthy, specific, emotionally elaborate memories that focus on the self as a central character. Chinese tend to give brief accounts of general routine events that center on collective activities that are often emotionally neutral" (**http://www.news.cornell.edu/Chronicle/6.28.01/memory-culture.html**). These differences do not, however, preempt our ability to reach some level of understanding with the appropriate expenditure of time and effort.

Ethnocentrism is very similar to assumptions of superiority. Ethnocentrism is the belief that one's own culture is at the center of the human experience, that it is of primary importance. This belief often includes the assumption that everyone agrees with this assessment, regardless of their own cultural background. Ethnocentrism is often most prevalent in people with little experience of other cultures. It can lead to an attitude of complacency in which we may not make an effort to understand or learn about other cultures than our own, because they aren't important, in our view.

Dialogic Communication and Strategy

As mentioned above, organizations are not in business to enable employees to construct productive, supportive relationships. Those relationships, however, are necessary to accomplish the organization's mission, which is generally to innovate, turn a profit, and survive. Successful organizations devise strategies to ensure their survival. For companies, crafting a strategy is a pure exercise in message design. Essentially, an organization must come up with a brief yet clear statement of why customers should choose it over its competitors (Eisenberg & Goodall, p. 302). Developing a strategy involves research; a company must learn what the demand is for its product or service, and analyze the target market and environment, and its competitors.

However, today's sophisticated customer does not make financial decisions based solely on competitive advantage. Customers are increasingly sensitive to a

communication  IN YOUR WORLD

A new challenge for many advertising and marketing executives is appealing to the the needs of the growing Hispanic population in the United States, particularly young people. Right now, Hispanic teens make up 20 percent of the U.S. teen market, with Hispanics in general representing more than 13 percent of the U.S. population, according to Rosa Serrano, senior VP and group account director of multicultural media for Initiative Media.

For example, marketers who use television as an advertising medium are trying to identify and target both Englishlanguage-dominant and Spanishlanguage-dominant Hispanic youth, with data that is hard to access. Figures from Initiative Media, a top-five, New York–based media agency, illustrate the difficulty of this endeavor. Of the 100 top-rated Hispanic youth television shows, 38 were from English-language broadcasters. But most of the top-rated shows among Hispanic viewers from 12 to 24 are still Spanish-language telenovelas—prime-time soaps, such as Univision's *Mariana de la Noche* and *Nina Amada Mia*.

But Jeff Valdez, CEO, chairman, and founder of SiTV, a Hispanic-themed, English-language cable network, said his channel can solve some of the challenges in finding young adults. "It's not about language; it's about culture," he said, summing up SiTV's marketing plan.

Targeting the 18-to-34 demographic hasn't been a primary focus of the bigger Hispanic networks, Univision and Telemundo. For years, U.S.-based marketers believed the young-skewing, English-language networks were adequately serving Hispanic youth.

Mr. Valdez said that such narrow thinking was bad for both viewers and marketers. "Traditionally, there have been no shows that targeted young [Hispanic] adults," he said. Since English-language programming was all that was offered to young Hispanics, that's what they watched. Now media analysts observe a swing back.

"Yes, there is some crossover," said David Joyce, senior equity analyst for cable and media for J.B. Hanauer & Co., a Miami-based stock brokerage that covers Univision. "But there is also a rise in pride among young adults to use the Spanish language."

Discussion

1. **Has ethnocentrism or assumptions of superiority influenced the approach of marketers and television programmers to the Hispanic youth market?**

2. **Has the assumption of universality had a similar influence on the attitudes of marketers and television programmers about the Hispanic youth market?**

Adapted from an article written by Wayne Friedman and entitled "A Bilingual Quandary: Young Viewers Elusive, but English-Language Nets Make Strides" that appeared in *TelevisionWeek*, Sept 6, 2004, 23 (36), p. 34.

company's reputation. Public relations thus has been developed as a functional area to manage a company's reputation. The public relations function is highly rhetorical because it involves communicating multiple messages with multiple goals to diverse audiences. Effective public relations strikes a balance 1) between developing a distinct image while simultaneously being recognized as a cooperative member of society and the business community; and 2) between shaping the external public's perceptions and maintaining credibility with internal publics and employees (Cheney & Vibbert, 1987).

In contrast to reputation, which is the view outsiders have of an organization, image and identity have to do with insiders' assessments: identity describes what an organization's members believe to be its character, while image describes insiders' assessments of what outsiders think about an organization (Dutton & Dukerich, 1991, p. 547).

For a company to succeed, then, it should invest resources into developing a strategy that distinguishes it from its competitors as well as helps it maintain an excellent reputation and image, and a clear identity. Like successful professional communicators, companies must also understand who they are and be able to communicate that effectively to their multiple audiences.

Like organizations, individual employees have also been affected by the increased pressures and competitiveness brought about by the forces of globalization. In fact, many writers in recent years, including business guru Tom Peters, have advised employees to take an "intrepreneurial" approach to their careers. In other words, employees should see themselves as their own business and market themselves as such. Like well-functioning organizations, employees should develop an excellent reputation and image, a clear identity that distinguishes them positively from others based upon their own unique strengths. But that is only one component of success; the interdependencies that have emerged with globalization extend down to the individual level. Your success also will depend upon your ability to develop relationships with others through the processes of effective communication.

In the table below, the steps of strategy formulation are explained. This process, called a SWOT analysis, an acronym that stands for strengths, weaknesses, opportunities, and threats, was initially designed to use in the formulation of a marketing strategy for a product or service. However, its basic principles are also applicable at the personal level. We should be aware of our own strengths and weaknesses; we should identify the opportunities in the market for someone with our skills, experience, and knowledge as well as the threats that exist for someone with those skills, experience, and knowledge.

TABLE 1-2. *Steps of Strategy Formulation.*

STEPS OF STRATEGY FORMULATION

1. **Identify opportunities and risks.** For a product or service, you must identify the opportunities that exist within a market or markets. But this is not enough, and it is at this point where critical thinking skills enter the picture. You also must determine what threats exist. For example, is a new company entering your industry that might take market share away? Are consumer patterns changing due to larger economic factors?

   These same considerations apply when developing personal strategies. What opportunities are there today? What is the job market in my field? Are there opportunities for advancement in my organization? What threats exist? Perhaps the job market is contracting, perhaps your company is facing a merger or downsizing. These opportunities and threats must be identified as part of a successful strategy.

Continued on next page.

TABLE 1-2. *Continued*

2. **Appraise weaknesses and strengths.** Just as you must analyze and identify opportunities and threats, you must be willing to assess the strengths and weaknesses of your organization if you are conducting a corporate strategy assessment; your product or service if you are doing a marketing strategy assessment; your department if you are performing a managerial strategy assessment; or yourself if you are preparing a personal or career strategy.

For example, if you are developing a marketing strategy you must identify the strengths of your product or service. Perhaps your product is the lowest-cost alternative in the market. If so, you have a strategic advantage. However, on the downside, your product does not offer all the features of comparable products. If this is the case, strategy formulation helps you identify your product's particular market niche: consumers who want the basic utility your product offers but who are unwilling or unable to pay for a wide array of product features.

The same is true for a personal career strategy. You should identify your strengths and weaknesses and determine your best path given these parameters. This exercise is useful when preparing an employment package: you should identify your skills, personality traits, and knowledge that best match the organization's needs.

3. **Identify resources.** From an organizational perspective, these consist of such elements as your relationships with suppliers, your reputation, and your distribution channels. From a personal or career perspective, these might be financial; you have the money or support to pursue an advanced degree, to move to a city with more opportunities, or to spend more time searching for just the right position rather than taking the first job available.

4. **Match opportunity and capability.** In plain English, this step involves considering what you *might do* with what you *can do*. This step of strategy formulation is critical to success, and it is the step often ignored by managers and individuals, since it involves critical analysis or the ability to look at both sides of a situation. Such a step generally involves a "reality" adjustment, and many are not at a point where they can deal with the reality of a situation, if it isn't completely positive. However, in order to devise a feasible strategy, you must weigh your or your organization's opportunities, strengths, and resources against the potential threats and existing weaknesses.

5. **Consider what you *should do*.** This final consideration is for those interested in creating ethical strategies. The omission of this last step may have led to the recent corporate meltdowns caused by questionable financial reporting practices.

critical **thinking**

How might using a SWOT analysis help you to create a plan to better achieve your career objectives? How might using a SWOT analysis help you to prepare, apply for, and obtain desirable jobs in your chosen field?

From this perspective, it should be clear that although employees are faced with competitive pressures to distinguish themselves, they must temper any urges that would harm their reputation and image as a professional. It is this combined attentiveness that helps meld the realities of the business world with a dialogic model of communication. In other words, we can deal with the competitiveness of the business environment by distinguishing ourselves as skilled, credible, dependable, and honest persons who have enviable abilities to interact with and unite people of diverse backgrounds, views, and opinions. That is the primary goal of this textbook: to help you negotiate the challenges and complexities of the modern business world in such a way as to exemplify yourself as a skilled and ethical communicator.

The Elements of Message Formulation

The remainder of this textbook will focus on explaining a systematic approach to formulating business messages. A systematic approach to message formulation requires excellent analytical and observational skills, since you must study a situation to determine an appropriate approach to best ensure communicative success. Each of the elements introduced below is covered more fully in a chapter devoted entirely to discussion of that element.

- **Purposes of Communication (Chapter 2):** You should identify the purposes of your communication, then devise a communication strategy that effectively achieves those purposes. The four purposes of business communication are to inform, to persuade, to convey goodwill, and to establish credibility. In the message that is the product of your communication strategy, it should be apparent to your audience what your purposes are, generally from the beginning of that message. In other words, business audiences generally want to know immediately what your message is about and why they should pay attention to it.

- **Audience Analysis (Chapter 3):** From the planning stages throughout the message formulation process, you should focus on your audience and its needs, expectations, and concerns. You should ask and answer such questions as: Who will read your document (now and in the future) or hear your message? What do they already know? What do they need to know to make a decision about the information in your message? In other words, your messages should be audience-centered.

- **Channels of Communication (Chapter 4):** Various channels and media exist through which you can communicate. Each of these channels and media is suited for particular types of messages to particular audiences. In other words, each channel has its advantages and disadvantages. Knowing this information can help you to select the appropriate channel or media to ensure the successful reception of your message.

- **Organization (Chapter 5):** Your messages should be logically organized, unified, and complete so your audiences can readily and fully comprehend your intended purposes and meaning. The **introduction** should provide the overall purpose of the message and preview its organization and contents. It should be clear to your audience why it is important for it to read or listen to your message. A **logical structure** of information should be evident from the beginning to the end of the message. The purpose or controlling idea should be logically developed, with each section of the message moving clearly to the next.

Coherence refers to the logical flow of ideas both throughout the message and within its subsections or paragraphs. You should provide a topic sentence for each paragraph, each paragraph should develop one main point, each sentence should clearly lead to the next, and clear connections should be provided between each point or sentence. **Transitions** assist your audience to move from one topic to another through your use of words and phrases that link the ideas you are developing. Presenting known information prior to new information can help make connections. **Forecasting,** like transitions, tells your audience what you will cover next. Bulleted lists, summaries, and preview statements are effective forecasting devices.

The **conclusion** is important for providing your audience a sense of closure. Three common types of conclusion are goodwill, summary, and sales or call to action. Goodwill conclusions are often included in short messages, such as e-mails, letters, or memos; summaries are used for more complex messages that cover several points; and sales conclusions are used to motivate audiences to act.

- **Content (Chapter 6):** Content has to do primarily with what you say or write, not how you say it. The ideas you include are important to the overall effectiveness of your message; they must be presented clearly, purposefully, and adequately in order to "state your case" convincingly. Content should be logical; thus, it is an indicator of your reasoning abilities or how well you present claims and establish their merit with supporting evidence. Content also includes **focus,** which refers to the message's effectiveness at maintaining a clear and consistent direction and goal. All information should support clearly related topics that are guided by a central purpose.

The evidence you provide to support your claims should be both relevant and sufficient. **Relevance of supportive information** addresses the quality of the evidence, or how applicable and appropriate it is for supporting the related claim you make. **Sufficient information** addresses the quantity of the evidence, or whether you have provided enough supporting evidence given the position of your audience(s).

- **Verbal/Vocal/Nonverbal Expression (Chapter 7):** This element is rather complex in that it deals with the verbal aspects of both written and oral messages as well as the nonverbal messages that are sent when we speak.

A writer selects the tone and style of verbal expression, depending on the purpose of the document, the audience's needs and expectations, the writer's relationship with the audience, and the situation within the company, the market, and the competition. **Tone** is the implied attitude of the writer toward the reader. When considering tone, you should think about language choices, level of formality or familiarity, the power relationship between you and your reader, and humor or sarcasm. **Style** is the level of formality of your document. Business documents should use business style, which is less formal than traditional academic writing and more formal than a conversation. Business style is friendly and personal.

Vocal Expression has to do with spoken or oral communication. Your voice plays an important role in the meanings listeners find in your words. By varying the rhythm, pace, emphasis, pitch, or inflection you can easily change these meanings. In addition, how your message comes across to your audience depends a great deal on the adequacy of your voice.

Nonverbal Expression is the effective use of nonverbal communication to reinforce your spoken messages. Nonverbal communication includes eye contact, posture, gestures, movement, and facial expressions. Other nonverbal cues include our understandings of and use of time and space as well as the way we dress and present ourselves.

- **Visual Impression (Chapter 8):** Visual impression is important to consider for both written documents and visual aids for presentations. For written documents, visual impression can often help or hinder how your audience receives and responds to the information presented. The design and layout of text, the use of space, and the addition of graphics all combine to convey an impression to the audience.

Visual aids for presentations should be **visible** from all parts of the room and **emphasize** the main points of your speech. They should be skillfully **integrated** into the presentation, and their use should be **practiced** so that they are not distracting or do not adversely affect your credibility by making you look unprepared.

The form provided below can be used to evaluate your own and others' oral and written messages regarding their effectiveness in addressing these elements of effective communication. The form includes an additional element that is not considered in great depth in this text. That element is the mechanical correctness of our language use. This element is important since it can affect the clarity of our messages as well as our credibility. If you have problems with mechanical correctness, it is recommended that you purchase a handbook that contains the rules of correct grammar, punctuation, and sentence structure to aid you in avoiding these errors.

CHECKLIST FOR EVALUATING MESSAGES

AREA OF FOCUS	+ ✓ –	COMMENTS
WRITING TASK Provides a clear purpose. Meets assignment criteria/purposes.		
AUDIENCE Is audience-centered. Answers audience's needs/questions/objections.		
CHANNEL Considers audience preferences. Considers situational preferences. Selects most appropriate channel.		

FIGURE 1-1. *Checklist for evaluating messages.*

Continued on next page.

ORGANIZATION Introduces the topic. Provides a logical structure. Provides coherent flow. Links with transitions. Forecasts. Provides a conclusion.		
CONTENT Focuses toward goal. Provides relevant supportive information. Provides sufficient information.		
VERBAL/VOCAL/NONVERBAL EXPRESSION Uses an appropriate tone. Chooses an appropriate style. Exhibits effective interpersonal skills. Exhibits effective oral presentation skills. Practices effective nonverbal communication. Practices effective listening skills.		
VISUAL IMPRESSION Considers overall appearance. Uses design features, i.e., headings/lists. Uses space/graphics.		
MECHANICS/ERROR INTERFERENCE Uses correct grammar. Uses correct spelling. Uses correct sentence structure. Achieves clarity and credibility.		
STRENGTHS AND AREAS FOR DEVELOPMENT:		

FIGURE 1-1. *Continued*

- Communication has become more important to the effective and efficient functioning of organizations because of the increased competition created by the global economy, the subsequent flattening of the hierarchical structures of organizations, and the resulting need for more effective interpersonal communication.

- Three models that have historically been used to explain the communication process are communication as information transfer, communication as transactional process, and communication as strategic control.

- The dialogic model of communication better meets the needs of today's organizations, because it recognizes the growing importance of interpersonal relationships upon our own success and happiness in the workplace as well as in our personal lives. According to the dialogic model, the strategies that we use to communicate must take into account how our messages affect others' perception of us as well as the effect of our communication upon others. The dialogic model also highlights the inherently ethical nature of communication as well as helps to address the challenges of communicating with others from different cultures.

- Like well-functioning organizations, employees should develop an excellent reputation and image, a clear identity that distinguishes them positively from others based upon their own unique strengths. However, because of the interdependencies that have emerged with globalization, our success also depends upon our ability to develop relationships with others through the processes of effective communication. Therefore, it is important to develop communication strategies that enable us to achieve our goals, and at the same time, maintain our relationships with others.

- When developing complex or important messages, seven aspects of communication should be considered. These are the purposes of communication; the audience's needs and expectations; the communication channel to be used; the organizational elements of the message; its content; expressive issues, such as style and tone in written messages and nonverbal and vocal cues in oral ones; and, finally, visual elements of the message and their impact.

KEY TERMS

Dialogic model of communication, 6
Intercultural communication, 8
Plurality, 8

Self-awareness, 9
Self-esteem, 9

DISCUSSION QUESTIONS

1. Why has communication become more important in today's business environment?

2. Explain each of the four models of communication and what distinguishes them. Why might the dialogic model better meet the needs of today's workplace?

3. What are the challenges to applying the dialogic model of communication? How might these challenges be overcome?

4. What are the elements of strategy formulation? How do they apply to the individual and his or her communication practices? How does the dialogic model fit into strategy formulation?

5. What are the seven elements that should be considered when formulating important or complex messages?

APPLICATIONS

1. Research the history and development of your career field as well as some of the companies or organizations that offer employment in your area. How have their business practices changed over the years? What has been the effect of technology on their business? What has been the effect of globalization on their business? How have their needs changed in terms of the skills and qualifications they seek in the employees they hire?

   Review the steps of strategy formulation on pages 13–14 of this chapter. Using an Internet search engine, identify the market for applicants seeking jobs in your chosen career field. Based upon what you have learned, explain the opportunities that exist for you, as well as the potential threats.

   Then, using a job listing Web site, find several job descriptions for a position like the one you will be applying for upon graduation. Identify the key qualifications that companies are looking for in applicants for this type of job. Then follow the steps of strategy formulation to identify the qualifications you now have and the qualifications you yet need to acquire. Ask yourself: What resources do I have at my disposal to help me acquire those needed skills?

   Based upon this analysis, create an action plan for what you need to do to achieve your goal of acquiring your desired professional position.

2. Find a recorded speech or a business document that is somewhat substantial in its content. Using the

   checklist provided on pages 17–18, analyze the message for its effectiveness in meeting each of the seven message criteria.

3. Identify and describe a miscommunication that you have had with a fellow college student, friend, family member, coworker, or representative of a company that you were dealing with. Explain the source or cause of the miscommunication and then discuss how using the dialogic approach to communication might have helped to eliminate these causes. Did any of the challenges to applying the dialogic model that were discussed in this chapter contribute to the misunderstanding?

4. Choose a culture that differs from your own, then describe your beliefs and attitudes about and perceptions of this culture. Now conduct research to find out as much about the culture and its values, beliefs, and practices as you can. You may also wish to interview someone from this culture, if this opportunity is available. After learning more about the culture, what misperceptions did you hold about it? Has your research changed your attitudes and beliefs about the culture?

5. Identify examples of the use of moral exclusion and describe the intent and effect of their use. Based upon this analysis, discuss whether such practices are ethical. Support your response with evidence.

INFOTRAC ACTIVITIES

1. Using the keyword option in InfoTrac College Edition, type in the search box the words "business ethics." After reviewing some of the articles that appear as a result of your search, identify some of the key concerns regarding ethical behavior in business and discuss how they apply to communication practices.

2. Using the keyword option in InfoTrac College Edition, type "diversity and business." After reviewing some of the articles that are identified by your search, discuss the importance of the ability to understand the differing values and perspectives of others in business situations and how these might be addressed using the dialogic model of communication.

Case Analysis

One result of increased competition in the business world has been a concomitant increase in merger activity. The number of mergers over the past two decades is too numerous to list here, but some examples of merger activity in the banking industry alone include:

- Citicorp with Traveler's Group.

- Wells Fargo & Company with First Interstate Bancorp and then with Norwest Corporation.

- BankAmerica with Security Pacific, then Continental, Robertson Stephens, and NationsBank. NationsBank itself had previously merged with Boatmen's Bancshares, Montgomery Securities, and Barnett Banks.

Mergers are not always successful. In the food industry, Quaker Oats purchased Snapple for $1.7 billion in 1994, only to sell it later for $300 million. Among software makers, Novell purchased WordPerfect for $1.4 billion and unloaded it two years later for $200 million.

Even successful mergers may result in negative effects to some stakeholders in the organization. Stakeholders are those individuals and groups who have a stake in an organization or are affected by its actions and its financial health. Stakeholders include shareholders, employees, customers, suppliers, competitors, the industry, the community, and the nation itself. For example, the recent financial accounting scandals have resulted in a discussion across the nation about ethics in business.

One group of stakeholders that was immediately affected by the merger of Wells Fargo and Norwest was employees. With the merger, 5 percent of the new organization's total workforce—or about 4,600 positions—were eliminated. Likewise, after Citicorp's merger with Traveler's Group, the new entity announced its intention to cut 5 percent of its 160,000-person workforce. The potential for such layoffs is just one of the realities facing employees in today's competitive global market.

Discussion

1. How might the application of a strategic approach to communication tempered by the considerations of the dialogic model of communication help employees better deal with the pressures of global competition, such as increased merger activity, that now affect business organizations at every level, including frontline workers?

2. How might employees, including potential ones like yourself, better prepare for this situation, by completing a SWOT analysis and revising it periodically?

The Purposes of Business Communication

GLOBAL MEDIA VENTURES, INC.: A MESSAGE TO SHAREHOLDERS

Kathryn Colter, the Chief Executive Officer of GMV, arrives at her Los Angeles office at 8 a.m. sharp. She has cleared her schedule today to devote her attention to planning a very important message: her annual speech to shareholders.

This past year has been a mixed bag for GMV. The company's newspaper and television holdings have suffered a drop in readers and viewers, while the film production unit seems to be holding its own. Surprisingly, GMV's publishing division has fared the best, with the release of several autobiographies by high-profile politicos and a couple of political diatribes by television pundits.

However, the biggest challenge the company has faced this year was the well-publicized lawsuit that was brought against one of GMV's division presidents for sexual discrimination and harassment. After the announcement, stock prices took a dive and have not yet fully recovered.

discussion...

1. Ms. Colter must decide how much time, if any, she wants to spend on each of these issues in her speech. What is your recommendation? How should she address each topic, if at all?

2. What should Ms. Colter's primary purposes be in her speech? How should she achieve these purposes?

3. What other topics might Ms. Colter address to help her achieve the purposes of her speech?

Identify the four purposes of business communication and explain their applications.

Explain the importance of self-awareness in helping you to achieve the purposes of business communication.

Discuss the basic types of business communication messages and how they correspond to the purposes of communication.

In this chapter, you will learn about the first element you should consider when devising a business communication strategy: purpose. After reading this chapter, you should have a good understanding of the importance of identifying the purposes of your communication, how to identify those purposes, and then how to apply what you have learned in communication practice.

Hundreds of years ago, the Greek philosopher and writer Aristotle (384–322 BC) identified three purposes of communication: to inform, to persuade, and to entertain. Although entertainment is the purpose of much of the communication that occurs in the culture of the United States today, it is not highly emphasized in communication for business purposes. In fact, communication that is intended to entertain can have a negative effect on the relationship you have with others or can damage your credibility. For example, if you use humor in oral presentations or e-mail messages at work, you take the risk of offending others who might not share your sense of humor or creating an image of yourself as unprofessional. Some attempts at humor may even violate the law if they are considered racist, sexist, ageist, or otherwise discriminatory of others.

For these reasons, entertainment will not be considered one of the foundational purposes of communication in organizational settings. However, four purposes of communication still exist in the professional workplace. These are:

- To inform
- To persuade
- To convey goodwill
- To establish credibility

Many writers group credibility and goodwill into a single category, but those purposes have been separated in this text to emphasize the importance of both aspects in achieving your purposes of communication and to help you better understand their nuances.

COMMUNICATING TO INFORM

When asked the purpose of communication, most of us respond with one simple answer: to inform. Our common sense tells us that we communicate to tell someone about something. To inform is to pass on information. In the world of work, you are informing when you explain something to your colleagues, your employees, or your customers and clients. If you tell an employee how to operate the copy machine, you are informing; if you tell a customer how to fill out a form, you are informing. You also inform when you tell another person what happened. Perhaps you received a phone call from a customer who is angry about his or her service, and you need to describe the call to your supervisor to learn what to do next. This situation is another example of communicating to inform.

COMMUNICATING TO PERSUADE

Although we may believe that most of our communication is intended to inform others, in the business world almost all communication is persuasive. In other words, you are trying to get another person to do or believe something. In business, you are almost always selling: selling your ideas, yourself, your products, or your services. Selling and persuading are nearly synonymous in the business world. You may be trying to persuade your supervisor to give you a raise, you may be attempting to persuade a colleague to change a portion of a project on which you are both working, or you may be trying to sell a customer your company's service or product. All of these are examples of persuasion at work.

In order to succeed at persuasion, you must generally give good reasons for the person you are communicating with to do or believe what you intend. That is one reason why it is generally important to identify your purposes for communicating in the workplace before you communicate. If you believe you are only informing, you may fail to provide the good reasons or evidence necessary to persuade, if that is indeed your primary purpose.

Evidence consists of a variety of types of information, such as facts, anecdotes, examples, and statistics. These types of evidence and their usage are discussed in more detail in Chapter 6: Content.

According to Conger (1998), persuasion is a difficult and time-consuming activity. But it is a skill that is necessary in today's business environment, since the old "command-and-control" managerial model now often results in poor or unwanted outcomes.

> As AlliedSignal's CEO Lawrence Bossidy said recently, "The day when you could yell and scream and beat people into good performance is over.

> *Today you have to appeal to them by helping them to see how they can get*
> *from here to there by establishing some credibility and by giving them some*
> *reasons and help to get there. Do all those things, and they'll knock down*
> *doors." (Conger, 1998, p. 86)*

According to Conger (1998), there are four essential steps to effective persuasion.

1. **Establish credibility.** For Conger, credibility has two aspects: expertise and relationships. People are considered to have high levels of expertise if they have a history of sound judgment or have proven themselves knowledgeable and well informed about their proposals (Conger, 1998, p. 88). On the relationship side, people with high credibility have demonstrated *over time* that they can be trusted to listen and to work in the best interest of others (Conger, 1998, p. 88).

2. **Frame for common ground.** In order to strengthen the appeal of your proposal to others, you must first identify its tangible benefits to the people you are trying to persuade. In order to accomplish this task, you must thoroughly understand your audience and its needs and concerns.

3. **Provide evidence.** According to Conger (1998), effective persuaders should use a variety of types of evidence—numerical data, examples, stories, metaphors, and analogies—to make their positions come alive (p. 92).

4. **Connect emotionally (convey goodwill).** In our culture, we may like to believe that people make decisions based upon reason; however, emotions always are at play (Conger, 1998, p. 93). In fact, Conger claims that emotions play a primary role in persuasion. To connect emotionally with an audience, Conger suggests that the communicators show their own emotional commitment to the proposal being made and that they adjust their arguments to their audience's emotional state. However, in showing their own emotional commitment to their proposal, communicators must use some restraint.

Conger attempts to reconceptualize our understanding of persuasion from simply the act of convincing and selling to one of persuasion as learning and negotiating. This claim is based upon his 10 years of observing people attempting to persuade. According to Conger's approach, persuasion involves stages of discovery of information, preparation, and dialog. Dialog must happen before and during the persuasive process. "A persuader should make a concerted effort to meet one-on-one with all the key people he or she plans to persuade" (Conger, 1998, p. 89). In some cases, through this dialog, effective persuaders may find that they need to adjust their positions in order to better achieve their goals. This approach supports and underscores the importance of the dialogic model discussed in Chapter 1 to achieve our communication purposes.

In Conger's approach, interpersonal communication is critical to effective persuasion. In interpersonal and small-group communication situations, persuasion is often referred to using another term: **influence.** Influence is defined in a very similar manner as persuasion: it is the power that a person has to affect other people's thinking or actions (Pearson, Nelson, Titsworth, & Harter, 2003).

Influence

Influence is the power to affect the thoughts or actions of others.

Compliance-gaining

Compliance-gaining refers to attempts a communicator makes to influence another person to do something that the other person might otherwise not do.

In the area of interpersonal influence, one area of research focuses on **compliance-gaining** and *compliance-resisting* behaviors. Compliance-gaining is defined as those attempts made by a communicator to influence another to "perform some desired behavior that the [other person] otherwise might not perform" (Wilson, 1998, p. 273). Compliance-gaining occurs whenever we ask someone to do something for us. For example, we may ask our supervisor to give us a raise or promotion or a coworker to switch days off with us. Like Conger's view that effective persuasion takes time and may consist of several stages, research into compliance-gaining shows that its success also often involves a series of attempts.

Research on compliance-gaining indicates that people generally prefer socially acceptable, reward-oriented strategies (Miller, Boster, Roloff, & Seibold, 1977). In other words, people are more apt to be persuaded or influenced if they are offered some kind of reward or benefit for doing so. Conversely, people do not respond well to negative, threatening, or punishing strategies to gain compliance. This is where some scholars draw the line on the similarities between persuasion, influence, and compliance-gaining. Compliance-gaining behaviors that rely upon coercion and threats can be seen as abuses of power rather than the ethical pursuit of persuasion or influence. Studies indicate that as more resistance is encountered, compliance-gaining efforts generally move from positive tactics to more negative ones. It is at this point that compliance-gaining efforts may move from persuasion to coercion.

Compliance-resisting

Compliance-resisting is the refusal to comply with another person's attempts at influence.

Compliance-resisting is defined as the refusal to comply with influence attempts (Pearson, et al, 2003). When resisting requests, people tend to offer reasons or evidence to support their refusal (Saeki & O'Keefe, 1994). People who are more sensitive to others and who are more adaptive are more likely to engage in further attempts to influence (Ifert & Roloff, 1997). They may address some of the obstacles they expect when they initiate their request and adapt later attempts to influence by offering counterarguments.

For example, if you are preparing to ask your supervisor for a raise, you might consider some of the reasons he or she might refuse. Your supervisor might respond by saying money isn't available, you don't deserve a raise compared to your peers' contributions, or you have not performed in such a manner as to deserve a raise. In such a case, a person who is adaptive and sensitive to his or her audience's needs and concerns will respond with information or evidence intended to counter these claims.

Interpersonal dominance

Interpersonal dominance is the relational, behavioral, and interactional state reflecting the achievement—by means of communication—of control or influence over another person.

Another term that is closely related to compliance-gaining is **interpersonal dominance.** Interpersonal dominance is defined as "a relational, behavioral, and interactional state that reflects the actual achievement of influence or control over another via communicative actions" (Burgoon, Johnson, & Koch, 1998, p. 315). Dominance is often viewed negatively, especially when the objective is to control others, but Burgoon argues that it may involve positive qualities that include aspects of social competence.

This idea is better understood by examining the four dimensions of interpersonal dominance. *Persuasiveness and poise* refer to a person's ability to act influentially and to behave with dignity. *Conversational control and panache* refer to the individual's presence and expressiveness. *Task focus* refers to an individual's ability to remain focused on the task at hand, and *self-assurance* refers to a person's level of confidence and ability to avoid either arrogance or timidity.

As discussed in Chapter 1, the recent flattening of organizational hierarchies and resulting interdependency of work tasks among employees have resulted in a greater need for excellent interpersonal skills. Because of these changes, Bernard Keys and Thomas Case (1990) claim that "influence must replace the use of formal authority in relationships with subordinates, peers, outside contacts, and others on whom the job makes one dependent" (p. 38). What this means is that since positional authority is no longer sufficient to get the job done, a web of influence or a balanced web of relationships must be developed. "Recently managers have begun to view leadership as the orchestration of *relationships* between several different interest groups—superiors, peers, and outsiders, as well as subordinates" (Keys & Case, 1990, p. 39).

Just as managers must learn how to foster and orchestrate relationships between people, often through the process of influence, so must subordinates. According to Keys and Case (1990), of the types of influence that subordinates use on superiors, *rational explanation* is the most frequently used type. Rational explanation includes some sort of formal presentation, analysis, or proposal. A host of other tactics—such as arguing without support, using persistence and repetition, threatening, and manipulation—were not found to be effective. In fact, Keys and Case (1990) found that subordinates who used these tactics usually failed miserably. Nevertheless, no one influence tactic will be best in all situations; instead, the subordinate must learn to tailor his or her approach to the audience he or she is attempting to influence and the objective that is sought (Keys & Case, 1990).

Similarly, Riley and Eisenberg (1992) claim that the primary skill individuals must cultivate in managing their bosses is advocacy—the process of championing ideas, proposals, actions, or people to those above them in the organization. Advocacy requires learning how to read your superior's needs and preferences and designing persuasive arguments that are most likely to accomplish your goals. (Analyzing audiences is discussed in Chapter 3: Audience Analysis.) Successful advocacy involves the following steps:

1. **Plan.** Think through a strategy that will work.

2. **Determine why your boss should care.** Connect your argument to something that matters to your boss, such as a key objective or personal value.

3. **Tailor your argument to the boss's style and characteristics.** Adapt your evidence and appeal to those things that are persuasive to your boss, not those things that are persuasive to you.

4. **Assess prior technical knowledge.** Do not assume too much about your boss's level of knowledge and vocabulary or jargon.

5. **Build coalitions.** Your arguments need the support of others in the organization.

6. **Hone your communication skills.** An articulate, well-prepared message is critical to build your credibility with your boss.

As you may notice, these steps mirror the elements of message formulation introduced in Chapter 1 and that are addressed in the chapters of this text. Analyzing your audience is discussed in further detail in Chapter 3, and selecting and adapting the evidence to meet your audience's needs is discussed further in Chapter 6.

An additional component of successful persuasion is the ability to sell yourself effectively. This latter idea is where the third purpose of business communication—goodwill—comes in.

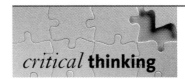

critical **thinking**

Think about a time that you were unsuccessful at persuasion. Why were you unsuccessful? In retrospect, what could you have done to improve your chances of succeeding?

COMMUNICATING TO CONVEY GOODWILL

According to *Merriam-Webster's Collegiate Dictionary*, goodwill has three definitions: "1. friendly disposition; kindly regard; benevolence; 2. cheerful acquiescence or consent; 3. an intangible, salable asset arising from the reputation of a business and its relations with its customers." For those of you who have taken accounting courses, you are probably familiar with the third definition of **goodwill;** in business contexts, goodwill is considered an asset. As a purpose of business communication, goodwill can be thought of as the ability to create and maintain positive, productive relationships with others.

Goodwill

In the business communication context, goodwill is the ability to create and maintain positive relationships with others.

As discussed earlier, Conger (1998) has studied how individuals use language to motivate people. His research indicates that people with high credibility on the relationship side have demonstrated that they can be trusted to listen and to work in the best interests of others. They also have consistently shown strong emotional character and integrity. In other words, they do not exhibit mood extremes or inconsistent performance. "Indeed, people who are known to be honest, steady, and reliable have an edge when going into any persuasive situation" (Conger, 1998, p. 88).

Many of you who have work experience probably would agree with this statement. The ability to establish and maintain relationships is indeed what makes the business world go around. Establishing and maintaining relationships with others, or networking, is one of the most successful forms of job hunting, for example. Likewise, the best form of advertisement is word-of-mouth, not only because it is inexpensive, but because you are more likely to trust the judgment of people you already know. When working with others or in groups, you are more likely to cooperate with people whom you know, like, and trust.

Having a positive relationship with another person or being an expert in a relevant field often enables us to be more successful at persuasion. As long ago as the middle of the fourth century BC, Aristotle made this assertion in *On Rhetoric*. For Aristotle, the problem of communication essentially boiled down to seeing the available means of persuasion in each particular case. According to Aristotle, in order to persuade successfully, communicators must know the extent to which they enjoy the trust, respect, and liking of the people with whom they are communicating. Aristotle recognized that the importance of the character of the speaker (or writer) is a legitimate concern in effective communication.

This idea is easy to see in practice in our day-to-day activities. You are more likely to trust someone you know, and that trust may make it easier for that person to persuade you. If your neighbor sees you leaving for the store and asks for a ride, you are probably more likely to take him or her along than a stranger who makes a similar request. You are also more likely to trust and believe an expert. If the server at the fast-food window tells you that your car sounds like it needs a new transmission, you will probably take the comment with a grain of salt. But if your auto mechanic makes the same statement, you will likely believe it, since he or she is presumably an expert in auto repair—someone with credibility (which is discussed in the next section, "Creating and Maintaining Credibility")—and someone with whom you may have established a relationship of trust based upon his or her past performance.

From an organizational perspective, relationships can play an important role in producing effective supervision, promoting social support among employees, building personal influence, and ensuring productivity through smooth work flow. The need for good interpersonal relationships in organizations is particularly important from both the standpoint of the individual, who requires social support in an increasingly turbulent world, and the organization, which must maintain high levels of cooperation among employees to meet customer demands and remain competitive.

As discussed in Chapter 1, the recent flattening of organizational hierarchies and resulting interdependency of work tasks among employees, as well as the increasing diversity of the workplace, requires a need for corporate cultures of trust built on respect for differences and mutual cooperation. According to Rosabeth Moss Kanter (1989), informal interpersonal relationships and communication networks are the most dynamic sources of power in organizations today. (Communication networks are discussed in more detail in Chapter 4: Channels of Communication.) In contrast, more formal relationships are slower and less trustworthy sources of information. Most decision makers rely heavily on verbal information from people they trust.

This need is echoed in the 2003 *Wall Street Journal* survey cited in Chapter 1, in which recruiters said that interpersonal skills and the ability to work well in a team were the top two characteristics they found most attractive in prospective employees. Interpersonal skills and the ability to work well in a team are founded upon trust. *Trust* can be understood as the confidence that our peers' intentions

The flattening of organizational hierarchies and increasing diversity of the modern workplace require corporate cultures of trust built on respect for differences and mutual cooperation.

are good (Lencioni, 2002). In other words, we must believe that those with whom we work will not act opportunistically or take advantage of us and others to narrowly pursue their own self-interest.

Recent studies indicate that trust has five components: integrity, competence, consistency, loyalty, and openness (Robbins, 2001). *Integrity* refers to a person's ethical character and basic honesty. In order to feel that our peers are *competent,* we must be convinced that they have the technical knowledge and interpersonal skills to perform their job. If you don't believe a coworker is competent, you are unlikely to depend upon him or her or respect her opinion on work-related matters. We are more able to trust those who appear *consistent* in their behavior or who are reliable, predictable, and demonstrate good judgment. We tend to trust others who are *loyal* and willing to protect and help others to save face. Finally, we tend to trust those who are *open* and conversely, find it difficult to trust those who appear evasive, deceptive, or secretive.

Additional factors affect our ability to forge the relationships businesspeople depend upon so much: valuing relationships, assertiveness, and active listening (Eisenberg & Goodall, 1993, p. 252). The first step in building interpersonal relationships at work is learning to *recognize the importance of relationships* in business—if you haven't already. For many individuals, interpersonal communication is the work, particularly among managers.

The importance of *assertiveness* becomes obvious when you consider the alternatives. On one hand, the avoiding, passive-aggressive individual whines, complains, and frets about problems at work, but when asked directly what is wrong, says nothing (Eisenberg & Goodall, 1993, p. 252). This strategy, known as **avoidance,** is defined as a conscious attempt to avoid engaging with people in the dominant group (Pearson, et al, 2003, p. 214). Avoidance is also considered *passive,* which is an attempt to separate by having as little to do as possible with the dominant group. The result of an avoiding, passive approach is a consistent inability to raise and resolve problems, needs, issues, and concerns.

At the other extreme, aggressive individuals sabotage their ability to meet their needs and to establish supportive relationships by creating defensiveness and alienating others (Eisenberg & Goodall, 1993, p. 252). **Aggressiveness** includes those behaviors perceived as hurtfully expressive, self-promoting, and assuming control over the choices of others (Orbe, 1996, p. 170). Aggressive individuals are also described as argumentative. Not only are such individuals more aggressive, they are more insecure and less likely to be well regarded or happy at work (Infante, Trebling, Shepard, & Seeds, 1984).

In contrast to avoidance and aggression, **assertiveness** is defined as "self-enhancing, expressive communication that takes into account both the communicator's and others' needs" (Orbe, 1996, p. 170). Assertiveness involves

Avoidance

Avoidance is the strategy of knowingly avoiding engagement with those in the dominant group.

Aggressiveness

Aggressiveness is a series of behaviors and characteristics including hurtful expressiveness, self-promotion, attempting to control others, and argumentativeness.

Assertiveness

Assertiveness is self-enhancing communication that takes into account not only the communicator's needs, but those of others as well.

clearly articulating what you want from others in terms of behavior. It is direct, yet not attacking or blaming. Assertiveness is associated with positive impressions and overall quality of work experience.

Like assertiveness, *listening* is a learned skill and one that very few individuals ever master. Talking to someone who really knows how to listen actively makes you feel valued, important, and free to speak your mind (Eisenberg & Goodall, 1993, p. 252). (Active listening is discussed in more detail in Chapter 7: Verbal, Vocal, and Nonverbal Expression.) In an ideal communication situation, assertiveness and active listening go hand in hand as people are able to express their own perceptions and desires and at the same time attend to the perceptions and desires of others. As you may recognize, these two skills are the foundation of the dialogic model of communication introduced in Chapter 1.

COMMUNICATING TO ESTABLISH CREDIBILITY

Aristotle recognized that the importance of the character of the speaker—or writer—is a legitimate concern in effective communication. In our time, when the facts are often complex and hard to determine for ourselves, and when television brings speakers "up close and personal" for our inspection, the importance of credibility has been magnified several times that of ancient Greece.

Credible people demonstrate that they have strong emotional character and integrity; they are known to be honest, steady, and reliable. Credibility is akin to reputation. Increasingly, at an organizational level, reputation is becoming more important. Sophisticated customers do not make financial decisions based solely on an organization's competitive advantage in the marketplace (Eisenberg & Goodall, 1993). Instead, customers are increasingly sensitive to a company's reputation. In fact, public relations has developed as a functional area to manage the reputations of companies.

In contrast to *reputation,* which is the view outsiders have of an organization, *image* has to do with insiders' assessments of an organization.

Although these terms are applied to organizations in management literature, they are equally applicable to individuals. Just as organizations understand that their reputation and image can affect their successful continuation, savvy employees are aware of the applicability of these concepts in their own careers. One study indicates that 92 percent of more than 2,300 executives said that if a person loses credibility with them, it would be very difficult to gain it back (Pagano & Pagano, 2004).

To make matters worse, most managers overestimate their own credibility considerably (Conger, 1998). In the worst-case scenario, they may revert to the old "command-and-control" style of leadership, which studies have shown damages productivity and morale in skilled, well-educated workers and creates frustrated, silenced employees who steal pencils and sabotage the company's computer system. Lack of or ignorance of the importance of credibility may ultimately lead to a Machiavellian game of terror and threats, in which strong tactics of domination and control are used to gain influence rather than softer, less destructive methods.

Factors that help to build credibility include:

- Expertise and competence

- Personal ethics and integrity, our trustworthiness

- Control of emotions

- Development and maintenance of a professional image

Expertise and Competence

Clearly, your relevant job knowledge and ability to perform your job well affect your credibility. Skill levels and competency are also important for the effective functioning and performance of small groups and teams. Attitude and personality characteristics can also improve your reputation as a competent, conscientious employee. For example, those who complain without offering solutions to the problem are perceived more negatively than those who discuss problems in terms of their solutions. The former may be seen as "whiners," while the latter become known as problem solvers. These perceptions contribute to your overall image within a company.

Competence also extends to communication skills. Speaking correctly and articulately generally enhances our credibility by indicating to others that we are well educated and intelligent. The same goes for our written communication. If our written messages are full of errors, we may be perceived as undereducated, lazy, or not detail-oriented. All of these negative judgments can affect our credibility. In one case, a résumé or letter with a grammatical error eliminated an applicant from consideration and in another, the same company asked an applicant with a doctoral degree to provide samples of reports and other documents he had written (Kroepels & David, 2003).

This situation provides an opportunity for those who can communicate well in today's competitive business environment. In other words, one way you can positively distinguish yourself from others is to demonstrate excellent communication skills. Employees who can write clearly can create a better impression of a firm with customers, suppliers, and outsiders than any public relations program ever devised. "If you send out a sales letter that is filled with errors, you're losing credibility. You send the message that your company is careless" (Tayler, 2003, p.87).

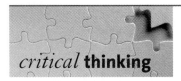

critical **thinking**

What competencies and areas of expertise do you possess that can help you to build your feelings of confidence as well as your credibility with professional audiences? What skills in communication can help you to do the same?

Effective business writing skills have become crucial for both personal performance and organizational productivity. With the proliferation of personal computing, more and more employees at all levels in the company are producing documents that represent an organization, and the quality of this written material can have a significant impact on both perceptions and performance. Technology has also created a problem of exposure. Voice mail, e-mail, faxes, audio-video conferencing, and other technologies expose businesses to an ever-growing array of diverse audiences.

E-mail is a particular problem because of its wide use. "Your company's voice is often judged by what pops into your client's inbox. That first impression better be a good one," says Adam Chandler, national account director for Yahoo! (Moerke, 2004, p. 63). Jonathan Herschberg, a communications developer based in New York, says, "If I get an e-mail that's full of errors and I know nothing else about you, there's no reason for me not to think you'll handle my business in the same way you handled that writing" (Moerke, 2004, p. 63).

critical **thinking**

Discuss your greatest challenges regarding the achievement of grammatical correctness in your written and oral communication. Have these affected your confidence or your credibility with your communication audiences? Have you taken steps to become more correct and confident in your written and oral communication? If not, what steps might you take?

Not all errors in writing are created equal, however. In the table below, writing errors are categorized from the most severe to the least in terms of their effects on message clarity and writer credibility.

TABLE 2-1. *The varying severity of mechanical errors in communication.*

THE VARYING SEVERITY OF MECHANICAL ERRORS IN COMMUNICATION

Mechanics/Error Interference: assesses if errors interfere with a writer's clarity and credibility.

A writer's communication may be judged partly on how closely the language follows conventions in sentence structure, grammar, usage, mechanics, spelling, and so on. Severe and frequent errors (and in some circumstances even milder forms and degrees of error) can negatively impact both clarity and credibility. All errors are not equally intrusive or offensive to all readers, however. Below, errors are categorized by severity, beginning with the most severe and ending with the least.

Disruptive **errors** may interfere with communication, preventing the reader from comprehending what the writer means. These include unintelligible sentences, unclear pronoun references, incorrect verbs, run-on sentences, fragments, and the use of wrong words.

Credibility **errors** don't usually disrupt communication, but tend to reflect negatively on the writer's credibility, reducing the reader's confidence in what a writer has to say. These include faulty subject/verb agreement, passive voice, and punctuation and spelling errors.

Continued on next page.

TABLE 2-1. *Continued*

Etiquette errors are errors that many readers—but not all—hardly notice, especially if reading quickly for meaning. However, etiquette errors can reduce a writer's credibility, especially with those readers who are concerned about professional image or those who believe that critical thinking is reflected in the observance of grammar rules. These include pronoun usage, false subjects, and misplaced apostrophes.

Accent errors commonly characterize the writing of nonnative speakers or the use of local idioms and dialects. Accent errors, which are nearly impossible for nonnative speakers to correct in the short term, may be ignored by readers. These errors rarely interfere with communication and usually do not damage the writer's credibility. These generally entail missing or wrong articles or prepositions.

Source: Rogers, P. S. & Rymer, J. (1996). Analytical writing assessment diagnostic program. Prepared for the Graduate Management Admission Council, p. 41.

Unfortunately, there is no quick fix for grammar and mechanical problems. Achieving correct grammar usage takes time and some effort; it takes practice. To improve the correctness of your writing:

1. Read—often and about diverse topics. Reading helps us to subconsciously recognize and internalize correct grammar usage in writing.

2. Solve word games and puzzles. These activities can help you build your vocabulary and learn the meanings of words.

3. Become aware of the common mistakes you make in your writing. This knowledge will streamline the process of proofreading if you can more quickly identify the areas that you need to double-check for correctness.

4. Edit others' writing. This activity can improve your analytical skills, which are necessary to proofread your own writing.

5. Learn how to properly use the spell-checking and grammar-checking tools available in most word processing programs. It is important to recognize that these computer tools do not recognize all writing errors. You will also need to proofread your written messages carefully, so it is essential to keep a good writing handbook and dictionary on hand.

6. For very important messages, it is often a good idea to ask a literate friend or colleague to review and provide feedback about their correctness.

As mentioned earlier, this attentiveness to accuracy should be reflected in a greater sensitivity to grammatical correctness in speaking, too. By exerting some time and energy toward the goal of achieving correctness, greater confidence, competence, and credibility will be your reward.

Personal Ethics and Integrity

The *Wall Street Journal* poll referenced earlier in this text also indicates that personal ethics and integrity are among the top five characteristics sought by recruiters. The attractiveness of ethical employees may be a result of the recent and continuing discovery of unethical and illegal practices by U.S. businesses:

- Enron was found to have improved its financial image by moving debt off its books and using other illegal accounting practices. As a result, thousands of Enron employees lost not only their jobs but their retirement investments, while company executives made millions of dollars from stock sales before the company's problems became public.

- WorldCom also engaged in illegal accounting practices, such as registering a single sale many times, thus overinflating company revenues by millions of dollars.

- Andersen Worldwide suffered financial collapse following disclosures that it failed to report widespread fraudulent accounting practices among its clients.

Such cases are not a recent development or the exception. "Between 1975 and 1985, two-thirds of the Fortune 500 firms were convicted of serious crimes ranging from fraud to the illegal dumping of hazardous wastes. A much larger number were convicted of misdemeanors after extensive plea bargaining, and a still larger number settled suits out of court" (Conrad, 1990, p. 15).

The causes of such unethical behavior have been widely studied. For example, Lehman and Dufrene (2002) claim unethical behavior stems from a number of causes, including:

- Excessive emphasis on profits by managers. According to Federal Reserve Chairman Alan Greenspan, "infectious greed" ultimately pushed companies, such as Enron, Global Crossing, and WorldCom, into bankruptcy.

- A misplaced sense of corporate loyalty may cause an employee to do what seems in the best interest of the corporation, even if it is illegal or unethical.

- An obsession by employees to gain personal advancement.

- An expectation that illegal or unethical actions will not be caught.

- An unethical tone set by top management.

- Uncertainty about whether an action is wrong.

- Unwillingness to take a stand for what is right.

Eisenberg and Goodall (1993) claim that another possible reason for the common practice of unethical communication behavior may be the increased pressure to compete. The increasing complexity of organizations may also lead to lies or distortion, turf building, and cover-up (Eisenberg & Goodall, 1993, p. 333).

Terence Mitchell and William Scott (1990) attribute unethical behavior to the United States' "ethic of personal advantage." This ethic has three themes:

- A present versus future orientation.

- An instrumental as opposed to a substantive focus.

- An emphasis on individualism contrasted with community.

Other scholars agree with this assessment. For example, Eisenberg and Goodall (1993) state that the "greatest weakness of businesspeople in the past two decades has been short-term thinking, or the willingness to trade off long-term value for immediate gain (p. 333).

Likewise, in his study of the Los Angeles riots, Michael Lerner (1992) contends that the looters were merely "living out the cynical American ethos" (p. B7). Lerner claims that we live in a culture of looting, where the highest goal is to "look out for number one" and to "get what you can when you can" (p. B7). This assessment echoes that of Mitchell and Scott, who advance the case that unethical behavior is caused in part by an emphasis on individualism and instrumentalism.

> *Any cost to others is acceptable as long as you don't get caught or don't hurt your own future chances. . . . Within this ethos, concern for the future—of the planet, of one's own country or even of one's own children—seems naïve and silly, something to be left to "do-gooders." The ethos of looting is the "common sense" of the society. (Lerner, 1992, p. B7)*

The unethical practices of corporations and their employees can have far-reaching consequences. Those affected by the decisions, the *stakeholders,* can include people inside and outside the company, as the Enron case indicates. Not only were employees negatively affected, but the entire citizenry of the state of California suffered from the company's illegal and unethical practices in the sale of electricity. Financial markets can suffer from an erosion of public confidence, as was the case after the recent spate of corporate scandals.

Even though the lapses in ethics that we see around us may seem overwhelming at times, you can do something to ensure that your communication is ethical. Putting ethical practices first will not only benefit your employer, colleagues, clients, and customers, it will also enable you to maintain your credibility and create a reputation of fairness and good judgment that can positively impact your ability to communicate and succeed in your career goals.

In the table below, you will find the "Nine Commandments" of the National Communication Association to help ensure ethical communication practices.

TABLE 2-2. *The national communication association credo for communication ethics.*

THE NATIONAL COMMUNICATION ASSOCIATION CREDO FOR COMMUNICATION ETHICS

Questions of right and wrong arise whenever people communicate. Ethical communication is fundamental to responsible thinking, decision making, and the development of relationships and communities within and across contexts, cultures, channels, and media. Moreover, ethical communication enhances human worth and dignity by fostering truthfulness, fairness, responsibility, personal integrity, and respect for self and others. We believe that unethical communication threatens the quality of all communication and consequently the well-being of individuals and the society in which we live. Therefore, we, the members of the National Communication Association, endorse and are committed to practicing the following principles of ethical communication:

- We advocate truthfulness, accuracy, honesty, and reason as essential to the integrity of communication.

Continued on next page.

TABLE 2-2. *Continued*

- We endorse freedom of expression, diversity of perspective, and tolerance of dissent to achieve the informed and responsible decision making fundamental to a civil society.
- We strive to understand and respect other communicators before evaluating and responding to their messages.
- We promote access to communication resources and opportunities as necessary to fulfill human potential and contribute to well-being of families, communities, and society.
- We promote communication climates of caring and mutual understanding that respect the unique needs and characteristics of individual communicators.
- We condemn communication that degrades individuals and humanity through distortion, intimidation, coercion, and violence, and through the expression of intolerance and hatred.
- We are committed to the courageous expression of personal convictions in pursuit of fairness and justice.
- We advocate sharing information, opinions, and feelings when facing significant choices while also respecting privacy and confidentiality.
- We accept responsibility for the short- and long-term consequences of our own communication and expect the same of others.

Communication is inherently ethical. This is because whenever people interact with one another, ethics invades every exchange because the manipulation of symbols involved in language use also involves a purpose that is external to, and in some degree manipulative of, the audience for or interpreter of the message (Barnlund, 1986, p. 40). Communication thus can be intended to prevent, restrict, or stimulate the cultivation of meaning. In the first case, messages can be intended to coerce others by choosing symbols that are threatening to the audience or interpreter of the message. The values of the listener are ignored in this type of communication. In the second, messages can be intended to exploit by arranging words to filter information, narrow the choices, or obscure the consequences, so that only one meaning becomes attractive or appropriate. The values of the listener are subverted in this type of message. Finally, messages can be facilitative. In such communication, words are used to inform, to enlarge perspective, to deepen sensitivity, to remove external threat, or to encourage independence of meaning (Barnlund, 1986, p. 41). The values of the listener are respected in this type of interaction.

Just as certain communicative behaviors are considered ethical, it is easy to identify those that are considered unethical. W. Charles Redding (1991) has developed a typology of unethical messages in organizations, which is shown in the table on the following page.

Messages can be used to harm or mislead others. Persuasive messages particularly always contain the potential for unethical practices. This is because persuasion involves:

- A person or group attempting to influence others by altering their beliefs, attitudes, values, and overt actions.

- Conscious choices among ends sought and means used to achieve those ends.

- A potential judge (any and all receivers of the message).

Responsible Communication

Have you been on the receiving end of the types of unethical messages listed in the table below? How did you feel? What might be appropriate responses to such unethical communication practices?

TYPOLOGY OF UNETHICAL MESSAGES

Type	Examples
Coercive	An employee criticizes the boss's "pet" development program in a meeting and is fired on the spot for her remarks.
Destructive	A supervisor makes a sexist joke at the expense of an employee.
Deceptive	Federal Aviation Administration (FAA) employees falsify employee work records to justify the firing of air traffic controllers during their 1981 strike.
Intrusive	Electronic surveillance of employees is conducted through hidden video cameras.
Secretive	The asbestos industry suppressed information that left little doubt about the health hazards posed by its product.
Manipulative/ Exploitative	Management threatens union members with a plant closing if they don't ratify a contract.

Source: Redding, W. C. (1991). Unethical messages in the organizational context. Paper presented at the Annenberg Convention of the ICA, Chicago, IL.

Because of the potential for unethical communication practices, both senders and receivers of messages hold responsibilities. Responsible communicators carefully analyze claims, assess probable consequences, and weigh relevant values (Larson, 1995, p. 29). In addition, responsible communicators exercise the ability to respond and are responsive to the needs and communication of others in sensitive, thoughtful, fitting ways (Larson, 1995, p. 29). More specifically, both parties in an interaction bear mutual responsibility to participate actively in the process. This active participation occurs through two steps: reasoned skepticism and appropriate feedback.

Reasoned skepticism involves actively searching for meaning, analyzing and synthesizing information, and judging its soundness and worth. **Appropriate feedback** requires that you are honest and reflect your true understanding and judgments. However, such feedback should also be appropriate for the subject, audience, and occasion or context, primary elements of business communication strategy.

Reasoned skepticism

Reasoned skepticism is the process of searching actively for meaning, analyzing and synthesizing information, and judging the worth of that information.

Appropriate feedback

Appropriate feedback is honest, reflecting the communicator's true understanding and judgment, and is appropriate for the subject, audience, and occasion or context.

Emotional Control

Employees are expected to maintain a professional demeanor while in the office, or when they represent their office in the field. Part of our ability to accomplish that goal often has to do with our ability to control our emotions. According to a study done by the University of Missouri–Columbia, "many employees do not want their coworkers to express any type of strong emotion—positive or negative" (Dealing with emotions, 2003, p. 1). In this study, the employees were asked to describe situations where they believed coworkers acted appropriately and inappropriately. The consensus of the employees was that negative emotion should never be expressed, and positive emotion should be shown in moderation.

Expressions of negative emotions, such as fear, anxiety, and anger, tend to be unacceptable except under fairly specific conditions. For example, verbal anger is direct, aggressive, and intentional. When you allow anger to control your communication, the results are generally unproductive. Outbursts of anger tend to make people uncomfortable, especially when the person exhibits irrational forms of anger. If construed as harassment in the workplace, excessive displays of anger can lead to disciplinary measures.

Anger can also be communicated in our written communication. We should never write a message when we are feeling a negative emotion but should wait until we have calmed down to express ourselves. Although it can feel good to vent negative feelings, we should immediately delete or erase messages written in anger. Unfortunately, with the popularity and proliferation of e-mail, it is easy to pound out our frustrations in an electronic message. "Then we click 'send.' In a frenzied span of 15 minutes we have managed to do some real psychological damage, usually more to ourselves than to anyone else" (Manley, 2001). That damage may come in the form of a loss of credibility and damaged relationships.

When we become angry, we are typically upset because we have not gotten our needs met. "We are blaming someone or something else for not getting what we want" (Rosenberg, 2003). Unfortunately, in these cases, we may speak or act in a way that guarantees we will not get what we want.

However, negative emotions can be tamed. Kristin Anderson, president of Say What? Consulting recommends that you maintain a neutral body and voice. Keeping your body loose and your voice tone neutral will help to maintain a calm demeanor (McCune, 2003, p. 1). A second tactic is to listen without trying to judge if the situation is good or bad.

Janice Arenofsky offers some additional suggestions:

1. Put yourself in the other person's shoes. See if you can imagine how he or she feels.

2. Exercise to get rid of the tension. Ride your bike, play soccer, or, if you are at work, go for a long walk.

3. Do not jump to quick conclusions. Listen carefully to what the other person says.

Following these simple techniques can help any aggressive situation turn positive. If confronted by anger, you may feel like retreating or become defensive. However, being defensive and yelling back may cause more harm. Instead, empathize with the person. Doing so will help you maintain your credibility by showing that you act reasonably, rationally, and respectfully in stressful situations.

Developing a Professional Image

All the aspects of credibility discussed thus far help us to cultivate a professional image: our expertise and competence in a variety of job skills, our ability to control our emotions, and our integrity. Our communication skills, both written and oral, can enhance our image as a professional. Personality traits can also contribute to a more credible and professional image. If we show ourselves to be dependable, reliable, careful, thorough, able to plan, organized, hardworking, persistent, and achievement-oriented, we are more likely to be perceived as professional and competent. (Personality is discussed further in the section that follows, "Self-Awareness and Communication.")

Our appearance, through dress and posture, also communicates to others. Every time you walk into a room, you communicate who you are before you speak, through your appearance (Buhler, 1991). For example, it would not be expected for your company president to walk into a business meeting wearing Bermuda shorts. On the other hand, a fishing guide would not show up for work in a three-piece suit. Dressing appropriately for a particular situation can affect whether others perceive you as professional and credible. It also sends the message that you are a part of the group, that you belong. This message can help you in the relationship area of communication.

Some people are better able to consciously cultivate a professional image. **Impression management** is the control (or lack of control) of communication information through a performance. In impression management, people try to present an "idealized" version of themselves in order to reach desired ends.

All of us attempt to manage the impressions we make to varying degrees in various situations. For example, when you are with your friends, you probably try to dress like them and act like them so as to be seen as part of the group. When you go out on a date, you are likely to be on your "best behavior" to reduce the risk of doing or saying something that may not be viewed as attractive by your date. In small-group situations, you often hold back during the forming stage of the group process for the same reason.

High self-monitors are those individuals who are highly aware of their impression management behavior (Snyder, 1979). On the other hand, **low self-monitors** communicate with others with little attention to the responses to their messages. They have little idea about how others perceive them and know even less about how to interact appropriately with others.

Impression management is one aspect of a natural and productive process called **anticipatory socialization.** Anticipatory socialization is the process through which most of us develop a set of expectations and beliefs concerning how people communicate in particular occupations and in formal and informal work settings

---

Impression management

Impression management is the attempt to control the impression of ourselves that we present to others in any communication situation.

High self-monitors

High self-monitors are people who are acutely aware of their impression management efforts.

Low self-monitors

Low self-monitors are people who have little awareness about how others perceive them, and little knowledge about how to interact appropriately with others.

Anticipatory socialization

Anticipatory socialization is the process we use to develop our expectations and beliefs about how people communicate in various formal and informal work situations.

(Jablan, 2001). The business communication course you are now enrolled in—as well as some of the other university courses you are now taking—is part of that process. If you are involved in internships or other job-related activities, these also contribute to that process. In fact, learning how to work in a position probably begins in early childhood.

Since anticipatory socialization is a process that probably begins in childhood, it is also a part of our self-concept. Most discussions of anticipatory socialization recognize that as people mature, they use the information they gather about jobs from their environment to compare against their self-concept. This comparison helps them to make judgments about choosing occupations and specific jobs (Jablan, 2001). This process may be likened to a self-inventory, such as the SWOT analysis that was discussed in Chapter 1, to determine career opportunities that best match an individual's skills and attitudes.

Some people believe that impression management is unethical or deceptive. However, according to the theory, impression management can help others and ourselves save face or avoid embarrassment. When we act in ways that are appropriate to the situation, we are respecting the expectations of others. In these cases, impression management is a matter of politeness. Like many matters of communication, the ethics of impression management come down to intent. If we change our behaviors and presentation style in an attempt to deceive or mislead others, such actions can be judged as unethical. Even in their least offensive form, we may be seen as superficial, pretentious, lacking integrity, or a "suck-up."

critical **thinking**

Discuss your own application of the four purposes of business communication. Do you agree that in business contexts, you generally should consider and apply all four? Why or why not?

SELF-AWARENESS AND COMMUNICATION

How you view yourself can make a great difference in your ability to communicate and achieve your purposes. Many scholars believe that communication also forms our self-concept. In other words, people are the products of how others treat them and of the messages others send them. Dean Barnlund (1970) introduced the idea that individuals "construct" themselves through the relationships they have, wish to have, or perceive themselves as having. Barnlund developed the idea that "six persons" are involved in every two-person communication. These six persons emerge from:

- How you view yourself

- How you view the other person

- How you believe the other person views himself or herself

- How the other person views you

- How the other person believes you view him or her

Barnlund's model emphasizes the relational nature of communication and the centrality of the self and our perception of the self in communication. From this model comes the notion of the **self-fulfilling prophecy,** or the idea that you behave and see yourself in ways that are consistent with how others see you (Wood, 1997, p. 383).

Another term that refers to the way you think about yourself is *self-awareness,* which is an understanding of the self, including your attitudes, values, beliefs, strengths, and weaknesses (DeVito, 1986, p. 274). As Barnlund's model indicates, self-awareness develops in our communication with ourselves as well as our interaction with others. Communication with ourselves is called **intrapersonal communication***,* which includes "our perceptions, memories, experiences, feelings, interpretations, inferences, evaluations, attitudes, opinions, ideas, strategies, images, and states of consciousness" (Shedletsky, 1989). According to Gardner (1993), **intrapersonal intelligence** is the capacity to form an accurate model of oneself and to be able to use that model to operate effectively in life.

Self-awareness is important for communication, since it can affect how well we communicate with others and how we are perceived by others. According to Gardner (1993), intrapersonal intelligence is a correlative ability to **interpersonal intelligence.** Interpersonal intelligence is the ability to understand other people: what motivates them, how they work, how to work cooperatively with them. Essentially, Gardner claims that we must have self-awareness in order to be able to understand others.

For example, if our self-concept does not match the perception that others have of us, we may misinterpret their responses to our messages. We may also misinterpret the way that our communication is interpreted by others. For instance, we may believe that we are highly reliable; however, others may believe the opposite about us. These contradictions can negatively impact our ability to work with others and in groups. If we are unaware of these contradictions, then we are unable to change our communicative behaviors, both verbal and nonverbal, to better correspond with the message we want to send about ourselves. It is important that the messages we send through our actions correspond to those we send verbally and in writing, since people are more likely to believe nonverbal cues.

A related concept and outgrowth of Gardner's and others' work is that of **emotional intelligence.** Emotional intelligence refers to an assortment of noncognitive skills, capabilities, and competencies that influence a person's ability to successfully cope with environmental demands and pressures. Emotional intelligence consists of five dimensions:

- **Self-awareness.** The ability to be aware of what you are feeling.

- **Self-management.** The ability to manage one's emotions and impulses.

Self-fulfilling prophecy

Self-fulfilling prophecy is the idea that we see ourselves in ways that are consistent with how others see us.

Intrapersonal communication

Intrapersonal communication encompasses our communication with ourselves, including memories, experiences, feelings, ideas, and attitudes.

Intrapersonal intelligence

Intrapersonal intelligence is the ability to form an accurate model of oneself and to use this model effectively.

Interpersonal intelligence

Interpersonal intelligence is the ability to understand others.

Emotional intelligence

Emotional intelligence is the assortment of noncognitive skills that influence our ability to cope with the pressures and demands of the environment.

- **Self-motivation.** The ability to persist in the face of setbacks and failures.

- **Empathy.** The ability to sense how others are feeling.

- **Social skills.** The ability to handle the emotions of others.

Emotional intelligence can help us to establish relationships with others as well as our credibility. As was discussed earlier, having the ability to control our emotions can contribute to the creation of a credible and professional image. Such an ability is also one aspect of emotional intelligence. Emotional control or the ability to delay gratification and resist impulses can greatly affect our career success and ability to communicate with others. Studies have shown that those who were able to resist temptation as small children are more socially competent as adolescents (Mischel & Peake, 1990). They were more personally effective, self-assertive, and better able to cope with life's frustrations. They were less likely to be negatively affected by stress or to become disorganized when pressured; they embraced challenges, were self-reliant and confident, trustworthy and dependable, and took initiative. More than a decade later, they were still able to delay gratification. Those who were less able to delay gratification were more likely to shy away from social contacts, to be stubborn and indecisive, to be easily upset by frustrations, to think of themselves as unworthy, to become immobilized by stress, to be mistrustful and resentful about not getting enough, to be prone to jealousy and envy, and to overreact to irritations with a sharp temper, thus provoking arguments.

Other personality attributes mirror many of the findings of research on emotional intelligence, including a person's proclivity to self-monitor. Another dimension, **locus of control,** has to do with how much control we believe we have over our lives. Those labeled as *internals* believe they control their own destiny, while those called *externals* believe their lives are controlled by outside sources (Rotter, 1966). Your behaviors and communication are clues to whether you are an internal or an external. For example, studies have shown that externals often do not believe they have control over the grades they earn in school, so they blame the teacher, their group members, the grading system, and so on.

The self-fulfilling prophecy also applies to locus of control. For example, internals tend to believe that their health is under their control, so they take more responsibility for their health and have better health benefits. Internals generally perform better on the job because they have a tendency to search more actively before making a decision, are more motivated to achieve, and tend to take action. Locus of control is a part of emotional intelligence, as is the ability to self-monitor. High emotional intelligence involves the ability to self-motivate, which is a characteristic of someone with an internal locus of control.

Another widely used measure of personality is the Myers-Briggs Type Indicator (MBTI). The test measures four characteristics: whether a person is introverted or extroverted (I or E), sensing or intuitive (S or N), thinking or feeling (T or F), and perceiving or judging (P or J). These classifications are then combined into 16 personality types. For example, the ENTP is a conceptualizer. He or she is innovative, individualistic, versatile, and entrepreneurial. ESTJs are organizers,

Locus of control

Locus of control is the degree of control we believe we have over our lives.

communication IN YOUR WORLD

Emotional intelligence is proving to be the deciding factor on who will win the dream job with Donald Trump on the hit NBC show *The Apprentice,* according to a leadership professor at the University at Buffalo School of Management.

"Success in today's business world depends not only on our training and expertise, but also on how well we handle ourselves and others and our ability to learn and adapt to new and changing situations," says Muriel T. Anderson, who teaches the School of Management's Leadership PACE (Personal Achievement through Competency Evaluation), a course designed to help MBA students identify their personal limitations and develop a plan to overcome them.

Anderson points out that the main difference between outstanding and average leaders is linked to emotional intelligence—the ability to manage one's emotions and those of others.

"Several of the contestants, namely Sam, Tammy, and Omarosa, were self-assured in their abilities, but they failed to recognize how their behaviors negatively affected others," says Anderson in her analysis of the 2004 season show. "It was this lack of emotional self-awareness that probably led to their firings."

"Emotionally intelligent leaders work well with others, remain calm under pressure, and can motivate themselves and others," she says, noting that most of the contestants who remained longer on the 2004 season show exhibited a higher level of emotional intelligence when appropriate.

"Nick doesn't hesitate to bring up ethical concerns and falls back on his values to guide him in his decision making. Troy has been chosen most often by his peers as project manager due to his strong communication skills and ability to encourage others. And Amy has shown that she can easily build bonds with team members and clients, as well as keep her emotions and impulses in check when faced with high-pressure situations," she explains.

After the worst offenders are eliminated, it becomes more difficult to predict who will succeed and who will fail, but Anderson expects, "It's going to come down to emotional intelligence." Then the real challenge begins: The winner must learn how to manage having "The Donald" as a real-life boss, Anderson says.

Discussion

1. Think about groups in which you have worked or been involved. Do Anderson's observations hold true in those situations?

2. How might you alter your own behaviors in group or other social situations to exhibit greater emotional intelligence?

Adapted from an article entitled "Emotional Intelligence Key to Winning on 'The Apprentice'" published by *AScribe Health News Service,* March 22, 2004, p. NA.

who are realistic, logical, analytical, and decisive. ESTJs make good businesspeople or mechanics. INTJs are visionaries, who have original minds and a great drive for their own ideas and purposes. They are skeptical, critical, independent, determined, and often stubborn.

Although there is no hard evidence that the MBTI is a valid measure of personality, it is a helpful exercise in giving you some insight into your strengths and weaknesses, your aptitudes, career preferences and fit, and how you communicate with and are perceived by others.

Many of these dimensions have already been discussed in this chapter in terms of their importance in helping you achieve your communication purposes. Studies also indicate that high levels of emotional intelligence are better indicators of job performance than academic IQ (Robbins, 2001).

critical **thinking**

Using an Internet search engine, look for Web sites that offer free self-assessments, including those for locus of control, self-monitoring, emotional intelligence, the MBTI, and other personality traits. One useful Web site for this purpose is http://www.queendom.com, which offers a variety of personality, career, and IQ assessments, many free of charge.

TYPES OF MESSAGES

Just as business communication can be broken into four purposes, it can also be categorized into types of messages that generally correspond to those purposes. Business messages can be categorized as being primarily informative, persuasive, or goodwilled in nature. For example, a simple e-mail telling your colleagues of the time and place of next week's meeting is considered a routine informative message. Not all informative messages are simple, however. A special type of informative message, the negative or "bad news" message, often requires additional considerations so as not to damage your credibility or relationship with the receiver. A memo intended to motivate your supervisor to give you a promotion, or an oral presentation intended to move a client to buy your company's product, are examples of a persuasive message. A thank-you note is an example of a message intended solely for goodwill purposes.

These different types of messages require, to some degree, unique considerations as to the kind of information each should contain. These considerations are discussed in more detail in Chapter 6: Content.

Summary

- The purposes of business communication are to inform, to persuade, to convey goodwill, and to establish credibility. These purposes should be considered whether you are planning to communicate in writing, in person, using the phone, or via e-mail. It is also important to recognize that most business communication is generally not intended solely to achieve one purpose. Since most business communication includes some aspect of sales or persuasion, and since successful persuasion also often depends upon your relationship with your audience, i.e., goodwill and your credibility, you should pay attention to achieving all four purposes in many, if not all, of your messages.

- Your ability to establish credibility and create and maintain relationships with others depends a great deal upon your perception by others. Consequently, to be an effective communicator, you must have a large measure of self-awareness as well as insight into how others perceive and respond to you. If you become aware of weaknesses in certain areas that may negatively affect your abilities to communicate with others and ultimately your attainment of career goals, you have an opportunity to change for the better.

- Many textbook writers like to group message types in the same categories as the purposes of communication. These broad types of messages are informative, persuasive, and goodwill. A special type of informative message is the "bad news" message. Formulating these messages is discussed in more detail in Chapter 6: Content.

KEY TERMS

Aggressiveness, 32

Anticipatory socialization, 42

Appropriate feedback, 40

Assertiveness, 32

Avoidance, 32

Compliance-gaining, 28

Compliance-resisting, 28

Emotional intelligence, 44

Goodwill, 30

High self-monitors, 42

Impression management, 42

Influence, 27

Interpersonal dominance, 28

Interpersonal intelligence, 44

Intrapersonal communication, 44

Intrapersonal intelligence, 44

Locus of control, 45

Low self-monitors, 42

Reasoned skepticism, 40

Self-fulfilling prophecy, 44

DISCUSSION QUESTIONS

1. What characteristics do you look for to determine the credibility of your classmates or other speakers? What strategies can speakers use to establish credibility?

2. Instructors use a variety of compliance-gaining tactics in the classroom. What are some of these tactics? What are some strategies that students use to resist instructors' compliance-gaining efforts? Have you seen examples of these tactics used in the workplace or in other organizations of which you are a part?

3. What are the five components of trust? What role do these components play in your

relationships with family members? Friends? Coworkers?

4. How can self-esteem affect communication in interpersonal, small-group, and public speaking situations?

5. Discuss examples of the use of informative, bad news, persuasive, and goodwill messages in your own life. What characterizes excellent examples of each?

APPLICATIONS

1. Observe a live or recorded speech or oral presentation in which the speaker is attempting to persuade. How credible was the speaker? What did he or she say or do that helped to enhance or to detract from his or her credibility? How effective was the speaker in conveying goodwill or establishing a relationship with his or her audience? What did the speaker say or do that helped to build or detracted from his or her goodwill? Finally, how persuasive was the speaker? What did he or she say or do that supported or detracted from the talk's persuasiveness? How did the speaker's credibility or ability to convey goodwill affect his or her persuasiveness?

2. Find a persuasive business message at least one page in length. Do the content and appearance of the document enhance or detract from the writer's credibility? Did the writer use language or style to establish or maintain a relationship with the reader? If so, how? Were there words or phrases that detracted from the writer's goodwill? How successful was the writer in his or her attempts to be persuasive? What contributed to that success or detracted from it?

3. Using the Internet, search for free online self-assessments of emotional intelligence, locus of control, and self-monitoring. One place to start is at http://www.queendom.com. After completing the assessments and reading the results, summarize them and then write three goals for self-improvement for each personality measure, including your plan for achieving each of them.

4. Observe a group or watch an episode of a television show that focuses on group dynamics, such as *The Apprentice* or *Survivor*. Identify each of the group members, then analyze their behaviors, looking for clues to their level of emotional intelligence, their locus of control orientation, and their ability to self-monitor. How do these behaviors affect their membership in and relationship to others in the group?

5. Find an example of each of the following types of written messages: informative, persuasive, goodwill, and bad news. How are they alike? How do they differ in tone, content, and organization?

InfoTrac Activities

1. Using the keyword option in InfoTrac College Edition, type "corporate reputation." After reviewing some of the articles that are identified by your search, discuss the importance of reputation in the business world.

2. Using the keyword option in InfoTrac College Edition, type "emotional intelligence." Find and read the article entitled "Immature Execs: Hurting Results? Emotional Intelligence: Some Firms Measuring Manager's Self-Awareness," which was published in the May 3, 2004 edition of *Investor's Business Daily* on page A09. How might the observations made in this article be applied to your own career preparation?

Case Analysis

Although the revelations of accounting fraud, executive greed, and other questionable behavior by such companies as Enron, WorldCom, Arthur Andersen, Boeing, Ernst & Young, and Merrill Lynch happened more than three years ago, the public's trust in corporations is still low. In fact, in 2002, a public opinion survey of corporate reputation found people incredibly cynical about the latter company. "In my opinion," one respondent said, "Merrill Lynch is ethically on a par with Las Vegas and the Mafia" (Alsop, 2004, p. 21).

And while these scandals have brought attention to the need for greater efforts aimed at managing and maintaining reputation, corporations have been slow to effectively respond. According to a Harris Interactive and The Reputation Institute study conducted in 2003, three quarters of the respondents judged corporate America's image as either "not good" or "terrible" (Alsop, 2004). One respondent said, "I'm very disappointed in how money can rob the goodness in people" (Alsop, 2004).

The illegal and questionable practices of some corporations can taint the reputations of all of them. Ron Sargent, the CEO of Staples, was surprised by the questions he received from students while visiting a high school in suburban Boston. One student, who had apparently heard of the WorldCom scandal, asked, "Do you have a $6,000 shower curtain?" (Alsop, 2004).

According to Ronald Alsop, author of *The 18 Immutable Laws of Corporate Reputation: Creating, Protecting, and Repairing Your Most Valuable Asset,* organizations must respond to this situation by making reputation management a fundamental part of the corporate culture and value system. Reputation must be central to the corporate identity. However, just creating an ethics code may not effect such a transformation, as is evidenced by Enron, whose code and its cover letter contained the following statements:

- "We want to be proud of Enron and to know that it enjoys a reputation for fairness and honesty and that it is respected";

- "Ruthlessness, callousness and arrogance don't belong here";

- "We work with customers and prospects openly, honestly and sincerely"; and

- "We are dedicated to conducting business according to all applicable local and international laws and regulations . . . and with the highest professional and ethical standards."

According to Alsop, companies in crisis could avoid damage to their reputations if they were honest from the start and willing to apologize for their indiscretions or mistakes (2004). However, organizations may be hesitant to make such statements, since it may increase their risk of legal liability.

Still, some organizations have been willing to take such a risk. Such was the case of Texaco, when employees alleged that CEO Peter Bijur made prejudicial racial and religious comments about his colleagues in 1996 (Alsop, 2004). "I want to offer an apology to our fellow employees who were rightly offended by these statements; to men and women of all races, creeds and religions in this country; and to people throughout America and elsewhere around the world," Bijur stated. "I am sorry for this incident" (Alsop, 2004).

Demonstrating corporate responsibility may pay even bigger dividends, as was the situation when the manufacturer of Tylenol pulled their product from store shelves to protect consumers, even though in the end, it was not responsible for bottles of painkillers that had been tampered with. Stock prices for the company rose shortly after the announcement.

As the Tylenol situation shows, such actions may be worth the risk when it comes to maintaining a company's reputation. A more recent study by Harris Interactive and The Reputation Institute found that demonstrations of sincerity are the strongest indicator of a positive corporate reputation (Alsop, 2004). Unfortunately, when it comes to sincerity, organizations that demonstrate it are in the minority. Only about one third of the respondents indicated that they believed the 60 companies reviewed in the study were sincere in their communications (Alsop, 2004).

Discussion

1. How important is corporate reputation to you in terms of its effects on the products you purchase or organizations you may wish to work for?

2. Like some of the respondents of the surveys cited above, are you skeptical of some of the messages sent by organizations accused of illegal or unethical dealings?

3. Do you agree that honest and sincere communication is the best way for companies to deal with mistakes and potential scandals? Why or why not?

3
chapter **Audience Analysis**

GLOBAL MEDIA VENTURES, INC.: MEETING SHAREHOLDERS' NEEDS

Faced with the challenge of addressing shareholders at the annual meeting of GMV, CEO Kathryn Colter has yet to complete a first draft of her speech. In her talk, she needs to address the company's current financial situation as well as a well-publicized lawsuit brought against a president of one of the company's divisions. Although she has been able to identify the purposes she hopes to achieve in her speech, she is still uncertain about the information to provide, particularly in terms of details, the order in which she should present this information, and the specific language she should use.

discussion...

1. How many audiences should Ms. Colter consider in preparing her speech? Although the intended audience is shareholders, will other important audiences be privy to this information?

2. What are the demographic features of each of these audiences? Do they differ in any significant way?

3. What are the concerns, expectations, and interests of each of these audiences?

Analyze various business audiences to help you identify the interests, concerns, and questions you need to consider in formulating your messages.

Discuss the general kinds of business audiences and their needs.

Describe the difference between messages that are focused on the audience's needs and expectations and those that are conveyed from the writer's or speaker's perspective.

In this chapter, you will learn about the second element of devising a communication strategy: audience. After reading this chapter, you should know about the importance of considering your audience's knowledge, demographics, concerns, and interests; how to do so; and how to apply what you have learned in your communication practice.

On its face, audience analysis may appear to be a simple task. However, in practice it is often the most difficult task to carry out. People often have difficulty understanding the complex and sometimes nuanced differences of seemingly similar individuals. This difficulty may in part be caused by the strong ethos of individualism present in the culture of the United States. This emphasis on the individual can cause us to be *egocentric,* which means we may have difficulty empathizing with or understanding others' points of view. Learning how to see through another's eyes can be a difficult yet important skill in communicating successfully with others in the workplace as well as our personal lives. Without the ability to empathize with others and understand their views and feelings, we are unable to enact a dialogic model of communication.

When you are crafting important business messages or those to new audiences, you should analyze your audience or audiences. You can do so by considering a number of characteristics about your audience. These include:

■ Its demographics, including age, ethnicity, socioeconomic status, education level, and regional culture, if appropriate.

■ Its knowledge of your company, product, service, or the situation—the topics— you address in your message.

- Its interests in and attitudes about the topic of your message.

- Its concerns, reservations, or questions about the topic of your message.

- Its relationship with you, the communicator, and/or your company.

Your audience's preferences and characteristics should always guide the decisions you make regarding the creation and communication of successful business messages. The most successful messages construct win/win situations for both you and your audience; therefore, it is of critical importance to invest time in the analysis of your audience in order to achieve this goal.

AUDIENCE DEMOGRAPHICS

Demographics

Demographics is the statistical data about a particular population, including its age, income, education level, and so on.

Pligari / language

For those of you who have taken courses in marketing, the term **"demographics"** is probably a familiar one. Marketing and business communication have a great deal in common, since both fields are generally concerned with sales or persuasion. Just as you should consider a potential market's characteristics before you can go about creating a successful marketing plan or campaign, you should also consider a potential audience's characteristics before creating a message that has the best chance of success.

For example, if you are marketing home health products to seniors, you would consider the preferences of older people regarding advertising media, distribution of the product, and pricing. In the selection of an advertising medium, for instance, you would be more likely to select the local newspaper for a senior market than for a product aimed at young adults. Older people are more likely to read the local newspaper than teenagers and college students.

© ANTONIO MO/ PHOTODISC/ GETTY IMAGES

When crafting messages intended for an older audience, you would probably create messages with a more formal tone by avoiding the use of slang words. When considering visual presentation of a written message intended for older people, you might select larger font sizes to make the message more readable and illustrate the document with pictures of older people so that they can more easily identify with the message you are sending.

Our audience's ability to identify with the content of our messages should also be considered. As mentioned above, it is easier for people to identify with messages that contain photographs of people like themselves. Likewise, using examples and anecdotes that are easier for your specific audience to identify with or relate to can help to make your communication more effective. If you are writing messages aimed at persuading a female audience to purchase your company's automobile, for example, you would probably focus on the vehicle's reliability and safety. In contrast, if your audience is a male one, you might instead focus on the vehicle's performance as an attractive feature.

One issue to consider when analyzing an audience with which you will communicate is its demographics or its characteristics in regard to gender, age, ethnicity, or socioeconomic status, among others.

Your ability to provide the appropriate amount of information for your particular audience can affect your ability to fulfill your intended communication purposes, the first element of communication strategy discussed in Chapter 2: The Purposes of Business Communication. If you don't provide sufficient or relevant information aimed at meeting your audience's specific needs, you will be less able to fulfill your purposes of informing, persuading, conveying goodwill, and establishing your credibility. For these reasons, the elements of communication strategy are inter-dependent; they depend upon each other for the success of your messages.

Audience Knowledge

Your audience's knowledge about the topic of your message should be considered before crafting it. For example, if you are communicating to your co-workers about a product on which all of you have been working for the past six months, it is probably safe to use acronyms related to the product and your company, since you can assume that your audience is knowledgeable about the meanings of those abbreviations. However, if you are crafting messages for new customers, you should avoid the use of acronyms, since they are probably not familiar with their meaning. If you ignore this fact, your message will probably not be as successful in clearly communicating the information you intended.

Likewise, when communicating with audiences who lack knowledge of a product, service, or situation, you should provide more explanation or information. One common characteristic of inexperienced business communi-cators is that they are often unable to recognize the difference between their knowledge of a particular topic and that of their audience.

As stated earlier, your ability to provide the appropriate amount of information for your particular audience can affect your ability to fulfill your intended communi-cation purposes. Without adequate or relevant information aimed at meeting your audience's needs and expectations, you are less likely to fulfill your purposes of informing, persuading, conveying goodwill, and establishing credibility.

Audience Interests and Attitudes

As discussed in the previous section, "Audience Demographics," providing information about which your audience is interested and to which it can relate, is one of the strategies of successful business communication. In an oral presentation, for instance, if you focus on information that does not address your audience's interests, you are likely to lose its attention and fail at your communication purpose. The examples and content you provide in an oral presentation aimed at college students should differ significantly from those you might use in a presentation delivered to college administrators and intended to achieve a similar purpose.

Likewise, it is important to consider the attitudes of your audience toward the topic of your message in formulating a successful communication strategy. If your audience is reluctant to agree with the content of your message or the position you present, you should give some thought to how to present your message in a way that might overcome this reluctance.

communication 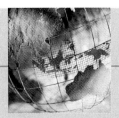 IN YOUR WORLD

One way of establishing credibility that is commonly used in popular media is through celebrity endorsements or *celebrity testimony*. Celebrity testimony is a statement made by a public figure known to the audience (Pearson et al, 2003, p. 436). Celebrity testimony has impact because we tend to identify with the people who are considered celebrities. In this regard, we see ourselves as having common ground with them.

Boon and Lomore's (2001) Canadian study of media figures as idols consisted mainly of actors (39 percent), musical artists (31 percent), athletes and dancers (15 percent), a few authors, and a number of other celebrities, such as Bill Gates and Oprah Winfrey. In the study, one fourth of the young people reported that they "engaged in efforts to change aspects of their personality to bring it more in line with that of their favorite idol," nearly 60 percent reported that "their idols had influenced their attitudes and personal values," and nearly half reported "that their favorite idol had inspired them to pursue one or more particular activities or pastimes—generally those in which their idols engaged" (p. 445).

Identification between celebrities and their fans is a powerful source of credibility and influence on thoughts and behaviors. However, such influence has its dangers, since celebrities may be used to endorse topics or products outside their areas of expertise.

Discussion

1. Who are the celebrities with whom you identify? Have you changed aspects of your personality, attitudes, or personal values to more closely mirror theirs?

2. Have you been influenced to buy products or services because celebrities endorse or use them?

One strategy is to think about the beliefs, values, or goals that you and your audience have in common. If you can begin your message by establishing agreement that you and your audience share the same interests or goals, you are attempting to show that you and your audience share some commonalities of belief that should reduce its resistance to the content and purpose of the remainder of your message. This strategy, which is referred to as establishing **common ground,** is generally effective in situations where your purposes include persuading and conveying goodwill. If you can focus your message on the benefits to your audience, you also are more likely to ensure a positive reception for your message. Again, this strategy is often used when your purposes are to persuade and convey goodwill.

Audience Concerns and Questions

You are not likely to be successful in attempts to persuade and convey goodwill if you do not effectively address your audience's concerns and questions. What is more frustrating than receiving a message that leaves you with many of your questions unanswered or your concerns completely ignored? Such lapses in

Common ground

Common ground is the interests, goals, and/or commonalities of belief that the communicator shares with the audience.

communication can negatively affect the relationship the communicator has with his or her audience, and his or her credibility. Such lapses can also negatively affect morale and productivity, both of which may impact a company's bottom line.

One of the biggest and most common concerns of business audiences is a lack of time. Most working people do not have enough time in their days to complete all the tasks that lie before them. Because of this problem, most businesspeople are challenged to find ways to do their jobs more quickly. One common strategy to make their use of time more efficient is to skim their written messages, whether delivered on paper or via e-mail.

One easy way to make your written messages more able to address your audience's concerns, at least regarding time pressures, then, is to make them easy to skim. To make written messages easier to skim, you should:

- Provide adequate "white space." White space is the blank space left in your written messages. Not only does white space visually cue the reader to a new topic, i.e., paragraph, it also makes a document look easier to read because you have provided "entry points" into the document. A message consisting of five short paragraphs appears much easier to read than the same message delivered in one large paragraph. Generally speaking, paragraphs should be kept short—seven or eight lines at a maximum—in business messages.

- Begin each paragraph with an accurate topic sentence. Readers can quickly skim the first sentence to understand the content of each paragraph. They can then make a decision about whether they want to read more of that paragraph.

- Use headings, if appropriate. Headings are generally reserved for more complex documents, i.e., those that cover several topics and require several paragraphs to adequately address each one. The proper use of headings will be discussed in more detail in Chapter 8: Visual Impression; however, it is important to remember that headings *do not* take the place of accurate topic sentences.

critical **thinking**

Identify an audience, an individual or group with whom you find it difficult to communicate. Describe the audience. What are its demographic features? What are its needs in the particular context that you communicate with it? Concerns? Expectations? How might taking these elements into consideration help you to communicate with this audience more successfully?

The Audience's Relationship with You

As discussed in Chapter 2: Purposes of Communication, an established, pleasant relationship with your audience can make successfully communicating with it much easier. As this chapter has addressed, you should also take into consideration your audience's concerns, interests, questions, and needs before communicating. However, understanding the value of these activities and how to accomplish them can be a challenge for us because of our cultural values, our awareness of our effect upon others, and knowledge of power differences between people.

Culture   From a communication perspective, cultures fall into two broad categories: collectivist or individualist. In fact, the individualism–collectivism continuum is thought by some scholars to be the most important dimension that distinguishes one culture from another (Hui & Triandis, 1986).

In **individualist cultures**, such as that of the United States, the autonomy of the individual is of paramount importance. Individualist cultures have an "I" focus in which competition, not cooperation, is encouraged; where decision making is predicated on what is best for the individual rather than the group; and individual initiative and achievement are highly valued (Samovar & Porter, 1995).

In contrast, in **collectivist cultures** commitment to the group is paramount. Therefore, these cultures prize cooperation rather than competition, individuals downplay personal goals in favor of advancing goals of the group, and privacy is sacrificed for the good of the group (Samovar & Porter, 1995).

All cultures have both individualist and collectivist tendencies, but one tends to predominate over the other (Gudykunst, 1991). The United States ranks number one in individualism. Venezuela is the most collectivist of countries, with Mexico, Thailand, Singapore, and Japan also ranking on the collectivist side of the continuum (Hofstede, 1980). Approximately 70 percent of the world's population lives in collectivist cultures. (Triandis, 1990).

These findings are important to business communicators for two reasons: 1) In our global economy, it is helpful to recognize that some people with whom we will communicate think about the world differently than we do; and 2) even within the United States, we often work in groups of various sizes, including larger organizations, in which their values must take precedence if we are to successfully achieve our goals. In fact, if groups are to succeed, individual goals and agendas should be of secondary, rather than primary, importance. Table 3-1 below summarizes the characteristics of individualistic and collectivist cultures.

Individualist cultures

An individualistic culture is one with an "I" focus, and in which competition is encouraged, rather than cooperation, and in which individual achievement is highly valued.

Collectivist cultures

A collectivist culture is one in which cooperation is encouraged, rather than competition, and in which individual goals are sacrificed for the good of the group.

TABLE 3-1. *Summary of cultural characteristics.*

SUMMARY OF CULTURAL CHARACTERISTICS

Individualistic Cultures	*Collectivist Cultures*
Value individual freedom; place "I" before "we."	Value the group over the individual; place "we" before "I."
Value independence.	Value commitment to family, tribe, and clan.
Value competition over cooperation.	Value cooperation over competition.
Value telling the truth over sparing feelings.	Value "saving face" by not causing embarrassment.
Examples: United States, Australia, Great Britain, Canada, Netherlands	*Examples:* Venezuela, Pakistan, Peru, Taiwan, Thailand

Individualist and collectivist values do not always conflict. They can be deployed in tandem to create win-win situations for the parties involved. If a group is successful in achieving its goal, that success should extend to the individuals who were part of making it happen.

This understanding is implicit in the recognition of the importance of goodwill and our relationship with our audiences to the achievement of our communication goals. However, since we live and work in an individualistic culture, it is sometimes difficult to adjust to this differing approach to the world and communicating with others. It takes a focus on the "we" and the "them" rather than the "I," although, as mentioned above, we generally can achieve our individual goals as well with an effective communication strategy and adequate communication skills.

Identify an audience from a different culture than your own. What cultural differences might affect the content of or your approach to a message intended for that audience?

Discrimination

A related issue is the development of an awareness of what constitutes discrimination. If we assume that others have the same experiences, beliefs, and values as ourselves, we suffer from what is called *ethnocentricism*. **Ethnocentrism** is the belief that your own cultural background, including ways of analyzing problems, values, beliefs, language, and verbal and nonverbal communication is correct. This belief can lead to an ignorance of and insensitivity to others, which, as has been discussed, can negatively affect your ability to communicate with others.

One result can be stereotyping. **Stereotypes** are generalized perceptions about certain groups of people or nationalities. These generalizations are often not useful for evaluating individuals, since they are prejudgments that are not based upon knowledge of a particular person. Therefore, these prejudices can damage your ability to communicate with specific individuals. Many prejudicial practices are also unlawful. Decisions based upon prejudiced views can be deemed discriminatory, and many states as well as the federal government have laws in place against discrimination based on race, age, ethnicity, religion, gender, and other characteristics. Language use can also be considered discriminatory or problematic in other ways. Telling off-color jokes in front of coworkers of the opposite sex can be seen as a form of harassment, which also can be considered unlawful.

Ethnocentrism

Ethnocentrism is the belief that one's own cultural background is correct, and that other cultures are somehow inferior.

Stereotypes

A stereotype is a generalized perception about a certain nationality or group of people.

What are some of the common stereotypes that you hold? Can you identify persons or situations in which those stereotypes do not hold? How might you gain more accurate knowledge about those persons you tend to stereotype?

Responsible Communication

Language can be used to exclude, denigrate, and discriminate against others. Language can also be used in more subtle ways that ignore or minimize the contributions of one sex in society. Such language use can be considered sexist and should be avoided in the professional workplace.

Some guidelines for avoiding sexist language use are provided below:

1. Replace *man* or *men* or words or expressions that contain either. For example, instead of *man* use human being, person, or individual.

2. Use gender-neutral terms when possible to designate occupations, positions, and roles. For example, instead of *businessman* use business owner, manager, executive, retailer, etc.

3. Refer to members of both sexes by parallel terms, names, or titles. For example, instead of man and wife use husband and wife. Rather than using men and ladies, use men and women.

4. Avoid the third person singular masculine when referring to an individual who could be of either sex. Instead of saying, "When a manager holds a meeting, he . . .", use the plural form of the pronoun when speaking generally, or the name of the person and the appropriate pronoun when communicating specifically. For example, "When managers hold meetings, they . . ." Or "When our manager, Ms. Johns, holds a meeting, she . . ."

5. Avoid language that disparages, stereotypes, or patronizes either sex. Avoid referring to adult females as *girls* or unmarried women as *spinsters* or *old maids,* for example. In addition, you should avoid terms such as *womanly, manly, feminine,* or *masculine* in ways that stereotypically associate certain traits with one sex or another.

Self-monitoring

As discussed earlier in this text, to be an effective communicator requires self-awareness and the ability to self-monitor to some degree. When you interact with others, it is helpful if you can be a participant as well as an observer in that process. In other words, you must be able to assume a detached view of yourself so that you can effectively perceive how others are responding to you, and adjust your communicative behavior if necessary to improve your ability to communicate with them. As discussed in Chapter 2, perception is an important part of communication because it affects the way we understand events, ourselves, and others.

The activity of observing ourselves in communicative situations is called self-monitoring. High self-monitors are those individuals who are highly aware of how others perceive them, while low self-monitors communicate with others with little attention to the responses they receive (Snyder, 1979). Impression management, or managing how others perceive us, can help us to achieve our goals through our communication practices, particularly in the image-conscious business world. When we use language that is appropriate for the occasion or situation, when we use nonverbal communication to demonstrate understanding or empathy, and when we wear clothing that is within appropriate guidelines for the situation, we increase the likelihood that we will be viewed as credible and professional, which can better enable us to achieve our goals.

Some believe impression management is unethical or deceptive. Another view is that impression management is necessary for successful communication in specific situations. It relies on the ability to develop an awareness of the appropriate behavior, communication practices, and self-presentation for a particular occasion or situation and adjust to meet those expectations to better ensure successful communication outcomes.

Three essential types of communication are used to manage impressions. They include manner, appearance, and setting (Wiggins, Wiggins, & Vander Zanden, 1993). Manner includes both verbal and nonverbal communication. Manner, for example, might be seen as indifferent, silly, businesslike, intelligent, immature, friendly, warm, and gracious. Your appearance may suggest a role you play, a value you hold, your personality, or how important you view the communication setting. Setting includes your immediate environment as well as public displays of who you are (your car, your clothes, your jewelry). (Verbal and nonverbal communication elements are discussed in more detail in Chapter 7.)

You are responsible for the effectiveness of your communication, and this responsibility entails being able to view your communication practices from your audience's perspective. To be an effective communicator, it is important to be able to perceive how others see us as well as whether they are interpreting our words and actions as we intend and to adjust our communicative behaviors to ensure understanding.

Power

Some of those who believe impression management is always unethical or deceptive may be subconsciously reacting to another element often present in business communication situations: a difference in the power distribution within particular relationships. In other words, you may believe it is unethical to adapt your behavior to the expectations of differing situations. But such a view not only ignores the fact that such adaptation may be a sign of respect for the practices and people involved in that situation, it may also ignore the workings of power in such situations.

It is important to recognize the existence of differing power relations, since it can severely impair our ability to communicate effectively. Power differences are systemic; that is, they are built into systems. Power differences are endemic to most organizations, institutions, and societies. In other words, a hierarchy of positions exists in most of these entities; some people have more prestige, more power, and sometimes more responsibility than others.

Because of these differences, it is important to identify who has the power and what that power is in any particular relationship or situation, because it can affect our choices and our ability to communicate effectively. One common error of judgment regarding power relations is that between an organization and its customers or clients. Many newcomers to an organization believe that the organization holds the power. However, that is not the case; without its customers or clients, an organization would cease to exist.

Being aware of differences in power is important, since being so may enable you to clarify your purposes for communicating. Is your intention to persuade your boss to see you as competent, or is it to undermine his or her effectiveness? You may not be aware of your intention for communicating, but your coworkers and perhaps your supervisor may. This knowledge can negatively affect your relationships with them as well as your credibility. In the end, it can negatively affect your ability to communicate to achieve your goals.

critical **thinking**

Identify a situation in which differences in power exist between the communicators. How do these differences affect the rules or expectations regarding how communication occurs in that situation? Have you seen instances where people failed to heed those rules or expectations? What was the outcome?

TYPES OF BUSINESS AUDIENCES

Business audiences are often quite different from those you may be familiar with in your academic experience. For example, most of your writing in school is probably intended for a teacher, who knows a great deal about the subject and who is required to read or listen to your message. However, this situation may not be true in the workplace. You may communicate with audiences who have little understanding of your topic, and it is very likely that you will write or speak to people who are not obliged to spend time reading or listening to your messages.

Another difference between communication in an academic setting and that in the workplace is that you may be communicating with a variety of people rather than a single person. If you are communicating with a number of people, they may have varying knowledge and needs. They may also differ in the strategies they use and skills they have for listening, reading, and processing information.

According to a typology devised by Olsen and Huckin (1991), in the workplace, you will generally be communicating with five types of audiences:

- Managerial.

- Non-expert.

- Expert.

- International or multicultural.

- Mixed.

Managerial Audiences

Managers are often the most important audiences you will communicate with, since they have decision-making ability and power over your future. According to Henry Mintzberg (1975), managers fulfill three types of roles that affect the way they communicate. These are *interpersonal, informational,* and *decisional* roles. The primary managerial role is interpersonal. Managers must lead and motivate a group of employees and often communicate with external audiences, such as suppliers, clients, and other departments. In this role, managers are also expected to disseminate information to these various audiences. Finally, managers must use information to make decisions that affect the various audiences with which they interact.

Because of the demands of these various roles, managers often have to deal with enormous time pressures. They have little time to listen or read carefully. Mintzberg's study found that 50 percent of the activities that executives engaged in lasted less than nine minutes. Many also treat message processing as a burden to be dispensed with as quickly as possible.

To ensure that your messages are received by managers, you can use a few strategies. For example, you can put key information up front where it is easily accessible. James Souther (1985) studied how managers read reports and found that all of them read the executive summary while most read the introduction, background, and conclusions sections. Only 15 percent read the body of the report. In general, managers look for the "big picture" and tend to ignore details.

Non-Expert Audiences

Non-expert audiences may be the most difficult to address, since they know little about a subject and will need more details. (Managers are also often non-experts, but they ignore details.) If you are communicating with a customer or client or perhaps a fellow employee from another department, you are probably communicating with a non-expert audience.

The problem with communicating with a non-expert audience is that you probably think like a specialist. That is, you may think about your topic differently than a non-expert and use different terminology than he or she might to discuss that topic. In addition, you may have difficulty identifying exactly what it is that a non-expert audience doesn't know, since you are so familiar with the topic.

As with managers, there are strategies you can use to communicate with non-expert audiences. These include:

1. Use a conventional mode of presentation.

2. Refer to common knowledge as much as possible without distorting the meaning of your message.

3. Provide an overview at the beginning of the document that explains what it is about and what it will cover.

4. Provide appropriate background information.

5. Include lots of definitions and explanations. For more complex concepts, you can incorporate examples, illustrations, and analogies to aid in clarifying their meaning.

Expert Audiences

Expert audiences are those who know as much about the topic as you do. Generally, expert audiences, who may be your peers, speak the same language as you do; that is, they understand the jargon associated with your profession. They also understand the same concepts, so you don't need to provide as much explanation and examples. In other words, they can fill in the gaps by making inferences about material that is common knowledge to both of you.

Strategies for communicating with expert audiences include:

1. Use standard technical terms.

2. Use a conventional format.

3. Emphasize data and display it in standard ways, using graphs, tables, equations, etc.

4. Make your points clear and easy to find.

5. Do not overstate your claims, since doing so may undercut your credibility.

International or Multicultural Audiences

The global economy and the growing diversity of the workplace mean that we will likely communicate with audiences whose first language may not be English and who have differing cultural interpretations of symbols and behaviors. When communicating with people whose first language may not be English, you should:

1. Avoid long or complicated sentences, since this may be more difficult for them to follow and comprehend.

2. Avoid slang, colloquial, or other idiomatic vocabulary uses. Such sayings as "in the ballpark," "under the weather," or "do an end run" may be interpreted literally by nonnative speakers of English, which will obviously cause confusion in terms of meaning.

Mixed Audiences

Even more difficult to communicate with are audiences who are composed of a variety of people: managers, non-experts, experts, and nonnative speakers or some combination of these. For example, you may be writing marketing literature that will be read by experts, non-experts, and nonnative speakers, or speaking to a group composed of the same individuals. There are two strategies for dealing with mixed audiences:

1. "Layer" a written document so that different sections are aimed at different audiences.

2. "Democratize" your message so that all audiences can understand all parts of it.

An example of the layered approach is a formal report. Such a report might include an executive summary, background information, and recommendation sections aimed at managers, while the body and appendices contain the details needed by specialists who are charged with implementing the report.

However, if you are speaking to a mixed audience, you may wish to use the "democratic" strategy. In this case, you aim your message primarily at the most important audience, but you add information in appropriate places that is needed for understanding by the other audiences. Although this approach is similar to the "layered" one, it differs in that you add in examples, definitions, and explanations throughout the message that are needed for understanding by all audiences.

AUDIENCE-CENTERED MESSAGES

Self-centered

Self-centered communication is that which fails to take into account the needs, concerns, or interests of its audience.

One of the most common manifestations of communication that does not take into account the needs, concerns, or interests of its audience is what is called **self-centered** communication. Although some of the reasons for self-centered communication might be attributed to cultural factors as well as developmental ones (i.e., the psychological maturity of the writer or level of self-awareness) another cause is our lack of awareness about our own message formulation process.

In the first draft of a document, for example, many of us write to ourselves in an attempt to figure out what it is we want to say. Such documents may begin without identifying a purpose or topic; in fact, in this process, we are often writing to identify the purpose or topic of our message for ourselves. In this stage of the writing process, beginning ideas may be general or abstract, or somewhat unrelated to the topic at which we eventually arrive.

In addition, such writing is generally not well organized. Paragraphs may cover several topics; they may lack topic sentences. But as we continue to write, we usually narrow our topic and then *voila!* We discover our purpose for writing. It is at this point that we may stop.

Much writing for school assignments, particularly essay exams, can often be described as self-centered writing. The writer begins to write about a general topic, perhaps making some detours along the way into related topics. In essay exams, the goal is often to get down on paper as many relevant ideas as possible—often in no particular order—to demonstrate to the teacher that you remember all the topics he or she discussed in class.

In this case, the teacher is required to read this jumble of thoughts, as it is part of his or her job, and interpret whether the jumble is adequate coverage of the topic. However, business people are not required to interpret such jumbles—they often don't have the time—and this is when it is important to recognize the difference between self-centered and audience-centered message formulation.

As indicated earlier, a self-centered message is generally the first draft of a document. The writer is writing to discover what he or she wants to say. In order to produce audience-centered writing, however, the writer must review the message to ensure that it contains the information that his or her reader needs to make sense of the message. In addition, the writer must ensure that the information is provided in a logical order and is easy to skim.

In self-centered messages, the main topic is often found at the end. As stated earlier, the writer—or speaker—may slowly narrow the topic, until he or she identifies the point he or she is trying to make. One of the first steps to create audience-based writing is to check whether the message should be turned upside down. Is the main topic or point at the end? If so, put it at the beginning of the second draft. Next, information that is not relevant to the main topic should be eliminated. Finally, what remains should be organized in a logical order and then proofread for correctness. (Creating well-organized messages will be discussed more fully in Chapter 5: Organization.)

Audience-centered

Audience-centered communication takes into account the needs, concerns, and expectations of the audience.

To achieve **audience-centered** messages, you should first identify your purposes for communicating; then ask what your audience's needs, concerns, and expectations are. These two steps are also the first in creating an effective communication strategy.

Résumés and application letters are excellent examples of the importance of audience-centered content and organization. Your planning for job application messages should always begin with analysis of your audience's needs, interests, questions, and concerns. Prospective employers want to know whether you can do the job they have to offer. To put it bluntly, they want to know what you can do for them. Employers are not offering jobs with the main objective of fulfilling your needs. Therefore, résumés and cover letters need to be focused on showing that you have the skills and experience for which they are looking. Employers want to know that you are the best-qualified applicant for the job.

The application letter below is a response to a job advertisement that asks for applicants who have a bachelor's degree in marketing and proven sales experience, as well as evidence of the ability to self-motivate. Ask yourself whether the letter focuses on providing the information an employer would need in making a decision about whether the writer is qualified for the position of customer service representative. How might the letter be improved?

FIGURE 3-1. *Self-centered employment letter.*

John Smith
234 Alabama St.
Worthy, TX 78000

January 5, 2005

Jane Summers
XYZ Parts Co.
Chicago, IL 30812

Dear Ms. Summers:

I am applying for the customer service representative position you advertised on the JOBLINE Web site. I believe the position will suit my personality and provide me the opportunities for which I am looking.

I am a fun-loving person who enjoys interacting with others. I believe the customer service position you are offering would enable me to meet a lot of new people. As the social chair of my fraternity, I excelled at creating fun ways for others to meet and interact.

I am looking for a position that will take advantage of my people skills and provide me opportunities for rapid promotion and pay raises. For those reasons, I believe your company will find me a good match for its needs.

Sincerely,

John Smith

FIGURE 3-1. *Self-centered employment letter.*

In your analysis, you should have noticed that it is not apparent that the applicant knows what the job qualifications are, nor does the letter clearly state that the applicant has those qualifications. More specifically, it does not provide evidence that shows that the applicant has all the qualifications for which the employer is looking. Rather than focusing on discussing the issues in which the reader is interested, it addresses only what the writer enjoys and wants. This letter is an extreme case of a message that is self-centered rather than audience-centered. The letter below is a better example of an audience-centered message.

FIGURE 3-2. *Example of an audience-centered employment letter.*

John Smith
234 Alabama St.
Worthy, TX 78000

January 5, 2005

Jane Summers
XYZ Parts Co.
Chicago, IL 30812

Dear Ms. Summers:

I am applying for the customer service representative position you advertised on the JOBLINE Web site. I am well qualified for the position, since I have the experience, education, and personal characteristics you are seeking.

Continued on next page.

FIGURE 3-2. *Continued*

My experience working for Teltek Manufacturing as a customer service intern will enable me to quickly become a productive member of your team. At Teltek, I used my interpersonal skills successfully to make six sales after one month of training.

I will complete my bachelor's degree in marketing this May. My education has provided me much useful knowledge that I can apply as a customer service representative for your firm. My courses in marketing, customer service, and business communication have provided me an excellent understanding of sales techniques and practice in the communication skills necessary to satisfy your business clients.

I am hardworking and have excellent time-management skills. While taking a full load of courses, I worked part time or interned during my entire college career. I was still able to participate in the Student Marketing Organization, eventually being elected president, and to maintain a 3.5 cumulative grade point average.

I will call you in a week to make an appointment to talk to you in more detail about how I might contribute to the continuing success of XYZ Parts Co.

Sincerely,

John Smith

In this letter, the writer addresses the specific skills that will help him to perform the job of customer service representative. The writer goes a step further in stating how his skills will contribute to the company's goals. This strategy, which focuses on the benefits that the writer provides, is a common one in persuasive messages. Finally, the document's organization also attends to the reader's needs. The document is easy to skim, since it is organized in short, concise paragraphs that are devoted to a single topic. The most important information is also provided first, to emphasize it. Typically, relevant work experience is the most persuasive evidence a job applicant can present to employers. The letter ends with a proactive statement by the writer that indicates he has high interest in the job as well as initiative.

The considerations you should make to create written messages that are focused on meeting your audience's needs can also be applied to oral communication. Oral presentations should be well organized so that your topics and content are clear, and the presentation is easy for your audience to follow. Your content should also be of interest to and meet the concerns and needs of your audience. By addressing your audience's needs, concerns, and interests you are more likely to achieve your own communication purposes.

critical **thinking**

Do you write to yourself to discover what it is you want to write? If so, have you recognized that this is just the first draft and that you may now need to edit the document heavily for others to read? Have you read writing that was clearly written from the writer's perspective and did not consider the reader? What were your reactions?

■ A second critical component of communication strategy formulation is the analysis of your audience or audiences. If your message is not tailored to meet the needs and expectations of your audience, it will likely not succeed in fulfilling its purposes. As simple as audience analysis appears, though, it can be difficult to perform effectively, because we often have difficulty understanding that others differ from us in many important and perhaps subtle ways. Because of the strong emphasis on the individual in United States culture, we may be egocentric, which means we have difficulty empathizing with or understanding others. To overcome this tendency, a systematic method for analyzing audiences exists. When analyzing an audience you should consider the following characteristics:

1. Its demographics, including age, ethnicity, socio-economic status, education level, and regional culture, if appropriate.

2. Its knowledge of your company, product, service, or the situation—the topics—you address in your message.

3. Its interests in and attitudes about the topic of your message.

4. Its concerns, reservations, or questions about the topic of your message.

5. Its relationship with you, the communicator, and/or your company. These considerations include the cultural background of the audience,

attempts to avoid discriminatory behaviors or language, efforts to pay attention to the power relationship between you and your audience, and the effects of your self-presentation and behavior on others.

■ Writing to business audiences differs dramatically from writing to an academic audience or teacher. Teachers are obliged to read your writing; they often are knowledgeable about the topic of your messages. However, this is not always true in a business setting, where people often face enormous time pressures. Because of these differences, you can use strategies to communicate more effectively with the various types of business audiences: Managerial, non-expert, expert, international or multicultural, and mixed.

■ It is important to recognize the difference between communication that is aimed at meeting your audience's needs and that is formulated from the perspective of the writer or the speaker. In the process of developing a message, we often create messages that help us to solve a problem or decide what we want to communicate. It is important to remember than this message probably is not structured in such a way as to best meet your audience's needs; it may also fail to contain the information for which the audience is looking. It is important to understand your own process for formulating messages, so that you can take the necessary steps to create audience-centered communication.

KEY TERMS

Audience-centered, 66
Collectivist cultures, 58
Common ground, 56
Demographics, 54

Ethnocentrism, 59
Individualist cultures, 58
Self-centered, 65
Stereotypes, 59

DISCUSSION QUESTIONS

1. When you are communicating with friends, what are their expectations regarding the content and delivery of messages that you convey to them, and how do you meet those expectations? How might you better meet their expectations?

2. When communicating with your parents, what are their expectations regarding the content and delivery of messages that you convey to them, and how do you meet those expectations? How might you better meet their expectations?

3. When communicating with your instructors, what are their expectations regarding the content and delivery of messages that you convey to them, and how do you meet those expectations? How might you better meet their expectations?

4. If you work or have worked part time, what have been the expectations of your supervisor regarding the content and delivery of the messages that you convey to him or her? How did you meet those expectations? How might you better meet them?

5. When you are applying for an internship or job, what are employers' expectations regarding the content and delivery of your employment messages? How can you meet these expectations?

APPLICATIONS

1. Using an Internet search engine, such as InfoTrac, identify an organization that was faced with a problem and needed to communicate how it was going to deal with that problem to various audiences who held different interests.

   a. Identify each audience that held an interest in the decision.

   b. Identify each audience's interests, expectations, beliefs, and concerns.

   c. Assess the effectiveness of the organization's messages in meeting each audience's concerns and addressing them in a satisfactory manner.

   d. In those cases in which the organization might have done a better job in addressing the audience's interests, explain how it might have better accomplished this task.

2. Your company is planning to announce a series of layoffs that will affect 10 percent of your employee population. Write an analysis that addresses the following issues:

   a. What audience concerns and questions would you need to address to attain the maximal communication outcome?

   b. To which purposes of communication would you need to attend?

   c. At what type of audience would the message be aimed?

   d. What would be the focus and content of your strategy to effectively communicate this decision to employees?

3. Using an Internet job search Web site, such as Monster.com, identify potential positions for which you might apply upon graduation. Review the job advertisements to identify the types of applicant qualifications and experience for which the organizations are looking. Choose one advertisement for which your skills best meet the organization's needs. Write an application letter that demonstrates that you understand the organization's needs and that you are qualified to fulfill those needs.

4. Identify a culture different from your own and using an Internet database, such as InfoTrac College Edition, research the beliefs, values, attitudes, and practices of its people. Write an essay in which you discuss these characteristics and compare them to those of your own culture. How

might these differences affect your communication with people of these cultures? What similarities do you hold that might provide opportunities for establishing common ground?

5. Interview a working professional in your intended field to discover how businesspeople's concerns, expectations, and communication practices differ from those of college students. Write an essay that discusses the results of your interview and concludes with a list of goals you intend to pursue to adjust your communication practices—written, oral, and nonverbal as well as those involving the use of technology—to better meet the expectations of the professional workplace.

InfoTrac Activities

1. Using InfoTrac College Edition, type in the words "audience analysis" in the keyword search engine. Visit some of the Web sites that you find to learn more about audience analysis.

2. Using InfoTrac College Edition, type in the words "demographic analysis" in the keyword search engine. Visit some of the Web sites that you find to learn more about how demographics are used to identify audience needs and preferences.

Case Analysis

In 2004, Dell Computer decided to move its product support for business accounts from India back to the U.S. in response to customer complaints about the service they were receiving.

The year before, the Central Texas Better Business Bureau logged 3,726 complaints against Dell from consumers throughout the U.S. That was up threefold from 2001, a period in which Dell's sales volume grew two and a half times. In comparison, Hewlett-Packard earned only 1,362 complaints nationwide for that entire three-year period, according to the Better Business Bureau of Silicon Valley. In 2003, the Texas attorney general's office logged 504 complaints against Dell and Dell Financial, more than double the pace of 2002.

According to a 2004 article in *Forbes* magazine, the reason for much of the discontent had to do with language and cultural rifts between disgruntled U.S. customers and Dell's bright but unseasoned Indian support staff. Another frustration was the reported unwillingness of Dell employees to depart from a script during customer service calls.

Dell was among the first computer makers to route customer service and technical support calls to India in an effort to cut labor costs. Dell set up its first center in Bangalore in 2001 and opened a second site in Hyderabad two years later. Complaints about Dell's telephone support from business customers began at that time.

M. D. Ramaswami, who helped establish Dell's Bangalore center, is proud of Dell's early hires. "We put them through eight weeks of training—four weeks around accent and culture and another four weeks around Dell products," says Ramaswami, who now runs his own consultancy in Bangalore. "The biggest challenge was working on the accent and culture. That challenge still remains—for all companies across the board."

Discussion

1. How might audience analysis have helped Dell executives avoid this problem?

2. What tools might have been used to conduct this analysis?

Adapted from an article written by Elizabeth Corcoran and entitled "Unoutsourcing: Dell Moves Product Support Back to US" that appeared in the May 10, 2004 edition of *Forbes* on page 50.

chapter 4

Channels of Communication

GLOBAL MEDIA VENTURES, INC.: MANAGING MEETINGS

Roberto Villanueva has been a manager at GMV's struggling television division for only three months. Villanueva's ten years of experience provides him with a breadth of knowledge of the types of challenges faced by the television industry as well as efforts to deal with such challenges. Villanueva also has worked in a variety of organizational cultures with many individuals of differing skill levels, attitudes, and objectives.

But such experience does not cancel out the fact that he is a newcomer to GMV's television operations. Some individuals resent the fact that he was chosen for the job over them; others are afraid that he may attempt to change current practices and policies with which they have grown comfortable. Others may just need time to develop a sense of trust in their new boss.

Villanueva has spent his short tenure with GMV talking to customers and employees in an effort to identify what is working and what isn't. He wants to hold a meeting with his staff members so they can discuss what changes may need to be made to meet some of the challenges the group is facing.

discussion...

1. To plan a successful meeting, what steps should Villanueva take to attempt to ensure cooperation from attendees?

2. During the meeting, what might Villanueva do to decrease any uneasiness that attendees may be feeling regarding his leadership, the direction of the division, and any changes that may affect them?

Learn about the elements that affect the quality of communication that occurs within an organization, including corporate culture and structure, and formal and informal communication networks.

Briefly revisit the basic communication model in terms of channel choice considerations. (Models of communication were discussed in more detail in Chapter 1.)

Learn about the considerations you should make in selecting a communication channel. Based upon this information, you will learn how to select the best channel and medium for delivery of your message.

Explore the challenges of establishing effective group communication, a critical channel of communication in today's business world.

Learn how to plan and execute effective meetings, another important channel of business communication.

After you have identified your purposes for communicating and analyzed your audience's needs, expectations, and concerns, the next step in formulating a successful business communication strategy is to decide which channel of communication is the best for delivering your message. Whether you choose to use a written or oral channel, you first should identify the purposes of your communication; analyze your audience's needs, concerns, and expectations; and consider the content, organization, and style and tone of your message in order to achieve your purposes and best meet your audience's needs.

ORGANIZATIONAL COMMUNICATION

"Communication is the lifeblood of any organization, big or small," says Ronald Gross, head of Censeo Corp., a Maitland human resources consulting firm (Wessel, 2003). However, a company's policies, programs, and structures can support or interfere with good communication. The context within which communication occurs can also affect how, what, when, and whether we should communicate. In short, the corporate culture of an organization can affect the quality of communication that occurs within it. In this section, these issues—in addition to the types of communication networks that exist in organizations, formal and informal—are discussed.

Context and Environment

All communication occurs within a particular context or situation. For this reason, it is important to spend some time analyzing the context, situation, or environment within which communication takes place to formulate an effective strategy for that particular set of circumstances.

There are several dimensions to context, including physical, social, chronological, and cultural. The *physical* context or setting can influence the content and quality of interaction. For example, if you were to ask your boss for a raise, the effect of the setting might dramatically affect your chances for success. How might the following settings affect such an interaction: In the boss's office? At a company picnic? Over lunch at a restaurant? In your work area, with others observing?

The *social* context refers to the nature of the relationship between the communicators, as well as who is present. In the same situation mentioned above, imagine how the relationship between your manager and yourself might affect your request for a raise if:

- You and the manager have been friends for several years, as opposed to a situation in which you and your manager have no personal relationship.

- You are the same age as your manager *or* she or he is 15 years older (or younger) than you.

- You and the manager have gotten along well in the past, compared to a situation in which you and the manager have been involved in an ongoing personal conflict.

The *chronological* context refers to the ways time influences interactions. For example, how might the time of day affect the quality of an interaction? How might the communicator's personal preferences regarding time affect an interaction? Is it a busy time of year for employees and managers? Has there just been a major layoff, downsizing, or profit loss? In this last case, you might want to put off your request for a raise until conditions improve.

Organizational culture

Organizational culture is the system of shared meanings and practices within an organization that distinguish it from other organizations.

The *cultural* context includes both the organizational culture as well as the cultural backgrounds of the people with whom you may be communicating. **Organizational culture** refers to a system of shared meanings and practices held by members that distinguish the organization from other organizations. Organizational culture can affect the means and style of communication that takes place in an organization. (Organizational culture is discussed more fully in the following section.)

A person's cultural influences also can affect the kind and quality of communication that takes place and can help to determine approaches that will be more effective. For example, young people have different expectations than seniors, Hispanics have different expectations than Asians, Californians have different expectations than people from the Midwest or East Coast, and men may communicate differently than women.

Environmental factors may also affect what should be communicated and how. For example, if the economy is doing poorly, some messages may be inappropriate or may have little chance for success. If you work in a highly litigious environment or one that is strongly regulated, constraints may exist for what you can communicate and how. Larger social, political, or historical events may affect whether certain messages are appropriate or have a chance of success.

Organizational Structure and Culture

Organizational structure and policies that affect organizational culture affect the quality of communication within an organization. The culture of a business provides part of the *context* (explained in the previous section) for interpreting the meaning of everyday organizational life, as well as determining what are considered appropriate messages and the proper or expected ways to convey them.

Research suggests that there are seven primary characteristics that, when taken as a whole, capture the essence of an organization's culture (O'Reilly et al, 1991; Chatman & Jehn, 1994). These are:

- **Innovation and risk taking.** The degree to which employees are encouraged to innovate and take risks.

- **Attention to detail.** The degree to which employees are expected to exhibit precision, analytical skills, and attention to detail.

- **Outcome orientation.** The degree to which management focuses on results or outcomes rather than on the techniques and processes used to achieve these outcomes.

- **People orientation.** The degree to which management decisions take into consideration the effect of outcomes on people within the organization.

- **Team orientation.** The degree to which work activities are organized around teams rather than individuals.

- **Aggressiveness.** The degree to which people are aggressive and competitive rather than easygoing.

- **Stability.** The degree to which organizational activities emphasize maintaining the status quo rather than focusing on change.

Each of these characteristics is listed in Table 4-1 and exists on a continuum from low to high. Appraising the organization on each of these characteristics can provide a picture of the organization's culture.

TABLE 4-1. *Primary characteristics of organizational culture.*

PRIMARY CHARACTERISTICS OF ORGANIZATIONAL CULTURE

1. The degree to which employees are encouraged to be innovative and take risks.

2. The degree to which employees are expected to exhibit precision, analysis, and attention to detail.

3. The degree to which management focuses on results or outcomes rather than on the techniques and processes used to achieve those outcomes.

4. The degree to which management decisions take into consideration the effect of outcomes on people within the organization.

5. The degree to which work activities are organized around teams or groups rather than individuals.

6. The degree to which people are aggressive and competitive rather than easy-going and cooperative.

7. The degree to which organizational activities emphasize maintaining the status quo compared to promoting change.

Source: O'Reilly, C. A. III, Chatman, J., & Caldwell, D. F. (1991). People and organizational culture: A profile comparison approach to assessing person-organization fit. *Academy of Management Journal*, Sept., pp. 487–516.

More generally speaking, the culture of business can be characterized as typically having a bias toward action, a demand for confidence, and a results orientation (Peters & Waterman, 1982). The culture of business can be seen in everyday office interactions. Being knowledgeable about an organization's culture can help you gauge the type and quality of communication that takes place as well as whether you are a good match with an organization.

Although what constitutes a healthy organizational culture can be debated, Spencer (1986) gives us a description of a good organization that includes communication behaviors and attitudes that contribute to positive communication. According to Spencer, good organizations are places where authentic (as opposed to pretentious) people:

- Listen well.

- Respect the validity of others' experience.

- Feel free to be assertive.

- Have a clear sense of direction and control.

- Get good feedback about their performance.

- Feel valued as intelligent human beings.

In addition, good organizations provide opportunities for employees to voice their opinions and concerns; encourage conversations that are simultaneously supportive and critical; promote a positive experience of work; and are able to remain profitable in a competitive marketplace. Many of the characteristics of good organizations are elements of communication, including the ability to listen well, provide good feedback, and communicate assertively yet respectfully with others.

Supportive climate

A supportive climate is one in which individuals do not feel threatened.

Such organizations have also been described as having a **supportive climate** (Gibb, 1961). An organization that exhibits a supportive climate is one in which you feel free from threat. You perceive that although the content of your communication may be evaluated and even rejected, no one is passing judgment upon your personal worth. In the absence of threat and perceiving that others are open and honest, you freely express your opinions and feelings, trust others, and are open to them.

In contrast, according to Eisenberg and Goodall (1993, p. 13), unhealthy work conditions include:

- Authoritarian and detailed supervision.

- Tasks characterized by restrictions on employees' abilities to use resources.

- Work production systems that do not provide opportunities to contribute initiative, responsibility, or personal knowledge to the job.

- Limited opportunities for employees to exercise influence in the planning and organizing of tasks.

- Tasks that deprive the individual of the self-determination of work rate and methods for carrying out the work.

- Tasks that limit human contacts during work.

Such an organization can be characterized as one that does not value its employees as intelligent human beings and does not trust them to make responsible, knowledgeable decisions. Although these characteristics have little to do with communication, they do concern a characteristic that is necessary for effective communication: trust.

Defensive

A defensive climate is one in which individuals feel threatened.

Just as healthy organizations are characterized as having supportive climates, unhealthy ones are characterized as having **defensive** ones. A defensive climate is one in which you feel threatened. You perceive that your communication can be used against you, carefully edit your comments to protect yourself from real or anticipated threat, and mistrust others, and therefore, are closed to them. The table below distinguishes those behaviors that characterize defensive and supportive organizational climates.

TABLE 4-2. *Climates of organizational communication.*

CLIMATES OF ORGANIZATIONAL COMMUNICATION

Defensive	Supportive
1. *Evaluation*. To pass judgment on another.	1. *Description*. Nonjudgmental. To ask questions, present feelings, refrain from asking the other to change his or her behavior.
2. *Control*. To try to do something to another, to try to change behavior or attitudes of others.	2. *Problem Orientation*. To convey a desire to collaborate in solving a mutual problem or defining it, to allow the other to set his or her goals.

Continued on next page.

TABLE 4-2. *Continued*

3. *Strategy.* To manipulate another, to engage in multiple and/or ambiguous motivations.

3. *Spontaneity.* To express naturalness, free of deception, straightforwardness, uncomplicated motives.

4. *Neutrality.* To express a lack of concern for the other, the clinical, person-as-object-of-study attitude.

4. *Empathy.* To respect the other person and show it, to identify with his or her problems, to share his or her feelings.

5. *Superiority.* To communicate that you are superior in position, wealth, intelligence, etc., to arouse feelings of inadequacy in others.

5. *Equality.* To be willing to enter into participative planning with mutual trust and respect, to attach little importance to differences of worth, status, etc.

6. *Certainty.* Dogmatic, to seem to know the answers, wanting to win an argument rather than solve a problem, seeing one's ideas as truths to be defended.

6. *Provisionalism.* To be willing to experiment with your own behavior, to investigate issues rather than taking sides, to solve problems, not debate.

Source: Gibb, J. (1961). Defensive communication. *Journal of Communication 11:* 141–148.

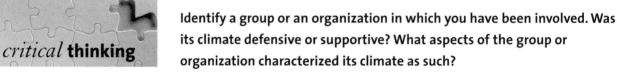

critical **thinking**

Identify a group or an organization in which you have been involved. Was its climate defensive or supportive? What aspects of the group or organization characterized its climate as such?

Formal Communication Networks

An organization's formal communication network is typically reflected in its structure or organizational chart. Such charts summarize the lines of authority; each position in the hierarchy represents a link in the chain of command, and each line represents a formal channel for the transmission of official messages. Information may travel three ways in an organization: down, up, and horizontally.

- **Downward flow.** Organizational decisions are usually made at the top and then flow down to the people who will carry them out. Most of what flows downward is intended to maintain the formal organizational culture and the company's overall profitability.

- **Upward flow.** Because the employees who perform the work of the organization often have the most information, managers should have access to their feedback to improve processes, productivity, morale, decision making, and ultimately, organizational profitability or sustainability. According to Wessell (2003), since upward communication may be less formalized than downward flow, it "has to be constantly fostered and reinforced, so that people see it's something that's valued."

- **Horizontal flow.** Communication also flows within and between departments. This information helps departments and employees share and coordinate their activities to improve productivity and the quality of decision making.

Informal Communication Networks

Every organization also has an informal communication network—the grapevine—that supplements formal channels. Most of this information is conveyed through casual conversations between employees. Although these conversations may also deal with personal matters, 80 percent of the information that travels through the grapevine deals with business.

Savvy managers will pay a great deal of attention to the informal communication network within an organization and will utilize it to disseminate accurate information to employees. If ignored, the informal communication network is another means by which managers can lose control of the flow of information within an organization.

However, awareness of the informal communication network should be tempered with recognition of the need for flexibility. According to Eric M. Eisenberg and H. L. Goodall, Jr. (1993), organizations must be flexible to remain competitive. Strict rules and procedures can be a hindrance to this needed flexibility in the current business climate, which is characterized by the constant of change. Without the time to formalize some relationships, their effectiveness often depends upon the trust that can develop over time between employees (Eisenberg & Goodall, 1993, p. 235). As you may recall from the discussion of organizational culture above, trust is the characteristic that was typically lacking in organizations that exhibited unhealthy working conditions.

CHANNELS AND THE BASIC COMMUNICATION MODEL

As discussed in Chapter 1, traditional models of communication identified a sender, a receiver, and the information being sent as the three parts of a message. One problem with this model of communication is that it assumes that information delivery is a one-way process: that a sender communicates information, which is then received unaltered by the person at the other end of the chain. The second problem with this model, then, is that it fails to take into account *interpretation* of the meaning of the message that is sent. In other words, the sender may intend to convey a piece of information, but that does not mean that the receiver receives that information with the meaning the sender intended.

For that reason, a more accurate model of communication recognizes that both parties in a communicative situation are always sending and receiving information at the same time. That means that the flow of communication is often continuous, simultaneous, and circular. In face-to-face situations, much of this information is delivered in the form of nonverbal communication cues. Some scholars claim that as much as 93 percent of the information we receive in face-to-face communication situations comes in the form of nonverbal information. The information that is sent is then *interpreted* by the person receiving it. This means that the sender should not assume that the information being sent was received as he or she originally conceived the idea in his or her head.

This is true for both oral and written messages. According to Lorand B. Szalay,

> *The idea itself does not really travel, only the code; the words, the patterns of sound or print. The meaning that a person attaches to the words received will come from his [sic] own mind. His [sic] interpretation is determined by his [sic] own frame of reference, his [sic] ideas, interests, past experiences, etc.— just as the meaning of the original message is fundamentally determined by the sender's mind, his [sic] frame of reference.*

This explanation underscores the importance of analyzing the audience for our messages, since it is its interpretation of the information that will ultimately determine our success. In addition, because interpretation of the information we receive is constantly occurring, it is the sender's responsibility to ensure that the receiver interprets the message as it was intended.

Information can be sent using a variety of means, which are known as the *channels* of communication, as shown in the diagram below.

FIGURE 4-1.
The Communication Model and Channels of Communication.

Choosing the right channel and medium for business messages is a communication skill that often should involve strategic planning. In the next section, considerations for selecting the best channel to communicate a message will be discussed.

CHOOSING A COMMUNICATION CHANNEL AND MEDIUM

Broadly speaking, three channels of communication exist: written, oral, and nonverbal. However, these broad categories can be broken down further; written communication can be disseminated using a variety of media or forms, including memos, letters, e-mails, faxes, press releases, company Web sites, and reports. Oral communication can also use various media or forms, such as face-to-face or interpersonal, the telephone, voice messages, teleconferences and videoconferences, speeches, and meetings. Typically, nonverbal communication supplements oral forms. The box below lists the issues that should be considered when selecting the channel and medium that best suits a particular communication situation.

TABLE 4-3. *Channel selection considerations.*

CHANNEL SELECTION CONSIDERATIONS

Richness vs. leanness

Need for interpretation (ambiguity)

Speed of establishing contact

Continued on next page.

TABLE 4-3. *Continued*

Time required for feedback

Cost

Amount of information conveyed

Permanent record

Control over the message

These considerations are discussed in more detail in the following sections.

Richness vs. Leanness

Some channels of communication provide more information than others. Generally the richest channels of communication provide nonverbal information in addition to that provided in written or oral form. For this reason, the richest channel of communication is face-to-face or what is often called *interpersonal communication*. Face-to-face communication provides participants a rich source of information, including vocal cues, facial expressions, bodily movement, bodily appearance, the use of space, the use of time, touching, and clothing and other artifacts.

In addition, face-to-face communication provides opportunities to facilitate feedback and to establish a personal focus. These aspects also contribute to the richness of interpersonal communication as a channel of communication.

Face-to-face communication is thus particularly useful for job interviews, where presumably the prospective employer is interested in gathering as much information as possible from applicants. Similarly, personnel issues involving single individuals may best be explored in a face-to-face communication situation, because such persons might provide more information about their feelings or attitudes, or nonverbal clues to issues that are preventing them from functioning at their highest levels.

Other channels of communication that provide access to nonverbal information are oral presentations, meetings, and group work. However, opportunities for checking the accuracy of interpretation of information may be more limited in these situations, because one person may exercise control over the exchange of information.

Written communication may provide less access to nonverbal forms of communication. However, tone can be communicated in writing and can be an indicator of the writer's attitude. For this reason, you should *never* write messages when you are experiencing negative emotions that may adversely affect your relationship with your audience. If you are experiencing negative emotions in response to a workplace situation, you should wait until you have calmed down before you respond in writing.

Perhaps one of the leanest channels of communication is a printed form, such as a job application form. Most forms ask for information that is very specific and limited in scope. Furthermore, forms oftentimes provide a limited amount of space in which to provide information. Because of the specificity and space limitations, forms often provide little opportunity to gather information other than the least amount needed to fulfill a particular task.

Need for Interpretation

Some channels of communication are more ambiguous or leave more room for interpretation of the message being sent than others. Nonverbal communication may be the most ambiguous channel of communication, since it requires the audience to interpret almost the entirety of the message. Nonverbal communication is difficult to interpret for a variety of reasons. First of all, one nonverbal code may communicate a variety of meanings. For example, you may stand close to someone because you are in a crowded room, you are having difficulty hearing him or her, or you are attracted to the person. Studies indicate that receivers of nonverbal cues can often only guess about the meaning of those cues (Motley & Camden, 1988).

Similarly, nonverbal communication can be difficult to interpret because a variety of codes may communicate the same meaning. This problem is particularly apparent when cultural differences come into play in a communication situation. In a public speaking situation, for example, you might show respect for the speaker by looking directly at the speaker, while in some cultures listeners show respect when they avert their eyes from the speaker.

A third issue that may affect a person's ability to interpret nonverbal codes accurately is intentionality. Some nonverbal codes are sent intentionally, while others are unintentional. If you smile at a friend, you are intentionally showing him or her that you are glad to see that person. However, the same nonverbal cue may be sent unintentionally yet interpreted as intentional. You might be thinking about a pleasant experience you had the night before and unintentionally smile. But if this occurs while you are walking down the street, the stranger approaching you may interpret this unintentional signal as an intentional cue of interest in him or her.

For this reason, face-to-face communication may be more ambiguous than other channels of communication. Furthermore, depending on our sensitivity to nonverbal communication codes, we may overreact to certain nonverbal messages or we may be somewhat or completely unaware of such information.

In contrast, written communication has the potential for being the least ambiguous channel of communication, particularly if it is prepared by a highly skilled writer who is able to precisely encode such a message. In other words, such a writer has an excellent command of the language and its correct usage. For this reason, many official or legal messages are delivered in the form of a written document. Similarly, instructions are often provided in written form.

Speed of Establishing Contact

Another important consideration, particularly in the business world, is the time it will take for a message to be delivered. As the old saying goes, time is often money. It is for this reason that electronic forms of communication have become so popular. Using the telephone, writing an e-mail message, or sending a fax are almost instantaneous channels of communication. In contrast, sending a written message or package by mail may take days. If you wish to communicate with someone who lives or works in another state or nation, it may also take days to arrange a face-to-face meeting. For these reasons, electronic channels of communication have become extremely useful in the modern workplace.

Time Required for Feedback

Just as we may need to contact someone immediately, we may also need a response from that person just as rapidly. The most rapid forms of communication, as explained above, are generally electronic. However, depending on the person with whom you are communicating, his or her personality, and your relationship, communicating with a person via an electronic channel does not guarantee prompt feedback. In other words, people generally have communication channel preferences and differing communication practices. Some people may prefer face-to-face communication and thus may be more responsive to messages delivered using this channel. Others may prefer the telephone, while still others may prefer to be contacted by e-mail. Just because you prefer e-mail does not mean that the person you are communicating with has a similar preference and will respond to your message immediately.

For these reasons, you should take into consideration your audience's preferences when selecting a communication channel. If you need a response immediately and your audience is in the cubicle next to yours, face-to-face communication may be the fastest means of receiving the information you need.

Cost

Many channels of communication are relatively inexpensive for business users. Mail, e-mail, telephones, and faxes are generally considered inexpensive forms of communication. Face-to-face communication, although the richest channel, can be quite expensive if those you wish to communicate with are located at a distance from yourself in another city, state, or country. If you wish to communicate with a large number of people who are not in close proximity, the costs of communicating interpersonally can be quite high. This is because such meetings involve the costs of travel, accommodations, and lost time.

Businesses have been exploring more cost-effective means of communicating with audiences who may be dispersed around the world. Some of these channels, such as teleconferencing, are relatively inexpensive since communication can occur over existing phone lines. However, teleconferencing does not provide all the information that face-to-face meetings might provide. For these reasons, numerous companies are experimenting with video-teleconferencing. Costs for such services are dropping and the quality of information transmitted is constantly improving, but for now, video-teleconferencing requires a capital outlay for which generally all but the largest companies have been unwilling to heavily invest, particularly since it is a medium that is still developing.

Amount of Information Conveyed

The best channel for conveying large amounts of information is generally a written one. One of the reasons is that most of us are generally poor listeners. Studies indicate that we retain only about 10 percent of what we hear. Therefore, if you want people to have the opportunity to process and remember the information you have to deliver, particularly if the message is long or complex, it is best delivered using a written channel.

You can see this channel choice consideration practiced in everyday news delivery. If you want more information about what is happening in your community, state, country, or the world, you will probably read a newspaper or newsmagazine or visit an Internet site devoted to news coverage. If you want the least amount of information about these issues, you might watch a television newscast or listen to a radio news program. Typically, less information is delivered by these electronic, oral channels, because they appeal to people who do not have much time to invest in such information or do not wish to invest much time, who have short attention spans, or who do not like to read. Bottom line, these channels generally deliver less information about the topics they address.

For these reasons, if you have a fairly large quantity of complex or detailed information to deliver, a written communication channel is the best, because it provides readers the opportunity to take the time necessary to process that information, oftentimes at their own convenience.

Need for a Permanent Record

A related consideration is the need to keep a permanent record. Businesspeople are often involved in situations where they must keep records of what occurred during various work activities throughout the day or week. These situations include the need to record what occurred at a department meeting, an employee's work history, the findings of an audit of a client's financial records, and an employee's travel expenses. Most legal documents, including contracts, use the written channel of communication for this reason: the need to maintain a record. E-mail messages, if stored and backed up properly, can also serve as a record.

Control over the Message

Written channels of communication also are the best choice when you wish to maintain greater control of the message that you send. The reason: if information is presented orally and interpersonally, you have a greater chance of persons who disagree with you or who wish to discredit you speaking out. That is why many negative messages are sent using a written channel of communication.

For example, if you must tell a job applicant that he was not selected for the position for which he recently interviewed, you can maintain control over the act of delivering that information by doing so in the form of a letter. Although calling the person to deliver the message might exhibit greater goodwill on your part, because you have taken the time to interact using a channel that enables you to utilize some nonverbal codes (vocal cues), you also risk a situation that might spin out of control if the person does not take the news well or wishes to take more of your time to find out why he was not selected. In this case, you also may be put in a position to explain the decision more fully. However, by sending a polite letter, you are able to convey the same basic message without the risk of losing control of the situation.

Similarly, in crisis situations, some companies refuse to speak to the media for fear of losing control of the message or releasing information that may be damaging. These situations may be handled by using the written communication channel to send a press release to the media. The press release delivers information but does not provide an opportunity for the receiver to question the communicator and potentially lose control of the message that the company intends to convey. Oral channels of communication are often riskier, because they expose the speaker to differences of opinion, conflict, and personalities that may be difficult to control.

SMALL-GROUP COMMUNICATION

During the 1980s, an explosion occurred in the use of teams in organizations. One of the goals of this use of teams was to do "more with less" in an era of shrinking resources and increased competition. Companies that have traditional, centralized, hierarchical structures are less efficient and responsive to rapidly changing market conditions.

Despite the widespread enthusiasm for teams, the definition of what constitutes a team remains ambiguous. However, there are two types of teams in organizations: project teams and work teams. *Project teams* are standing groups that help coordinate the successful completion of a particular project, product, or service. One type of project team is comprised of people working to design and develop a new product. Members of such a team may include engineers, manufacturing experts, marketing specialists, and quality assessment personnel, among others. In such teams, each member is an expert in one aspect of the project necessary for its success.

Work teams are intact groups of employees who are responsible for a "whole" work process or segment that delivers a product or service to an internal or external customer. For example, an eight-member work team at a southern California aerospace firm is responsible for all metallizing of components in the company. The team is housed together, has mapped its internal workflow, and is continually improving its work process. Work teams are characterized by their degree of empowerment or ability to self-direct or self-manage their work processes. However, true self-directed work teams are rare in the United States because of our history of use of the classical, hierarchical organizational structure. In other words, such teams would require a radical reframing of the power relationships in organizations, which few members of management are genuinely prepared to examine (Eisenberg & Goodall, 1993, p. 286).

Regardless of whether an organization uses teams, group communication skills are necessary in any organization, because the group is the fundamental unit of social organization. Yet achieving effective group communication is generally a challenge not only because of issues of empowerment and self-direction but because of our cultural legacy. "This [increased use of groups] is perhaps the most difficult principle to adapt to Western, particularly U.S., organizations. Our romantic obsession with rugged individualism, our cultural preoccupation with individual initiative, achievement, and reward, and our philosophical and moral belief in the value of the individual all mitigate against our willing participation in groups" (Eisenberg & Goodall, 1993, p. 187).

Christopher M. Avery, author of *Teamwork is an Individual Skill* (2001), agrees with this sentiment. "It's a social design problem. Teams are not unnatural, but we've made it difficult by the way we've socialized and organized ourselves [in our culture]."

However, according to Patrick M. Lencioni, author of *The Five Dysfunctions of a Team* (2002), the challenges of creating effective groups can be overcome. Lencioni's five dysfunctions of a team are:

- **Absence of trust.** Without the willingness to be vulnerable to one another—to admit weaknesses, to acknowledge failures, to ask for help, to genuinely apologize from time to time—team members will suspect one another of being disingenuous and protective, Lencioni says.

- **Fear of conflict.** Team members who don't trust one another can't engage in meaningful debate. Although some conflict is destructive, other types of conflict lead to improved processes, products, and services.

- **Lack of commitment.** Commitment, according to Lencioni, is a function of two things: clarity about the task and buy-in to goals.

- **Avoidance of accountability.** Without commitment, team members often struggle to hold each other accountable for problems and to call attention to counterproductive behavior. Communication of expectations of team members is critical at the beginning of a relationship.

- **Inattention to results.** Without accountability, team members tend to put their own needs (such as ego, career development, and recognition) before those of the team. When this occurs, achievement of the team's goals may obviously suffer.

In the remainder of this section, the issues that help contribute to effective group communication will be discussed. These include group structure and development, cohesiveness, influence, performance, decision making, and conflict.

Forming Groups

Groups form for a variety of reasons, including the need to collaborate to achieve particular tasks and because of interpersonal attraction. In organizational settings, the first of these reasons is typically the reason we work in groups; however, the interpersonal attractiveness of group members can contribute to successful group formation.

Collective Endeavors Groups are the means to achieve goals that would be beyond the reach of a single individual. In a workplace setting, groups are often used because some goals can only be accomplished when several individuals pool their unique talents in a coordinated effort. Other tasks can be accomplished by an individual, but a group may be more efficient.

Interpersonal Attraction A number of factors increase attraction between individuals and can contribute to group formation. These include the following:

> **Proximity.** Proximity increases the opportunity for interaction and the likelihood a group will form. For example, students sitting in adjacent seats in a classroom often form cliques.
>
> **The Similarity Principle.** We like people who are similar to us in some way. This occurs for several reasons. First, people who adopt the same values and attitudes that we do reassure us that our beliefs are accurate (Festinger, 1954). Second, similarity serves as a signal to suggest that future interactions will be free of conflict (Insko & Schopler, 1972). Third, once we discover that we are similar to another person, we tend to immediately feel a sense of unity with that person (Arkin & Burger, 1980). Fourth, disliking a person who seems similar may prove to be psychologically distressing (Festinger, 1957; Heider, 1958).
>
> **The Complementary Principle.** According to this principle, we are attracted to people who possess characteristics that complement our own personal characteristics (Kerckhoff & Davis, 1962; Levinger, Senn, & Jorgenson, 1970; Meyer & Pepper, 1977). For example, if you enjoy leading groups, you will tend not to be attracted to other individuals who strive for control of a group. Instead, you will probably respond more positively to those who accept your guidance.

We probably respond positively to both similarity and complementarity. We may prefer people who are similar to us in some ways, but who complement us in other ways (Dryer & Horowitz, 1997). Schutz (1958) distinguishes between **interchange compatibility** and **originator compatibility.**

Interchange compatibility exists when group members have similar expectations about the group's intimacy, control, and inclusiveness. Originator compatibility exists when people who wish to act on their needs for control, inclusion, and affection join in groups with people who wish to accept these expressions of control, inclusion, and affection. A good example of originator compatibility would be a group in which one member wanted to perform the leadership functions and the remainder of the group members were happy to grant those responsibilities to that person.

Interchange compatibility

Interchange compatibility exists when the members of a group have similar expectations about the group's intimacy, control, and inclusiveness.

Originator compatibility

Originator compatibility exists when people who wish to act on their needs for control, inclusion, and affection join in groups with people who wish to accept these expressions of control, inclusion, and affection.

Schutz found that 1) cohesiveness was higher in compatible groups than in incompatible groups; and 2) compatible groups worked on problems far more efficiently than incompatible groups.

The Reciprocity Principle. Liking tends to be met with liking in return. When we discover that somebody accepts and approves of us, we usually respond by liking them in return. Negative reciprocity also occurs in groups: we dislike those who seem to reject us. In terms of the purposes of business communication, the ability to convey goodwill by establishing relationships with others might improve the process of group formation.

The Minimax Principle. People will join groups and remain in groups that provide them with the maximum number of valued rewards while incurring the fewest number of possible costs (Kelley & Thibaut, 1978; Moreland & Levine, 1982; Thibaut & Kelley, 1959). Rewards include acceptance by others, camaraderie, assistance in reaching personal goals, social support, exposure to new ideas, and opportunities to interact with people who are interesting and attractive. Again, as with the Reciprocity Principle, the ability to convey goodwill by establishing positive relationships with others may help in group formation.

People are usually attracted to groups whose members possess positively valued qualities and avoid groups of people with objectionable qualities. We prefer to associate with people who are generous, enthusiastic, punctual, dependable, helpful, strong, truthful, and intelligent (Bonney, 1947; Thibaut & Kelley, 1959). We tend to dislike and reject people who possess socially unattractive qualities—people who seem pushy, rude, or self-centered (Gilchrist, 1952; Iverson, 1964). Boring people are particularly unappealing. Such people tend to be passive, but when they do interact, they speak slowly, pause before making a point, and drag out meetings. Bores also sidetrack the group unnecessarily, show little enthusiasm, and seem too serious and preoccupied with themselves.

Comparison level

The comparison level is the standard by which individuals evaluate the desirability of group membership and which is based upon our past experiences in groups.

However, we do not join just any group that promises a favorable reward/cost ratio. Our decision to join a group is based on two factors, according to Thibaut and Kelley (1959): our **comparison level** and our **comparison level for alternatives.** Comparison level (CL) is the standard by which individuals evaluate the desirability of group membership; CL is strongly influenced by previous relationships. If previous group memberships have been positive, a person's CL should be high compared to someone whose previous experience with groups has been one of higher costs and lower rewards. However, comparison level only predicts when we will be satisfied with membership in a group.

Comparison level for alternatives

Comparison level for alternatives is the lowest level of outcomes a member will accept in light of available alternative opportunities.

If we want to predict when people will join groups and leave them, we must also take into account the value of other, alternative groups. Comparison level for alternatives (Cl_{alt}) can be defined as the lowest level of outcomes a member will accept in light of available alternative opportunities. Entering and exiting groups is largely determined by Cl_{alt}, whereas satisfaction with membership is determined by CL.

Commitment to a group is in many cases determined by the availability of alternative groups. Members who feel that they have no alternative to remaining in the group are often the most committed. Members also become more committed to a group the more they put into it.

In summary, people often form groups to achieve certain tasks or objectives. However, a variety of interpersonal issues that determine the attractiveness of the group members can also cause groups to form or help to facilitate the group formation process.

Group Roles

Roles in groups structure behavior by dictating the "part" that members take as they interact. Once cast in a role, such as leader, outcast, or questioner, a group member tends to perform certain actions and interact with group members in a particular way. Sometimes groups deliberately create roles; this is called a formal group structure. But even without a deliberate attempt to create a formal structure, the group will probably develop an informal group structure.

Broadly, there are three types of group roles: task roles, socioemotional or social maintenance roles, and individualistic roles. People who fulfill task roles focus on the group's goals, its task, and members' attempts to support one another as they work.

A group may need to accomplish its tasks, but it must also ensure the interpersonal and emotional needs of the members are met. Such roles as "supporter," "clown," and even "critic" help satisfy the emotional needs of the group members. For a group to survive, it must both accomplish its tasks and maintain the relationships among its members.

A third set of roles, individualistic roles, are taken up by people who emphasize their own needs over the group's. Those who adopt individualistic roles may do little work and demand that others take care of them. Typically, individualistic roles do not contribute to the proper functioning of a group. Group roles and their functions are listed in the table below.

TABLE 4-4. *Roles in groups.*

ROLES IN GROUPS

Role	Function
Task Roles	
Initiator/Contributor	Recommends novel ideas about the problem at hand, new ways to approach the problem, or solutions not yet considered.
Information seeker	Emphasizes getting the facts by calling for background information from others.
Opinion seeker	Asks for more qualitative types of data, such as attitudes, values, and feelings.
Information giver	Provides opinions, values, and feelings.

Continued on next page.

Elaborator	Gives additional information—examples, rephrasings, implications—about points made by others.
Coordinator	Shows the relevance of each idea and its relationship to the overall problem.
Orienter	Refocuses discussion on the topic whenever necessary.
Evaluator/critic	Appraises the quality of the group's methods, logic, and results.
Energizer	Stimulates the group to continue working when discussion flags
Procedural technician	Cares for operational details, such as the materials and machinery
Recorder	Takes notes and maintains records
Socioemotional Roles	
Encourager	Rewards others through agreement, warmth, and praise
Harmonizer	Mediates conflict among group members
Compromiser	Shifts his or her position on an issue to reduce group conflict
Gatekeeper and expediter	Smoothes communication by setting up procedures and ensuring equal participation from members
Standard setter	Expresses, or calls for discussion of, standards for evaluating the quality of the group process
Group observer/commentator	Points out the positive and negative aspects of the group's dynamics and calls for change if necessary
Follower	Accepts the ideas offered by others and serves as an audience for the group
Individualistic Roles	
Aggressor	Expresses disapproval of acts, ideas, feelings of others; attacks the group
Block	Resists the group's influence; opposes group unnecessarily
Dominator	Asserts authority or superiority; manipulative
Evader and self-confessor	Expresses personal interests, feelings, opinions unrelated to group goals
Help seeker	Expresses insecurity, confusion, self-deprecation
Recognition seeker	Calls attention to him- or herself; self-aggrandizing
Playboy/girl	Uninvolved in the group; cynical, nonchalant
Special-interest pleader	Remains apart from the group by acting as a representative of another social group or category

TABLE 4-4. *Continued*

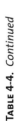

critical **thinking**

What group roles do you tend to play? What roles would you like to introduce into your repertoire? What roles should the competent communicator avoid?

Intermember relations

Intermember relations are the relations of group members to one another.

Group Member Relations

Intermember relations also affect group structure. Intermember relations or the relations of the group members to each other are determined by patterns of status, attraction, and communication.

Status Hierarchies Variations in dominance, prestige, and control among group members reflect the group's status relations. Status patterns are often hierarchical and centralized. Status differences in groups violate our expectations of "equal treatment for all," but in the microsociety of a group, equality is the exception and inequality the rule. Initially, group members may start off on equal footing, but over time, status differentiation takes place. Who rises to the top of the heap and who remains on the bottom is partly determined by the individual and partly by the group. The individual must communicate his or her claim to higher status, and the other group members must accept it. Individuals who deserve status are not always afforded status by their groups. Individuals who speak rapidly without hesitation, advise others what to do, and confirm others' statements are often more influential than individuals who signal submissiveness.

Attraction Relations Just as members of the group can be ranked from low to high in terms of status, so, too, can the members be ordered from least liked to most liked (Maassen, Akkermans, & Van der Linden, 1996). Popular individuals are the most liked, rejected members are the least liked, neglected members are nominated neither as most nor least liked, and average members are liked by several others in the group (Coie, Dodge, & Kupersmidt, 1990; Newcomb, Bukowski, & Pattee, 1993). Cliques also form in groups; these subgroups usually display homophily. In other words, members of cliques are often more similar to one another than they are to the members of the total group.

Individuals are generally considered more attractive if they possess socially attractive qualities, such as cooperativeness and physical appeal, but social standing also depends on the degree to which the individual's attributes match the qualities valued by the group. This match is referred to as person-group fit.

Communication Networks People of higher status and attraction often stay in close communication, while those on the bottom may be cut off from communication. The most important feature of a communication network is its degree of centralization. Networks can be centralized (one person controls the flow of information) or decentralized (all members can communicate with each other). The amount and type of information to be delivered, or what is called "information saturation," determines the best communication network for any task. If the information is simple, centralized networks work best; if the information to be transmitted is complex, decentralized networks are more efficient (Shaw, 1964).

A person's position in a communication network can also have effects. For example, those who are more peripheral in a communication network are usually those who are least satisfied, while those in central positions are most satisfied. Since the overall number of peripheral positions in a centralized network exceeds the number of central positions, the overall satisfaction in a centralized group is lower than the level of satisfaction in a decentralized group.

In summary, relations among group members can be affected by three things: a member's status within the group, a member's popularity within the group, and the type of network used within the group to disseminate information and a person's position in that network.

Stages of Group Development

Group cohesion, or unity, develops over time. It is the result of group development. There are five stages of group development: Forming, storming, norming, performing, and adjourning (Tuckman, 1965; Tuckman & Jensen, 1977).

The major processes in the forming stage include members becoming familiar with one another and the group; members dealing with issues of dependency and inclusion; the acceptance of a leader; and the development of group consensus. The characteristics of this stage include tentative, polite communications, concern over ambiguity and group goals, and an active leader and compliant members.

In the storming or conflict stage, the major processes include disagreement over procedures, expression of dissatisfaction, tension among members, and antagonism toward the leader. The characteristics of this stage include criticism of ideas, poor attendance, hostility, polarization, and coalition formation.

In the norming stage, major processes include the growth of cohesion; establishment of roles, standards, and relationships; and increased trust and communication. This stage is characterized by agreement on procedures, reduction in role ambiguity, and increased "we-ness."

In the performing stage, the major processes include goal achievement, high task achievement, and emphasis on performance and production. This stage is characterized by decision making, problem solving, and mutual cooperation.

In the adjourning phase, the major processes include termination of roles, completion of tasks, and reduction of dependency. This stage is characterized by disintegration and withdrawal, increased independence and emotionality, and regret.

Groups do not always develop in this order. Some groups manage to avoid particular stages, others move through the stages in a unique order, and others develop in ways that cannot be described by this five-stage model. In addition, the demarcation between stages is often not clear-cut.

critical **thinking**

Where do group norms come from? Why do we tend to conform to group norms? Is tension in a group desirable?

The Effects of Group Cohesion

People are usually more satisfied with their groups when the group is cohesive rather than noncohesive. A cohesive group creates a healthier workplace, at least at the psychological level. Because people in cohesive groups respond to one another in a more positive fashion than the members of noncohesive groups, people experience less anxiety and tension (Myers, 1962; Shaw & Shaw, 1962). People in cohesive groups more readily accept the group's goals, decisions, and norms.

Membership in a cohesive group can prove problematic for members, however, if they become too dependent on the group. Furthermore, pressure to conform is also greater in cohesive groups, which also can potentially create problems. Evidence suggests that members of cohesive groups sometimes react very negatively when a group member goes against group consensus, and they take harsh actions to bring dissenters into line (Schachter, 1951). Cohesion can also increase negative group processes, including hostility and scapegoating (French, 1941; Pepitone & Reiching, 1955). Cohesive groups vent their frustrations through interpersonal aggression: overt hostility, joking hostility, scapegoating, and domination of subordinate group members. In contrast, noncohesive groups tend to form coalitions among members.

communication   IN YOUR WORLD

Groups will sometimes go to great lengths to foster cohesiveness. Hazing rituals of college fraternities are examples of the sometimes extreme activities in which groups will participate to test the limits of an individual's commitment. Such extremes were documented by Cialdini (1993), who found instances in which pledges were forced to swallow quarter-pound hunks of raw liver; repeatedly punched in the stomach and kidneys if they forgot parts of ritual sayings; incarcerated in locked closets with only salty foods, no fluids, and a plastic cup in which to urinate; and abandoned on mountaintops or in remote areas in bitter cold conditions without proper clothing. Other well-publicized examples of hazing include forcing pledges to drink large quantities of alcohol. Such cases have led to hospitalization and even death. Because of the negative publicity such practices have drawn, 17 states had outlawed hazing by 1986.

Such initiation rites are not limited to fraternities. Clubs, gangs, and some businesses also subject new members to hazing. For example, one Japanese bank forced new employees to meditate and fast, perform community service, complete a 25-mile hike, and participate in basic training at an army base (Rohlen, 1973).

Moreland and Levine (1989) suggest that groups participate in such rituals for four reasons. First, groups initiate newcomers because the harder it is to gain membership to the group, the greater will be the loyalty and commitment. Some groups believe that the more severe the hazing ritual, the more desirable the group appears to be. Second, the group gains valuable information about the new member from initiation rituals. If newcomers resist or fail the initiation, it may be a sign that they will not conform to group norms. Third, extreme initiation practices discourage new members who may have a weak commitment to the group. And finally, such initiation rites may be used to send the message that newcomers are dependent upon the older members for their survival in the group. Such a belief may lead to increased conformity.

Discussion

1. Do you agree with Moreland and Levine's assessment of the effectiveness of hazing rituals in weeding out less committed members and gaining conformity from those who are committed to the group?

2. When do such attempts at compliance-gaining cross over to become an abuse of power? Are such practices ethical?

Generally speaking, though, groups that succeed tend to be more cohesive, and groups that fail tend to be less cohesive. The cohesion-performance relation is strongest when group cohesion is based on commitment to the task rather than attraction or group pride (Mullen & Copper, 1994). Cohesion also counts more when the group's task requires high levels of interaction and interdependence (Gully, Devine, & Whitney, 1995). These findings explain why some groups, even though they are cohesive, are not productive: the members are not committed to the group's performance goals. Surveys indicate that fairly low standards of performance can develop within highly cohesive groups. In sum, as long as group norms encourage high productivity, cohesiveness and productivity are positively related.

Sources of Influence Within a Group

Three types of influence can be exercised in group situations. Through **informational influence,** the group provides members with information that they can use to make decisions and form opinions. When **normative influence** occurs, group members tailor their actions to fit the group's standards and conventions. **Interpersonal influence,** in contrast, occurs when the group uses verbal and nonverbal influence tactics to induce change.

Informational influence is not immune to the effects of social influence. In other words, we may discover new information by observing others' responses. Social comparison theory assumes that group members treat other people's responses as data when formulating opinions and making decisions. In some cases, groups actively gather information about members' opinions, but generally, individuals gather information about others' views through routine discussion (Gerard & Orive, 1987; Orive, 1988a, 1988b). Unfortunately, this intuitive approach tends to be biased. Members of the majority, for example, tend to underestimate the size of their group, while minority members tend to overestimate the degree to which others agree with them.

People who consistently violate their group's norms are often reminded of their duty and told to change their ways. They are often disliked, assigned lower-status jobs, and in some cases dismissed from the group (Schachter, 1951). Normative influence explains why certain people, such as those with a high need for social approval and those who tend to be more authoritarian, conform more than others (Bornstein, 1992). Nonconformists tend to be more self-confident, while counter-conformists actively resist majority influence.

Interpersonal influence tactics include complaining, demanding, threatening, pleading, negotiating, pressuring, manipulating, and rejecting. The occurrence of rejection is more pronounced in more cohesive groups. In extreme cases, group members will eventually stop communicating with "disliked deviants," at least in cases where cohesive groups are working on relevant tasks (Schachter, 1951).

Informational influence

Informational influence is information the group provides to members that they can use to make decisions and form opinions.

Normative influence

Normative influence occurs when group members tailor their actions to fit the group's standards and conventions.

Interpersonal influence

Interpersonal influence occurs when the group uses verbal and nonverbal influence tactics to induce change.

critical **thinking**

How does communication influence how a team performs? Please provide examples that illustrate your point from your own work or group experiences.

Group Performance

First of all, to perform well groups must have the resources they need. They must have the skills, talents, and energy needed to successfully complete tasks. Secondly, the group must combine its resources effectively. Even if members have the resources that the task requires, the group may fail if it does not marshal these resources successfully. Performance depends on the group's resources and the methods it uses to combine these resources to meet the demands of the group's task.

A group's performance depends, in part, on its members' knowledge, skills, and abilities. On the task side, groups whose members are more skilled at the work to be done outperform groups comprised of less skilled workers. On the interpersonal side, members must be able to work well with others on joint tasks. Communication skills, leadership abilities, and a talent for managing conflicts are some of the qualities possessed by members of successful work teams. Some groups fail because they simply do not include members with the qualities and characteristics needed to complete their task.

Diversity can also help a group's performance. Much of the advantage of diverse groups occurs when members are all highly skilled but these skills do not overlap. Diverse groups may be better at coping with changing work conditions, because their wider range of talents and traits enhances flexibility. Diversity can help groups seek alternative solutions to problems and enhance creativity and innovation.

Diversity can also create problems in groups. Diverse groups may lack cohesion because of perceived dissimilarities. In addition, diversity in skill level—some members are competent but others are incompetent—does not appear to boost productivity (Tziner & Eden, 1985).

Groups that bring together people with similar personalities tend to outperform groups whose members have dissimilar personalities (Shaw, 1981). Classroom groups performed best when they were composed of individuals whose personality characteristics were similar and focused on goal attainment (Bond & Shiu, 1997).

Another negative effect on group performance is **process losses,** or reductions in performance effectiveness or efficiency caused by faulty group processes, including motivational and coordination problems. Although a group obviously produces more than an individual, groups usually do not work at maximum efficiency. As more and more people are added to a group, the group becomes increasingly less efficient. Secondly, people may not work as hard when they are in groups. This reduction of effort by individuals working in groups is called **social loafing** (Williams, Harkin, & Latane, 1981).

Process losses

Process losses are reductions in performance effectiveness caused by faulty group processes.

Social loafing

Social loafing describes the phenomenon of people working less hard as group members than as individuals.

Social loafing occurs when individual input is not identifiable. When our individual contributions are clearly known, evaluation apprehension sets in as we worry about how others will evaluate us. But when we are anonymous and our contributions are unidentified, the presence of others reduces evaluation apprehension and social loafing becomes more likely (Harkins and Jackson, 1985; Harkins & Szymanski, 1987, 1988; Jackson & Latane, 1981; Szymanski & Harkins, 1987; Williams et al, 1981).

Another cause of social loafing is the fact that group work often causes social dilemmas. Group members may want to do their share to help the group reach its goals, but at the same time they are tempted to concentrate on their own personal goals. So they engage in **free-riding.** People are most likely to free-ride when their contributions are combined in a single product and no one is monitoring the size of each person's contribution. Free-riding also increases when group members worry that their coworkers are holding back.

A third reason for social loafing is what is called the illusion of group productivity. Members of groups working on collective tasks generally think that their group is more productive than most (Polzer, Kramer, & Neale, 1997). Group members also generally do not feel that they are doing less than their fair share.

Groups can improve productivity in several ways. First, personal stake in the group's outcome should be increased. When individuals feel that a poor group performance will affect them personally, they do not loaf (Brickner, Harkins, & Ostrom, 1986). Second, groups that set clear, attainable goals outperform groups whose members have lost sight of their objectives (Weldon & Weingart, 1993). Third, groups that set high goals tend to outproduce those with lower levels of aspiration. Fourth, groups with realistic expectations about their chances of success also perform better. However, unrealistic goals can undermine motivation (Hinsz, 1995). Finally, increased unity can improve performance. However, increased cohesiveness improves performance only if group norms emphasize productivity.

However, a group can take steps to discourage social loafing. Rothwell (1998, p. 84–85) suggests the following:

1. **Establish a group responsibility norm.** From the beginning, group members should state the expectation of individual responsibility to the group and the importance of equal contribution by members to the group task.

2. **Note the critical importance of each member's efforts.** The leader of the group should communicate the importance and essentialness of each individual's effort and contribution to completion of the group task.

3. **Identify and evaluate individual contributions.** Each member should be provided specific and identifiable tasks, and the group should set aside time to evaluate each member's contribution to the project.

4. **Talk to the problem individual privately.** This step calls for the leader, the group, or a designated member to approach the loafer and ask why his or her

Free-riding

Free-riding describes the phenomenon of group members working less hard on collective tasks than when they are working for themselves.

contribution is less than expected. Asking the problem individual to suggest ways that he or she might improve her performance may help in getting buy-in to the group task.

5. **Confront the loafer as a group.** Group members should identify and describe the problem behavior in detail. The loafer should be asked how the problem can be solved. This step is effective only if group members avoid name-calling or personality attacks on the offender.

6. **Consult someone with more power.** When all the above steps fail, the group should consult a teacher, supervisor, or someone with greater authority than the group members and ask for advice or help. The authority figure may need to discuss the problem with the loafer.

7. **Fire the slacker.** This step should be taken only when all other attempts to obtain the loafer's cooperation have failed.

8. **Sidestep the loafer.** The group may decide to reconfigure the individual responsibilities and tasks so that even if the loafer does not contribute, the group can still accomplish its task. In the workplace, this step might result in a demotion or reassignment to another job or department.

Group Decision Making

Groups can be useful in making decisions because more people potentially bring more information to the task. In addition, groups tend to process the information they have more thoroughly through discussion. For effective decision making, groups should ensure that the process they use is a productive one. Although groups can be useful for decision making, they also face some challenges.

Stages of Group Decision Making Groups process information in four or more stages appearing consistently in many groups:

- **Orientation stage.** The group identifies the problem to be solved and plans the process to be used in reaching the decisions.

- **Discussion stage.** The group gathers information about the situation, identifies and weighs options, and tests its assumptions.

- **Decision stage.** The group relies on an implicit or explicit social decision scheme to combine individual preferences into a collective decision. Common schemes include delegating, averaging inputs, voting with various proportions needed for a decision, and consensus.

- **Implementation stage.** The group carries out the decision and assesses its impact. Members are more likely to implement decisions when they were actively involved in the decision-making process.

The Challenges of Group Decision Making Although group decision making can have productive outcomes, group members should be aware of some of the challenges and limitations of such a process. One problem is the tendency for groups to spend too much of their discussion time examining shared information—details that two or more of the group members know in common—rather than unshared information (Stasser, 1992; Stasser, Talor, & Hanna, 1989; Wittenbaum & Stasser, 1996). This tendency is called **oversampling.** Oversampling of shared information leads to poorer decisions when useful data might be revealed by considering the unshared information more closely. Oversampling of shared information increases when tasks have no demonstrably correct solution and when group leaders do not actively draw out unshared information.

In addition, the usefulness of group discussion is limited, in part, by members' inability to express themselves clearly and by their limited listening skills. Not all group members have the interpersonal skills a discussion demands. When researchers asked 569 full-time employees what happened during a meeting to limit its effectiveness, they received 2,500 answers, which are provided in the table below (Di Salvo, Nikkel, & Monroe, 1989).

Oversampling

Oversampling is the tendency for groups to spend too much of their discussion time examining shared information.

PROBLEMS WHEN GROUPS MAKE DECISIONS

Problem (Frequency)	Description
Poor communication skills (10 percent)	Poor listening skills, ineffective voice, poor nonverbals, lack of effective visual aids, misunderstanding or not clearly identifying topic, repetitiveness, use of jargon.
Egocentric behavior (8 percent)	Dominating conversation and group, behaviors that are loud and overbearing, one-upmanship, show of power, manipulation, intimidation, filibustering, talk to hear self talk, followers or brownnosers, clowns and goof-offs.
Nonparticipation (7 percent)	Not all participate, speak up, or volunteer; are passive, lack discussion, silent starts.
Sidetracked (6.5 percent)	Leave main topic.
Interruptions (6 percent)	Members interrupt speaker, talk over others, socialize, allow phone calls and messages from customers/clients.
Negative leader behavior (6 percent)	Unorganized and unfocused, not prepared, late, has no control, gets sidetracked, makes no decisions.
Attitudes and emotions (5 percent)	Poor attitude, defensive or evasive, argumentative, personal accusations, no courtesy or respect, complains or gripes, lack of control of emotions.

TABLE 4-5. *Problems when groups make decisions.*

Sometimes, groups use discussion to avoid making decisions. In addition, judgment errors that cause people to overlook important information and overutilize unimportant information are often exacerbated in groups. These errors occur more frequently when group members are cognitively busy (i.e., they are trying to work on too many tasks at once).

Common sense suggests that groups are more cautious than individuals, but early studies found that group discussion generates a shift in the direction of the more risky alternative. When researchers later found evidence of cautious shifts as well as risky ones, they concluded that the responses of groups tend to be more extreme than individual members' responses (the group polarization hypothesis) (Myers & Lamm, 1976). Polarization is sustained by the desire to evaluate one's own opinions by comparing them to others' (social comparison theory), by exposure to other members' pro-risk and pro-caution arguments (persuasive-arguments theory), and by groups' implicit reliance on a "risk-supported wins" social decision scheme (Clark, 1971; Myers & Lamm, 1975, 1976; Goethals & Zanna, 1979; Myers, 1978; Sanders & Baron, 1977). This approach is adopted by groups whose members are initially more risk-prone than cautious. In such groups, if one person supports a risky alternative, the group will not adopt it. But if two people support it, the group often accepts the risky recommendation (Davis, Kameda, & Stasson, 1992; Laughlin & Earley, 1982; Zuber, Crott, & Werner, 1992).

Group decision making can be challenging because it requires the ability to consider and accommodate multiple interpretative frameworks—multiple versions of reality—and to emerge with a single recommendation or course of action (Eisenberg & Goodall, 1993). This means that we must be willing to accept the inevitability of differences and to make a commitment to dialog. Groups also can be more effective at decision making if they pay more attention to the procedure that they use to solve problems (Hirokawa & Rost, 1992).

Sources of Group Conflict

There are three types of group conflict: personal conflict, substantive conflict, and procedural conflict. Conflict can also be increased by other factors, such as competition within a group and the social dilemmas that groups can create for their members. Just as there are various types of conflict, there are several approaches that group members use to resolve conflict.

Personal Conflict Personal conflict is rooted in individuals' dislike of other group members. For example, group members who treat others unfairly or impolitely create more conflict than those who are polite (Ohbuchi, Chiba, & Fikushima, 1996).

The relationship between dislike and conflict explains why groups with greater diversity sometimes display more conflict than homogeneous groups. Just as similarity between members increases interpersonal attraction, dissimilarity tends to increase dislike and conflict (Rosenbaum, 1986). Groups whose members have dissimilar personalities (e.g., differences in authoritarianism, cognitive complexity, and temperament) generally do not get along as well as groups composed of people whose personalities are similar (Haythorn, Couch, Haefner, Langham, & Carter, 1956; Shaw, 1981). Groups whose members vary in terms of ability, experience, opinions, values, race, personality, ethnicity, and so on can capitalize on their members' wider range of resources and viewpoints, but these groups often suffer high levels of conflict (Moreland, Levine, & Wingert, 1996).

Substantive Conflict When people discuss their problems and plans, they sometimes disagree with one another's analyses. These substantive conflicts, however, are integrally related to the group's work. Substantive conflict does not stem from personal disagreements between individuals but from disagreements about issues that are relevant to the group's real goals and outcomes. In other words, of the three types of conflict, substantive conflict has the potential to provide the most positive outcomes, such as making plans, increasing creativity, solving problems, deciding issues, and resolving conflicts of viewpoints (McGrath, 1984). Substantive conflict, in fact, is one of the reasons that groups are used to complete tasks.

Even though substantive conflicts help groups reach their goals, these impersonal conflicts can turn into personal ones. Members who disagree with the group, even when their position is a reasonable one, often provoke considerable animosity within the group. The dissenter who refuses to accept others' views is less liked. Group members who slow down the process of reaching consensus are often responded to negatively. Such pressures to conform can lead to what is called **groupthink.** To avoid this aspect of groupthink, groups should encourage members to take on the role of devil's advocate.

Procedural Conflict While substantive conflicts occur when ideas, opinions, and interpretations clash, procedural conflicts occur when strategies, policies, and methods collide. Many groups can minimize procedural conflict by adopting formal rules that specify goals, decisional processes, and responsibilities (Houle, 1989). Rules, however, can be overly formalized, which can hinder openness, creativity, and adaptability to change.

Groupthink

Groupthink is the pressure on individuals in a group to conform to the extent that critical analysis and discussion are avoided or abandoned.

critical **thinking**

Of the three types of group conflict—personal, substantive, and procedural—which is the easiest to avoid? How might you use these strategies to avoid conflict in your groups? Your workplace?

Conflict and Competition Conflict is more likely when group members compete against each other for such resources as money, power, time, prestige, or materials, instead of working with one another to reach common goals. When people compete, they must look out for their own interests instead of the group's interests or their co-members' interests. Because competing members can succeed only when others fail, they may even sabotage others' work, criticize it, and withhold information and resources that others might need (Franken & Brown, 1995; Franken & Prpich, 1996; Steers & Porter, 1991; Tjosvold, 1995).

In contrast, members of cooperative groups enhance their outcomes by helping other members achieve success. Work units with high levels of cooperation have fewer latent tensions, personality conflicts, and verbal confrontations (Tjosvold, 1995).

Few situations involve pure cooperation or pure competition; the motive to compete is often mixed with the motive to cooperate. Furthermore, as the **norm of reciprocity** suggests, cooperation begets cooperation while competition begets competition.

People's personalities contribute to conflict. Some people seem to be natural competitors whereas others are more cooperative or individualistic (Kelley, 1997; McClintock, Messick, Kuhlman, & Campos, 1973; Swap & Rubin, 1983). **Competitors** view group disagreements as win-lose situations and find satisfaction in forcing their ideas on others.

Individuals with competitive value orientations are more likely to find themselves in conflicts. Furthermore, competitors rarely modify their behavior in response to the complaints of others because they are relatively unconcerned with maintaining smooth interpersonal relations.

Norm of reciprocity

The norm of reciprocity suggests that any behavior tends to result in that same behavior in return.

Competitors

Competitors are people who view group disagreements as win-lose situations and find satisfaction in forcing their views on others.

Responsible Communication

In the United States, there is a long-held belief that competition builds character. Such an assumption manifests in the pressure for children to compete in sports and the proliferation of baseball and soccer leagues across the suburban landscape. But such an assumption has been questioned by researchers, who claim that competition does not build character but instead creates frustration, aggression, or apathy (Hocker & Wilmot, 1995). This assertion would seem to be supported by the growing phenomenon of unsportsmanlike behavior in parents at their children's games. In one such extreme situation, one father killed another at their children's hockey scrimmage in July 2000.

In fact, evidence shows that competition does not create character, but in some cases, results in cheating. In education, cheating among students has reached epidemic proportions (Derber, 1996). One study found that about three quarters of students admitted to cheating (Yates, 1985). The number one reason for cheating cited by students involved in that study was competition for grades.

Given the number of recent events making headlines from the corporate world involving fraud and other illegal activities, it may not be surprising that research by Baird (1980) and McCabe and Trevino (1993) suggests that college students who are business majors cheat more often than students from other disciplines. These studies are reinforced by the findings of Crown and Spiller (1998) that business students are more tolerant of unethical behavior than are non-business students.

Questions for Thought

1. **Do you agree with the assertion that increased pressure to compete also leads to increased pressure to cut corners to ensure success?**

2. **What are the goals of cooperative groups? Do such goals work against the pressures to be dishonest and to cheat that arise from competitive situations?**

Two other value orientations are those of cooperator and individualist. **Cooperators** value accommodative interpersonal strategies, while **individualists** are concerned only with their own outcomes. They make decisions based on what they personally will achieve, with no concern for others' outcomes. They neither interfere with nor assist others' attempts to reach their goals. It should be noted that this definition of individualist differs from the conception of individualistic roles in groups in that in a group situation, the latter inclination can negatively affect others. In the schema discussed here, competitive behavior is more akin to the individualistic roles that can arise in groups.

Cooperators

Cooperators value accommodative interpersonal strategies.

Individualists

Individualists care only about their own outcomes.

Social values vary across cultures. As was discussed in Chapter 3: Audience Analysis, Western societies, such as the United States, tend to value competition, while more cooperative and peaceful societies devalue individual achievement and avoid any kind of competitive games (Bonta, 1997; Fry & Bjorkqvist, 1997; Van Lange, De Bruin, Otten & Joireman, 1997).

Social Dilemmas Groups create social dilemmas for their members. The members, as individuals, are motivated to maximize their own rewards and minimize their costs. Conflicts arise when individualistic motives trump group-oriented motives and the collective intervenes to redress the imbalance.

One cause of conflict is the division of resources. When group members feel they are receiving too little for what they are giving, they sometimes withdraw from the group, reduce their effort, and turn in work of lower quality. Group members who feel that they are receiving too much for what they are giving sometimes increase their efforts.

Many studies of groups working on collective tasks find that members do not work as hard as when they are working for themselves. Such free-riding occurs most frequently when individuals' contributions are combined in a single product and these products aren't monitored. Free-riding can cause conflict in a group. In addition, some individual group members, to counter the inequity of working in a group with free riders, may reduce their own contributions or withdraw from the group.

As conflicts escalate, group members often become more committed to their positions instead of more understanding of the positions taken by others. Conflict is exacerbated by members' tendency to misperceive others and to assume that the other party's behavior is caused by personal rather than situational factors. This tendency is called the **fundamental attribution error.** As conflict worsens, group members will shift from weak to strong influence tactics, such as threats, punishment, and bullying.

Fundamental attribution error

The fundamental attribution error is the tendency of group members to misperceive others and to assume that personal rather than situational factors cause other members' behavior.

Conflict Resolution In group and team work situations, the first dysfunction that occurs is a lack of trust, according to Patrick M. Lencioni (2002). Lencioni defines trust as the confidence among group members that their peers' intentions are good. In other words, we must believe that those with whom we work will not act opportunistically or take advantage of us and others to narrowly pursue their own self-interest. Without trust, individuals are unable to use what is generally considered the most effective approach to conflict resolution: collaboration. Collaboration is built on trust. Collaboration is one of the five styles of conflict resolution illustrated in the figure below. Blake and Mouton (1964) initiated the styles approach to conflict resolution and Kilmann and Thomas (1977) elaborated and modified the styles approach.

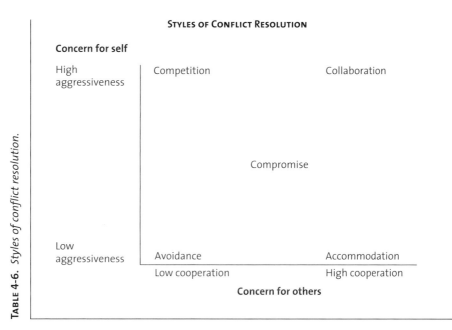

TABLE 4-6. *Styles of conflict resolution.*

As the table above indicates, the styles of conflict resolution can be understood by comparing how each relates in the areas of concern for others and concern for self as well as level of aggressiveness and cooperation.

- **Competition.** This style is characterized by high aggressiveness and low cooperation. Some people see conflict as a win-lose situation and use competitive and aggressive tactics to intimidate others. Fighting can take many forms, including authoritative mandates, challenges, arguing, insults, accusations, complaining, vengeance, and even physical violence (Morrill, 1995). An individual who uses a competing style exhibits a high concern for self and low concern for others.

- **Collaboration.** An individual who exhibits this style shows a high concern for others and for self. Because of this orientation, this style is characterized by assertive communication and high levels of cooperation. As such, it is considered a "win-win" approach, since a solution should be found that satisfies both parties.

- **Compromise.** This style is a middle ground. The emphasis is on achieving workable but not necessarily optimal solutions. Some consider this a "lose-lose" approach to conflict resolution.

- **Avoidance.** Individuals who practice this style show little concern for relationships or for task accomplishment. By avoiding conflict, they hope it will disappear. When students in small groups talked about their disagreements, they often said they adopted a "wait-and-see" attitude, hoping the problem would eventually go away (Wall & Nolan, 1987). Sometimes, however, avoiding is appropriate if you are a low-power person and the consequences of confrontation may be risky and harmful.

■ **Accommodation.** This style is characterized by a high concern for relationships but a low concern for task accomplishment. Like avoiding, this can be a useful approach in groups that have shown a high degree of conflict. Accommodating others in this situation provides for an opportunity for tempers to cool and steps toward resolution to occur. It can also be appropriate if the risk of yielding is low. For example, a group of your friends may disagree about where to eat dinner. The choice may be between two of your favorite restaurants; however, the one that most of your friends prefer is your second choice. Even so, since you like that restaurant, too, you have little to lose by yielding.

Of these five basic ways of resolving conflict, collaborating is more likely to promote group unity.

critical **thinking**

Describe a recent conflict you had with someone where you believe that poor communication on one or both parts was the culprit. What can be done to make sure this conflict does not occur again?

Our dislike of conflict and the need to promote cohesiveness can lead to an additional danger: *groupthink*. Groupthink occurs when group members dominate interaction, are intimidated by others, or care more about social acceptability than reaching the best solution. Groupthink occurs at the highest levels and can have serious consequences. It has been cited as causing the Bay of Pigs fiasco in the 1960s, the *Challenger* disaster in the 1980s, and the lack of effective preparation and response by the United States government to terrorism in the 21st century.

To avoid groupthink, Jane Gibson and Robert Hodgetts (1986) suggest:

1. The leader should encourage participants to voice objections and critically evaluate ideas.

2. Members should take an impartial stance and not get wrapped up in ego and emotions, affording a more objective view of the decision.

3. More than one group can work on a problem, which may lead to radically different recommendations.

4. Each member can be encouraged to discuss the group's deliberations with people outside the group and get their feedback.

5. Outside experts can be invited into the group for their input and feedback.

6. One of the group members can be appointed devil's advocate to ensure that all sides of each issue are explored.

7. The group can be divided into subgroups, each of which works the problem separately and then reports back.

8. A "second chance" meeting can be held after preliminary consensus is reached to allow members to express doubts and concerns that may have come up.

In summary, it is useful to understand the benefits and potential problem areas of group work, since we will all work in groups throughout our lives. The issues surrounding such concerns as group structure and development, cohesiveness, influence, conflict, performance, and decision making should be understood and considered when working in groups or deciding whether a group approach is appropriate for a task.

MEETING MANAGEMENT

Managing meetings is an important part of facilitating effective group communication. Meetings are a common means of communication within organizations, since they provide the potential for employees to ask and answer questions in an efficient manner. They also provide communicators access to nonverbal cues, which enable those with good observation skills to check and respond to messages that are not verbalized. Just as with most communication channels, though, meetings present challenges, the primary one being the cost in time. There are 11 million meetings in the United States every day, according to the National Statistics Council. Furthermore, professionals attend an average of 61.8 meetings a month and say that fully half of that time is wasted (Ethridge, 2004, p. 1). With such numbers, it is no easy task to make each meeting both productive and efficient. In this section, the common types of meetings will be discussed and the steps for ensuring a successful and efficient meeting will be explained.

With more than 11 million meetings taking place in the U.S. each day, it is important to understand and apply the practices of effective meeting management.

© RYAN McVAY/ PHOTODISC/ GETTY IMAGES

Types of Meetings

Defining the purpose of a meeting can help you to prepare for it. There are three key reasons to hold a meeting: to inform, to discuss or evaluate decisions, and to discuss performance.

■ Informative meetings focus on giving or receiving information. They may incorporate discussions, demonstrations, or lectures to aid in the exchange of information. The group size for these types of meetings can vary from as few as two to as many as 100 individuals.

■ Discussions are held to form decisions or agree on a plan of action. These meetings are successful if participants actively brainstorm, discuss, and evaluate ideas. These meetings work best with small groups of three to nine participants.

■ Performance meetings are held to accomplish a specific task or to plan an event. The key to making these meetings successful is to make sure everyone understands their particular responsibilities. Performance meetings are more effective when limited to six or fewer participants.

Steps in Meeting Management

After you have identified the primary purpose of your meeting, you should spend time on the three phases of meeting management to ensure that the discussion is productive and efficient. The three steps of meeting management are 1) Planning the meeting; 2) conducting the meeting; and 3) following up after the meeting has been held.

Planning the Meeting When considering a meeting, you must recognize that you have an obligation to show respect for all participants and their time spent attending this meeting. This is why preplanning a meeting is the most critical step in conducting a meeting. Before you send out notifications to initiate any type of meeting, you should answer the following questions:

■ What participants are essential to achieve the purpose of the meeting? What are the key roles each participant will have in the meeting? Will the setting be formal or informal? Meetings are productive only when attended by the right people. It may not be in the best interest to invite those who are simply interested. Your team should be comprised of individuals who have direct experience with the issues to be discussed or decided and who have a stake in the outcome of such discussions.

■ What agenda will be most effective and efficient for the purpose of the meeting? You will need to decide how to bring the participants together in terms of when and where you will meet. Will the meeting be by teleconferencing, video-conferencing, e-mail, on-site, or off-site of the business location?

■ What information, equipment, and tools are required to conduct the meeting?

■ How much time will be needed for decision making or to obtain the information needed to achieve the results of your objectives? Allow enough time to have questions answered and clarity established for the meeting.

Although the arrangements may be complex and the nature of your meeting will vary, the following suggested guidelines apply in most cases in conducting a successful meeting:

■ Give advance notice to all participants.

■ Provide information, such as the date, time (both start and predicted ending) and location, (include travel arrangements, if needed), and include the names of participants, their key roles, titles, and business affiliations.

- Design a structured agenda with the stated objectives, a list of the main topics of interest, and time allotted for each topic of discussion. Group related topics together to avoid having to backtrack on a subject in order to keep the meeting flowing in an orderly fashion. An agenda should be limited to one page in length. (A generic format for an agenda is provided in Figure 1 below.)

- Make sure all participants are prepared by providing the agenda in advance. Inform them of what is expected from each attendee in preparing for the meeting. Confirm that all participants have received the notice of the meeting agenda.

FIGURE 4-2. *Formal generic agenda for meetings.*

Agenda for [name of group] Meeting
Prepared on [date agenda created]
By [name of author of agenda]

Attendees: [those invited to attend, often in alphabetical order]
Date and time of meeting:
Location of meeting:
Subject: [major issues to be discussed or purpose of meeting]
Agenda items:

1. Call to order.
2. Routine business [procedural or administrative matters]   (10–15 mins.)
   a. Approval of agenda for this meeting.
   b. Reading and approval of minutes of last meeting.
   c. Committee reports.
3. Old business [unfinished matters from previous meeting]   (15–20 mins.)
   a. Discussion of issue(s) carried over from previous meeting.
   b. Issue(s) arising from decision(s) made at previous meeting.
4. New business.   (20–25 mins.)
   a. Most important issue.
   b. Next most important issue.
   c. Other issues in decreasing order of importance.
   d. Business from the floor not included on the agenda [only as time permits; otherwise, these issues should be addressed in the next meeting].
5. Adjournment.

Conducting the Meeting Meetings have four major stages: the introduction and vision statement, the meeting kickoff, the summary of accomplishments and the management presentation, and an evaluation exercise and closing remarks (Friedman, 1996). The facilitator is responsible for making sure these steps are followed and completed. The success of the meeting largely depends upon the facilitator's communication skills.

The facilitator's first goal is to set a positive, professional tone from the very beginning that is intended to make attendees say, "I'm glad to be here." Creating a welcoming atmosphere can be accomplished by encouraging open communication. Effective facilitators promote individual participation to gain the benefit of diverse points of view. To gain the most information, facilitators should ask open-ended questions to avoid simple "yes" or "no" responses. Facilitators are responsible for getting attendees to participate. They can do so by asking such questions as "What do you think about the topic?" "Can you tell me what we can do to make this better?" or "What other suggestions do you have?" The best solutions are always the result of input from many people.

The facilitator needs to be aware of the time and with that in mind, keep the conversation on topic. It has been estimated that executives spend an average of 7.8 hours a week in meetings that are unnecessary (Messner, 2002). Many inefficient or unnecessary meetings can be directly tied to a late start time, poor facilitation, or a late ending time. Good facilitators keep a meeting on schedule and on topic. Everyone's time is valuable. It's very important to respect others' time; it shows you value the presence and schedules of those who were prompt. Not only does keeping a meeting on schedule establish goodwill and your credibility as a facilitator, it will have a positive effect for future meetings.

Facilitators and presenters should avoid lecturing. According to a study by the MPI Foundation, meeting attendees do not care for "speakers who have poor presentation skills" (Clark, 1998, p.12). Speakers who wish to catch the attention of listeners should try to involve the participants emotionally in the meeting (Clark, 1998, p.12). Speakers should be spontaneous, but that does not mean that such discussions should not be planned. Just as with other types of presentations, speakers should plan what they have to say but deliver their message as extemporaneously as possible.

Holding a difference of opinion about the same subject is typical in meeting discussions. But proving a point or being right is secondary to your team's objectives. By following the suggestions below, facilitators can demonstrate leadership, and most importantly, focus everyone's energy on a solution that will progress the group.

■ Try to see things from each participant's point of view.

■ When someone is speaking, never say, "You're wrong."

■ Avoid right or wrongs; treat different opinions as a different way of looking at the same issue.

■ Remember that you and others are all working toward the same goal.

Meeting conflicts can be harder to solve than some of the toughest mathematical problems. One of the ways to handle conflict is to turn the point of conflict into a question and get other opinions on the topic. Another strategy is to try to lighten the situation with humor. Facilitators can also ask the person what is wrong in order to show concern. If the person is standing, the facilitator can ask him or her to sit down. It is harder to be mad when sitting. More generally, facilitators should try to make it a win-win situation for everyone involved in the conflict. They can do so by staying neutral and avoiding taking sides. Most importantly, facilitators and participants should not get angry and argue back by saying things like, "Don't feel that way," or "Yes, but . . ." Facilitators should not ridicule or criticize others' statements or tell others to just be quiet and to listen to their explanation. Any of these actions will probably maintain the conflict or make it worse (Successful meetings, 1997, p. 2).

As the meeting draws to a close, facilitators should summarize the main discussion points and any decisions that are made during the meeting. This information can help pull all of the information together for attendees.

After the Meeting After the meeting has concluded, minutes should be posted as soon as possible, within two days at the latest. The memo should include key topics covered, any decisions or conclusions that were drawn, any projects due and the deadlines, and specific information on future meetings. More specifically, the meeting minutes should include:

- Time, date, location.

- Names of attendees.

- Agenda items and any other items discussed.

- Decisions made.

- Assignments and person responsible.

- Length of meeting.

- Time, date, and location of the next meeting.

It may also be appropriate to communicate to participants progress that is made on the implementation of decisions or plans of action arrived at during the meeting.

- The context of communication should be considered when formulating a message. Context includes various internal and external environmental factors. The culture of the corporation as well as the communication climate can affect whether messages are communicated and how they are conveyed.

- After considering the context for communicating and the culture in which you will communicate, you are in a better position to select the appropriate channel or media to convey your message. In order to select the most appropriate channel or media for communication, you might consider such factors as the amount of complex information you wish to convey. Or, you might select a written channel, because this also serves as a record to which the receiver can refer back and because the information is less costly to deliver using your company mail service. Likewise, you might select an oral channel to communicate with your colleague in the next office because you want the additional information it provides ("richness" in the form of nonverbal communication), and you also desire immediate contact and feedback. After you have identified your purposes of communication and analyzed your audience's needs, expectations, and concerns, you are better

prepared to select a communication channel that will enable you to create an effective business communication strategy.

- One channel of communication that has received a lot of attention in recent years in both the workplace and academic settings is group communication. Although the purposes of business communication and the importance of audience analysis apply to group communication just as they do to other channels of communication, the complex dynamics that arise from group situations require additional knowledge for strategy formulation. Much of the research about and many of the practices involved in interpersonal communication are applicable to group communication situations. Paying attention to group formation and group processes can help ensure that groups are productive. Special attention may need to be paid to decision-making processes and conflict resolution to ensure that the potential benefits of groups are achieved.

- Group meetings are notorious for negatively affecting individual productivity. However, this problem can be avoided through careful planning, skilled facilitation, and proper follow-up of meetings.

KEY TERMS

Comparison level, 90
Comparison level for alternatives, 90
Competitors, 103
Cooperators, 104
Defensive, 79
Free-riding, 98
Fundamental attribution error, 104
Groupthink, 102

Individualists, 104
Informational influence, 96
Interchange compatibility, 89
Intermember relations, 92
Interpersonal influence, 96
Norm of reciprocity, 103
Normative influence, 96
Organizational culture, 76

DISCUSSION QUESTIONS

1. You want to ask your supervisor for a raise. What channel or channels of communication would you use and why?

2. You are the salesperson for a company and have unknowingly sold faulty product to a dozen customers. What is the best channel of communication for dealing with this problem and why? Would you use more than one channel? If so, in what order?

3. What are group norms, and how do they structure interactions within a group?

4. What are group roles and which roles occur most frequently in groups? Which roles are productive and why? Which roles are destructive and why?

5. What are the sources of conflict in groups? How can conflict be managed effectively?

APPLICATIONS

1. **Analyzing Communication Networks and Channel Choice.** Identify an organization of which you are a part. This organization can be your workplace, or a church, sports, or university organization in which you participate. Identify the formal communication network the organization uses and answer the following questions: Does it primarily use upward, downward, or horizontal flow, or some combination of these? Does it use its formal communication network as effectively as it might?

   Then give some thought to its use of the informal communication network. What role does the "grapevine" play in this organization?

   Finally, what are its favored channels or media of communication? Are these effective or not, and why?

2. **Writing a Group Contract.** One way to ensure that a group has the discussion that is necessary to begin on the path of performing is to create a group contract. Creating a group contract ensures that you have discussed your expectations of each other, assigned task responsibilities, created deadlines, and talked about group member roles. In addition, a group contract details the procedure for dealing

with the failure to meet these agreed-upon expectations. To complete a group contract, follow the steps below.

   a. You and your group members should discuss and identify your expectations of each other regarding the completion of your team project. These expectations generally include concerns about participation; the meeting of deadlines; attendance at in-class group meetings and at other group meetings; and the revision of individual sections of your presentation or paper to meet group standards. Group standards regarding the quality of work expected or the grade desired are also often useful.

   In addition, you may want to agree upon deadlines for the various components of your project as well as assign group roles and responsibilities.

   b. You and your group members should discuss and identify the consequences for not fulfilling these expectations. Specifying consequences is important for two reasons: 1) it provides an opportunity to empower group members; and 2) it mitigates against the enabling of free-riding and social loafing. Examples of consequences include percentage reductions in an individual's group grade if deadlines are not met, or if revisions are not made to individual assignments as expected by the team. Another example of consequences might be the termination of an individual's membership in the group if a certain number of contract transgressions occur.

c. Each group should write a contract that specifies its expectations of individual members as well as the consequences for not fulfilling these expectations. You should be as specific as possible. For example, you should specify what constitutes poor attendance, inadequate participation, and low-quality work. Consequences for not fulfilling expectations should be as specific as your group's expectations. As discussed above, your contract might also include a schedule as well as the assignment of group members' responsibilities.

3. **Planning a Team Meeting: Creating an Agenda.** Your team should prepare an agenda for an actual meeting it plans to hold. Your agenda for this meeting should include the following introductory items:

- The primary purpose of your meeting. Is it to generate ideas, narrow a field of options, or to make a decision?

- The time, date, and place of your meeting.

- The names of those attending.

Following this information, you should provide a list of *specific* topics you intend to discuss during your meeting that are organized in the order of their importance (the most important first). You may wish to include a time limit for the discussion of each item.

4. **Analyzing the Effectiveness of a Team Meeting.** After your team holds a planned meeting, you may wish to analyze its effectiveness by discussing what you observed, including the communication behaviors and roles each team member tended to play. In providing this assessment, you might consider the following:

- What did we do in this meeting that worked well?

- What happened that we would not want to repeat? Are there bad habits into which we keep falling?

- What roles did different team members take on? Were these helpful in achieving group goals? Why or why not?

- What type of communication behaviors did team members display? Were these helpful in achieving group goals? Why or why not? Other issues to consider include how well your group was able to attend to both the task and social functions of a team. More specifically, you might wish to consider whether:

- You were able to keep the discussion of a particular topic within a reasonable amount of time.

- You were able to keep the discussion focused on the agenda topics.

- Participants felt valued and respected because others listened to them and responded to what they said in a way that fostered participation.

- You were able to deal with conflict and individualistic behaviors effectively and productively.

- You were able to reach your goals for the meeting.

5. **Team Member Evaluations.** Use the following template to generate an internal team review. Please rank team members according to their value to the team. Additionally, provide each team member with a short paragraph outlining this individual's strengths, and an additional paragraph outlining an area where this individual needs to improve.

To begin this process, record each team member's name and score him or her on a scale of 1–5 (1 being lowest and 5 being highest) next to each of the team-related activities, using the template on the next page.

Team Member:

Establishing decision-making policies	
Setting meeting agendas	
Setting timelines and meeting deadlines	
Identifying team needs	
Defining project goals	
Planning strategies to meet group goals	
Facilitating problem solving	
Developing conflict resolution rules	
Organizing collaborative sessions	
Assigning task responsibility	
Flexibility and accommodating group	
Recommending action	

InfoTrac Activities

1. Using InfoTrac College Edition, type in the words "project teams" in the keyword search engine. Visit some of the Web sites that are found to learn more about how project teams are used in the workplace today.

2. Using InfoTrac College Edition, type in the words "teleconferencing in business" in the keyword search engine. Visit some of the Web sites that are found to learn more about how organizations use teleconferencing to meet their long-distance communication needs.

Case Analysis

Due to a behavior change process developed by Lynn Dorsett, program director, Global Teaming Services, IBM Management, and her team, more than 4,500 IBM teams worldwide do their work in shared digital spaces (Dorsett, 2001). Being able to collaborate electronically is now considered a critical skill for IBM employees and one that benefits the bottom line. Each team, on average, increased sales revenue by $3 million during the first six months of use (Dorsett, 2001).

Before the digital teams were developed, it was common for IBM sales teams to take nearly two months to produce a complex business proposal (Dorsett, 2001). The only alternative for speeding up the process was often to send drafts of the proposal by fax, with each recipient adding his or her corrections and updates and then sending the fax on to the next person. Such a process was so slow that IBM often lost bids to its competitors.

The success of digital collaboration at IBM depends not on the technology but on people's ability to adopt a new way of working, according to Dorsett (2001). What is important is the process that is used to help people make the required behavior changes. The process, which can take as long as two months, starts with one-on-one coaching of the team leader. Then in a two-day, face-to-face meeting, the facilitator helps the team:

- Align its mission.

- Clarify each member's role.

- Understand members' differing communication and work styles.

- Decide how the team will make decisions in the TeamRoom.

- Document and agree on team norms (Dorsett, 2001).

What IBM has found during the six years its teams have been collaborating in shared digital spaces is that teams that invest in basic teamwork skills and team leadership succeed in working electronically. Teams that concentrate only on the enabling technology fail.

According to Dorsett (2001), the benefits of properly trained digital teams include the following:

- When team members receive the same information at the same time and quickly, the conflict that comes from selective or secret information flow is avoided. Departmental politics are minimized.

- Accountability of team members to each other and to the work increases significantly. Participation and individual contributions by members are evident to everyone on the team.

- Even though members may be remote, decisions can be made with the knowledge and participation of the entire team.

- Since team members have the most current information, they can make high-quality decisions quickly.

- The digital space serves as a record. There are two benefits: 1) a record of any decision stays in the shared digital space, ensuring it will stick; and 2) relevant documents reside in that space and can be easily accessed. This ability also eliminates any ambiguity about which version is current.

- Important information stays with the team through changes in membership. New team members can become contributors faster because the team's history and intellectual capital reside in the shared space.

Discussion

1. Do you agree with the assessment that the success of teams often depends upon changing team members' behavior?

2. How might IBM's procedure for building effective digital work teams be applied to the groups in which you are involved?

chapter **Organization**

GLOBAL MEDIA VENTURES, INC.: THE CHANGING FILM MARKET

Bill Locke is vice president of GMV's film production company. For years, the division has produced big-budget epics and almost equally big-budget romantic comedies because of their reliance on A-list actors who command top salaries. But the costs of producing such films are seriously threatening the company's bottom line as it competes with comparatively low-budget independent films and those that rely upon relatively less expensive computer-generated special effects.

Locke believes that the division should diversify its product offerings by moving into a potentially lucrative yet lower-cost area: animated films for children and teenagers. Such films do well in the DVD market and cost much less to produce, since they don't involve high-priced actors or filming on location.

Locke's problem is that most of the employees in the division have worked there for years and are personally highly invested in its current product line. For many, the thought of doing "cartoons" for children is unthinkable.

discussion...

1. What are the purposes of Locke's message to his employees?

2. What are the interests of his audience? What are audience members' concerns and objections?

3. What channel(s) of communication should Locke use to best ensure that he achieves his purposes of communicating?

4. In organizing his message, what considerations should Locke make to ensure that his audience remains open to his message and will continue listening, giving him the opportunity to achieve his purposes?

After studying this chapter, you will be able to

Understand how good organization helps you to better meet your audience's needs and thus helps you to establish a good relationship with your audience.

Explain how good organization helps you to establish your credibility.

Use the process of writing to achieve these purposes.

Organize a message logically and clearly.

Organize a persuasive message, using the AIDA strategy.

Organize persuasive messages for resistant or hostile audiences.

The purpose of this chapter is to discuss the importance of good organization and explain how to achieve it. Good organization helps you to achieve two objectives: 1) it helps your audience to understand your oral as well as your written communication; and 2) it demonstrates the quality of your thinking. From a strategic perspective, the first objective is aimed at meeting your audience's needs, which may help you achieve one of the purposes of communication—conveying goodwill—while the second objective performs a second purpose: it reflects upon your credibility or image as a professional.

MEETING YOUR AUDIENCE'S NEEDS

Few of us read for enjoyment anymore. We all seem to lack enough time in our days. The few moments we may get to sit and relax are probably spent in front of a television, computer, or video game. However, just because we have little time for leisurely reading doesn't mean that we don't read. We carry pounds of "junk" mail from our mailboxes each week and are faced with dozens of e-mails, both personal and professional, perhaps on a daily basis. We still may receive paper documents to read at work or at school. We may periodically be required to read and fill out legal or government documents for personal and professional reasons.

Even though we may spend little time reading and writing for pleasure, most of us still spend a significant amount of time reading and writing if for no other reason than our jobs or schooling require it. And with the proliferation of personal computing and e-mail messaging, the amount of time spent creating and reading messages has increased dramatically. In fact, the amount of paper crossing a person's desk has increased 600 percent in the past ten years. (Watson, n.d., p. 2).

With this increase in the number of written messages in the workplace has come a greater demand for good writing. A few years ago, there was little call for good writers in the workplace. In fact, writing skills took a backseat to work experience. Now, employees whose jobs never included writing are now at minimum required to communicate with customers through e-mail. According to a survey conducted by Clearswift, the American Management Association, and the ePolicy Institute, the average U.S. employee spends about one hour and 47 minutes a day dealing with e-mail. Goizueta Business School claims this figure is even higher; a study of 1,200 managers found that more than half of them spend over two hours a day dealing with e-mail (Crainer & Dearlove, 2002, p. 23).

Unfortunately, studies also indicate that much of this writing is poor and difficult to read, decreasing company productivity and increasing costs. According to an article in *HR Focus,* American businesses generate an estimated 30 billion pieces of writing each year (Write On, 1993, p. S4). A great deal of this writing tends to be pointless, ambiguous, and redundant. "To make matters worse, employees receiving these communiqués have to sift and read through this grammatical litter" (Write On, 1993, p. S4). However, this problem can be overcome if employees know how to write well-constructed messages. In one study of military personnel, researchers discovered that Navy officers took up to 23 percent less time to read documents that were written in a clearly organized, concise manner. The researchers concluded that the Navy could save over $26.5 million in wasted person-hours by constructing documents that were written in a style that was easy to read (Crainer &Dearlove, 2004, p. 23).

As these studies indicate, the amount of information with which we must contend and the limited amount of time we have to do so causes us to search for ways to process messages more efficiently. We may use such strategies as skimming to quickly determine whether a message is important to read or not. If we determine that a message is important, we probably continue to skim to determine which parts of the message to read and which to skip.

The strategy of skimming may be so automatic that you don't even consciously recognize that you use it. But when was the last time that you sat down and read every word of every piece of "junk" mail you received in a day? We may get no further than the name on the envelope or that of the e-mail sender before we decide whether to open and read a message. Just a name may provide enough information to decide whether to read the message immediately or whether we can set the message aside for a more convenient time. Part of this decision may have to do with the credibility of the writer or our relationship to him or her. If the person has a tendency to send poorly written messages or those that are of low importance, we may choose not to waste our time attempting to decipher them.

communication IN YOUR WORLD

People are spending more time at their jobs and doing more work. Over 25 million Americans work more than 40 hours each week. Of that number, nearly 25 percent spend 49 to 59 hours weekly at the office; another 8.5 percent say they spend 60 hours or more (Fraser, 2001).

But working professionals aren't the only ones feeling the time squeeze. Rising college costs have also placed greater time pressures on students, more and more of whom are working to pay for the price of an education. Of full-time college students with jobs, 20 percent worked 35 hours or more each week. Another 26 percent reported working 25 to 34 hours a week, while 25 percent worked 16 to 24 hours, and 29 percent worked 1 to 15 hours (King & Bannon, 2002).

These time pressures are increased by the proliferation of technology that enables us to communicate with anyone anywhere: e-mail, Internet, cell phones, laptop computers, and wireless capabilities. It isn't unusual for professionals to work during their commute time or at home at night or on weekends, sometimes even during vacations, because of the availability and use of these technologies.

Students have availed themselves of the same technologies and with it may be exposed to the overwhelming number of messages—voice and text—that such capabilities deliver.

Discussion

1. **How much of your day in terms of minutes or even hours is used to communicate via electronic technologies, such as the Internet, voice mail, cell phones, and instant messaging (IMing)?**

2. **Have you begun to find ways to make your processing of such information quicker, such as sorting voice mail messages or skimming e-mail ones?**

3. **Have you given thought to the number of messages you send using such technologies, and how they might be received and processed by your audience(s)?**

critical **thinking**

How do you read messages? Do you skim or use the "name test"? What is your reaction to messages that are poorly organized or that do not clearly state their topics and purposes?

For those messages that get past the "name test," good organization is important. A document that is well organized enables readers to skim it easily and provides obvious signposts as to the contents and locations of its various parts. If a message does not provide these signposts, the reader may set it aside because it takes too much time to grasp its overall meaning quickly or to find the location of the information that he or she needs.

Good organization is important not only for written messages but for oral ones as well. The sad truth is that most of us are poor listeners. In fact, researchers have found that individuals recall only 50 percent of a message immediately after listening to it and only 25 percent after a short delay (Gilbert, 1988). However, there is a good reason for this fact: our minds work more rapidly than most people can speak. Therefore, when listening to an oral message or presentation of any duration, we often find our minds wandering to other subjects. For this reason, it is also important to take extra care to provide cues for our listeners so that they don't become confused about the contents of our oral messages and if they do "zone out," oral organizational cues can help them to more easily pick up the conversation.

There are two ways to provide these organizational cues in an oral presentation: visually and verbally. Visually, we can provide aids that communicate the main topics we will cover and indicate the topic that we are currently discussing. This subject will be covered more thoroughly in Chapter 8: Visual Impression. Verbally, we can provide overviews of the topics we will cover in our presentation as well as clear, complete transitions that indicate when we are moving from one topic to the next. Including a summary conclusion, to ensure that your listeners do not miss any important points, is also a good idea. These aspects of good organization will be covered in more detail later in this chapter in the section entitled "Developing Good Organization."

Establishing Your Credibility

Have you ever tried to read a document for which you could not identify its main topic or purpose fairly quickly? In such situations, you might feel frustration and stop reading because it takes too much time and effort to figure out what it is the writer is attempting to communicate. Your thoughts may then turn to the writer. What could bring someone to write like this? You might judge the writer as a poor thinker, as too lazy to write a clearer message, or as unaware and insensitive to the needs of his or her audience.

In addition to reflecting upon your concern or knowledge of your audience, your communication skills are a direct reflection of your ability to think in a logical, well-organized way. In fact, in order to create logical, well-organized documents, you must have excellent analytical skills. In other words, you must be able to break down a message into its component parts, organize those elements logically, and then construct a message so that the connections between your ideas are clear and easy to understand. Another way to think about your messages is that they are a "road map" or direct reflection of the quality of your analytical thinking abilities. If your messages are disorganized, illogical, and confusing to your readers or listeners, they may believe that this is an indication of the quality of your thinking as well.

When a reader or listener encounters disorganized, illogical, and confusing messages, he or she may believe that it is a waste of time to attempt to interpret the message. This decision may have two negative consequences: 1) the writer or speaker's credibility has been damaged; and 2) his or her attempt to communicate has failed. However, even if the audience attempts to figure out the meaning of the disorganized message, it might be a waste of time since the audience may interpret it incorrectly.

In addition, businesspeople read messages differently than teachers. You may have been in an academic environment for nearly two decades and become accustomed to your teacher's obligation to read your written messages, regardless of how disorganized they might be. But a busy professional is not obliged to read poorly written messages. If you write such a message to your supervisor, he or she is likely to enter your office and confront you about your confusing message. If this occurs, your credibility has been damaged.

Good writing skills are critical to your success in the workplace. One survey of the 1,000 largest employers in the United States reported that 96 percent say employees must have good writing skills to get ahead (Fisher, 1998, p. 244). Unfortunately, *The Wall Street Journal* reports that 80 percent of businesses surveyed believed that their employees' biggest weakness was written communication (Price, 2004, p. 13). This finding presents an opportunity, however, for those who can communicate well in writing. They can positively distinguish themselves from their peers through their written communication skills.

Poor organization can also have negative consequences in an oral presentation. Because we are poor listeners, the most important goal of any oral presentation is to keep your audience's attention. This goal can partially be accomplished through your delivery style and your content, but if your message is difficult to follow and to make sense of, then chances are, your audience will become confused and stop listening. In such a case, not only were you unsuccessful at delivering your message, but you may also have damaged your credibility, as mentioned earlier.

critical **thinking**

Have you listened to oral presentations that did not take the listener's needs into account? What were your reactions? How might you avoid such mistakes?

Messages that lack clear organization often reflect poorly on the communicator and may negatively affect his or her relationship with the audience. In a business situation, if disorganized writing is interpreted by your supervisor as laziness on your part or as evidence of poor thinking, these judgments may affect your ability to receive raises or to be promoted. Your supervisor may not want you to represent the company to outside suppliers, vendors, or customers because your inability to communicate clearly may reflect poorly on the company. More immediately, though, it may affect your ability to achieve your business communication purposes.

THE PROCESS OF CREATING AUDIENCE-CENTERED MESSAGES

Part of the reason for disorganized messages lies in our own lack of awareness about the process we use to formulate messages. In the first draft of a complex document, for example, many of us write to ourselves in an attempt to figure out what it is we want to say. Such documents may begin without identifying a purpose or topic; in fact, in this process, we are often writing to identify the purpose or topic of our message for ourselves. In this process, beginning ideas may be general or abstract, or even somewhat unrelated to the topic at which we eventually arrive.

As discussed previously in this text, such writing is generally not well organized. Paragraphs may cover several topics; they may lack topic sentences. But as we continue to write, we usually narrow our topic and discover our purpose for writing. Along the way, we may make some detours into topics that are tangentially related to our central topic but that are not particularly relevant to our purpose. Once we finally figure out our main goal for writing, we may stop, believing we are finished. Such messages are *self-centered*.

One of the reasons that such a process is used initially to formulate messages may be the way that our minds work. Each of our brains is unique in the sense that it is a storage place for our memories. Our brain creates links between these memories that are unique to each of us. When we think of one memory, the link to other memories may be highly dependent upon our own individual experiences of these events. Consequently, topics that may seem totally unrelated to others may be strongly connected in our own minds. This is called *associative thinking,* a process by which our minds link associated events stored in our memories. This process of linking associated ideas is typically outside of our consciousness.

Associative thinking might occur when your teacher asks you to write a paper about your summer vacation. Let's suppose that during your summer vacation, you took a road trip to the East Coast with your family. As you are writing your paper, however, you touch upon the topic of the family car. This discussion of the family vehicle may remind you of the car you would like to own, and suddenly you are writing not about your summer vacation, but about cars in general. This detour occurs because the topic of family car is related to other information stored in your brain about vehicles. However, your teacher, upon reading your essay, might give you a poor grade because you did not narrowly address the topic of the assignment, but instead wrote about the car you would like to eventually own.

Although associative thinking is natural for many of us, in Western cultures we prefer and generally expect academic, journalistic, and professional writing to be presented in a linear, logical form. In other words, we expect the topics that are covered to be clearly related and focused on a single stated topic that we can all understand.

Consequently, self-centered messages are generally considered first drafts. In other words, the writer is writing to discover what he or she wants to say. In order to produce audience-centered writing or speaking, however, the writer or speaker must review the message to ensure that it contains the information that the audience needs to make sense of the message. Not only does this include relevant and explanatory content, but it also requires that the information is logically ordered and that connections are made between topics. Another way to think about audience-focused messages is that you are attempting to provide a clear road map of your thoughts. As stated earlier, your messages are also a reflection of the quality of your thinking.

critical **thinking**

Are you a self-centered or audience-centered writer? In other words, do you write to yourself to discover what it is you want to write? If so, have you recognized that this is just the first draft and that you may now need to heavily edit the document for others to read? Specifically, what procedure might you use to ensure your messages are audience-centered?

Self-centered messages are not a bad thing in themselves, for they can be considered the first step in the process of message creation. The important thing to remember is that the formulation of messages to important audiences or to audiences with whom you are unfamiliar should be a multi-step process. The steps of this process are listed below:

1. Research and plan your message, which includes identifying your purposes and analyzing your audience(s).

2. Draft the message.

3. Edit for organization, content, and style and tone.

4. Proofread for correctness.

After reading this step list, it is probably apparent that much of the message creation that we may have done in the past and continue to do today has not involved all the steps of the process. Because of this, many of our messages may have lacked good organization, content, and style as well as correctness. For example, if we had thoroughly performed step 1, we might have avoided the creation of self-centered messages in the first place. That is because good research and planning involve identifying relevant topics and those that would be of interest to your audience and organizing them in a logical order, perhaps using an informal or formal outline.

Informal outlines are usually sufficient for less complex messages, such as an informal report in which you use a memo format. (Formatting is discussed in Chapter 8: Visual Impression.) For example, if you are proposing the offering of a flex-time policy at your organization, you might produce an informal outline that consists of the topics listed in Figure 5-1.

FIGURE 5-1. *Example of an informal outline.*

Introduction: Statement of purpose and overview of the contents of the message.

1. Explanation of the flex-time policy and how it would work.

2. Explanation of how a flex-time policy would benefit the organization and its employees.

3. Explanation of how to implement the new flex-time policy.

Conclusion: Restate benefits of the new policy to the organization and employees.

FIGURE 5-1. *Example of an informal outline.*

A formal outline is used for longer messages, such as reports and proposals. It is usually a detailed, time-consuming endeavor. When creating a formal outline, you place your thesis or purpose statement at the beginning, then list your major points and label them with roman numerals (I, II, III). These main points are broken down further into subpoints, which are listed below their respective main points and labeled with indented capital letters (A, B, C). These subpoints can be further subdivided and labeled with indented Arabic numerals (1, 2, 3). Finally, these can be further subdivided and labeled with indented lowercase letters (a, b, c). The organization for a formal outline is from general to more and more specific. In the figure below, the format of a formal outline is illustrated.

FIGURE 5-2. *Format of a formal outline.*

I. First-level heading
   A. Second-level heading
      1. Third-level heading
      2. Third-level heading
        a. Fourth-level heading
        b. Fourth-level heading
   B. Second-level heading
      1. Third-level heading
      2. Third-level heading
        a. Fourth-level heading
        b. Fourth-level heading

II. First-level heading
   A. Second-level heading
      1. Third-level heading
      2. Third-level heading
        a. Fourth-level heading
        b. Fourth-level heading
   B. Second-level heading
      3. Third-level heading
      4. Third-level heading

In the figure above, you will notice that you must have at least two headings at each level. It is not logical to have only one subheading under a major point; in that case, the subpoint is an integral part of the main point. This format can also be used for visualizing the organization of headings in complex documents, such as formal reports and proposals. Headings are discussed in more detail in Chapter 8: Visual Impression.

Although organization should be part of the first step in message creation, editing for organization generally occurs once again after the draft stage of a message. If you draft without creating an outline, you may discover that your message is self-centered in its organization. In other words, you may find when editing that the main topic is at or near the end of the message. The next step in creating an audience-centered message is thus to check whether the message should be turned upside down. In other words, if the main topic or point is located at the end of the draft, you should generally put it at the beginning of the second draft. The second step in this editing process is then to identify topics that are not clearly related to the main topic, and eliminate that information. Finally, what remains should be organized in a logical order at the global level and then at the paragraph level. (These steps are explained in more detail in the section that follows.) After editing for content and style and tone, a written message should be proofread for correctness. Content, style, and tone are discussed in more detail in subsequent chapters of this book.

DEVELOPING GOOD ORGANIZATION

Essentially, good organization comes down to providing clear beginnings, middles, and ends. As stated earlier, another way to think about organization is to compare a message to a road map. As a writer or speaker, you should be consistently telling your readers or listeners where they are going, where they are at, and where they have been so they don't become confused or have to expend a lot of their own energy trying to figure out the puzzle you may have inadvertently created for them. If done well, good organization also shows your readers or listeners the relationship between all of a message's parts.

Good organization occurs at the global as well as at the paragraph level in written messages. This section describes how to achieve good organization at both of these levels for both written and oral messages.

Before You Communicate

Analysis

Analysis, in a message, is the ability to identify the message's main topic and break it down into its component parts.

Before you deliver a message, you should identify your main topic and the subtopics you will address in the body of your message. The ability to identify a main topic and break it down into its component parts is called **analysis.** Analytical thinking skills are critical to the development of good organization and are often apparent to the audience for a message. In other words, your ability to analyze is communicated to your audience by the quality of the message you deliver.

As discussed above, some messages require considerable time spent in the planning stage. In addition to identifying the topics you will cover, you may need to spend time creating a logical structure through the process of outlining and gathering additional information, perhaps by conducting research, as discussed earlier in this chapter.

Regardless of whether such complex messages will be delivered in writing or orally, the planning stage is important. Below, a template for planning oral presentations is provided.

PRESENTATION PLANNER

Introduction

Attention-getting material:

Purpose Statement:

Overview of presentation:

    Subpoint:

    Subpoint:

    Subpoint:

  Transition to body of presentation:

Body

Main point 1:

  Transition to main point 2:

Main point 2:

  Transition to main point 3:

Main point 3:

  Transition to conclusion:

Conclusion

Summary:

Concluding remarks:

Each of the main parts included in the Presentation Planner is discussed in more detail in the sections that follow.

The Beginning

After identifying the main topic of your message and its subtopics, you should develop an introduction that states the purpose of the message and provides an overview of those subtopics. This step is important in professional messages because businesspeople are typically pressed for time and bombarded with information. Given these pressures, they often try to find ways to process information more rapidly or to cull out messages that are not of high importance. In fact, you have only one to seven seconds to convince a reader that the information is relevant and only 90 seconds to confirm and keep the reader's interest (Watson, n.d., p. 2).

An introduction should indicate to your audience why it is important to listen to or read your message. It should also provide your audience with a road map of what the message contains to either aid in skimming a written document or to better follow the logic or contents of your oral message.

For example, an introduction for a message intended to persuade your audience— perhaps an employee in the human resources department or a supervisor— to adopt a new company policy might state, "I am writing to ask you to consider the adoption of a new policy that will allow employees to work on a flex-time schedule. I will first discuss the need for this change, then the benefits it will provide to the company and its employees, and finally, my ideas for implementing the new policy."

In this example, the first sentence states the purpose of the message and also implies why this message is important to read: you are proposing a change to company policy. The second sentence provides a road map of the primary topics that will be covered, which also may pique the reader's interest, since you mention that your proposal will provide benefits.

In oral presentations, gaining your audience's attention and arousing its interest may be a more challenging undertaking. Many techniques exist for gaining an audience's attention at the beginning of an oral presentation. These include:

- Bringing to the presentation the object or person about which you will speak. For example, if you are going to be speaking on a product, you would bring it and perhaps demonstrate its use.

- Briefly stating the benefits your audience may receive.

- Inviting your audience to participate by asking relevant questions about your audience or topic.

- Starting with a sight or sound that is related to your message. These might include slides containing pictures or other images, a short film or video, and music or a sound clip. This technique should be used with care; you don't want the film or video to become your presentation, just to introduce and highlight your message.

- Arousing audience curiosity by telling an engaging, yet related story.

- Role-playing a relevant situation or event in front of the group with an audience member. For example, you might ask an audience member to play the role of a customer who is interested in buying a product.

- Stating striking facts or statistics that are related to your topic. For example, in a presentation to discuss the popularity and potential of a new soft drink introduced in the United States, you might state: "The average American drinks more carbonated soft drinks—56 gallons per year—than citizens of any other country in the world."

When selecting an attention getter for an oral presentation, it is helpful if you first identify the theme of your presentation, the main point you want to convey, or the action you want your audience to take, and ensure that your attention getter is clearly related. Some speakers think that every public speech should begin with a joke, but if a joke is inappropriate or irrelevant, or you are poor at telling jokes, skip it.

Some messages, however, may require slightly different openings. For example, if you are writing a persuasive message to an audience that is resistant or even hostile to your proposal, you might start your message with a statement of common ground or a point of agreement that you both share. Your intention is to send the message that you and your audience are not that far off in terms of your respective positions, and consequently should be able to agree upon a common goal or solution with sufficient discussion and openness to each others' perspectives and suggestions.

Most presentations that take place in the workplace are informal. Even in these cases, presenters should take care to engage their audience and maintain its attention.

Indirect opening

An indirect opening to a message is one that does not explain the specific proposal you are addressing.

In the example above, the introduction could be altered to include a statement of common ground: "In our past discussions, we have both agreed that efforts should be made to provide benefits to employees that do not negatively impact the company's bottom line. This memo will detail a proposal to do just that. I will first explain the need for this change, then the benefits it will provide to the company and its employees, and finally, my ideas for implementing the new policy."

This strategy is called an **indirect opening,** since it does not explain the specific proposal you are addressing. In this type of message, the body would contain information intended to show that there is a need for change and that other solutions aren't the best. It is only after providing this information that you specifically name and present the details of your proposed solution. This ordering is used when you fear that sharing the specifics of your proposal too early in the message will cause your audience to stop listening to you or reading your message. This organizational pattern is discussed in more detail in a later section, "Organizing Persuasive Messages."

The beginning and the end of a message are considered its most important parts because they are the most memorable. For that reason, you should make it clear in the introduction why your message is important to your audience.

critical **thinking**

Do you always immediately state the purpose of your message in such a way that it is clear to your reader or listener why your message is important to him or her? Do you also provide a brief yet clear overview of the topics your message will address?

The Middle

In the middle, or body, of your message, a variety of elements exist that can help make your message clear and easier to follow. These include the use of:

- A logical structure.

- Topic sentences.

- Coherent paragraphs.

- Transitions and forecasting.

- Headings, if appropriate.

Each of these is discussed in the sections that follow.

Use a Logical Structure Depending upon the purposes, the audience, the situation, or the information you are providing, the ordering of your message may affect its success. Several strategies are available to make your messages more logical and understandable for your audience. You can choose to:

- Present new information before old.

- Organize information chronologically.

- Use a general-to-particular pattern.

- Use a problem-solution pattern.

- Use a cause-and-effect pattern.

> **Present old information before new.** One organizational strategy is to present information that is known to your reader or listener prior to presenting new information. This strategy makes the new information easier to understand because your reader or listener has a basis of understanding—the old information—on which to draw to comprehend the less familiar material.

> **Organize information chronologically.** Chronological ordering arranges ideas in the order of their occurrence over time. Such a pattern might also be used to explain the steps for a procedure. In this case, each step must be performed in a particular order to achieve the desired result. Chronological ordering is easy to achieve, easy to recognize, and easy to follow. One reason is that such ordering is similar to a narrative pattern, which is used in storytelling of all kinds, including that found in movies, novels, and television sitcoms. Because of our exposure to such media, we are all familiar with chronological ordering.

Use a general-to-particular pattern. Another common organizational strategy is to arrange your ideas from the general to the particular. General-to-particular is a common organizational arrangement in persuasive messages. The general statement is considered your claim. For example, you might state that "Our company has made a number of changes to benefit our employees." The particular information would then include the specifics of those changes as well as the benefits. Another way to think about the general-to-particular strategy is in terms of levels of abstractness. In other words, the general statement is more abstract than the particular information, which is more concrete.

Use a problem-solution pattern. The problem-solution pattern is common in business because it is highly persuasive and can include other patterns of reasoning, such as question-and-answer. When using this pattern, the communicator begins with a shared, recognizable problem, situation, or question and progressively moves to a solution supported by information or evidence. Such a pattern typically begins with a definition of the problem that proceeds to an analysis of the problem or evaluation of the solutions, and then concludes with a redefinition of the problem or suggestion for action.

Use a cause-and-effect pattern. The key to using the cause-and-effect pattern successfully is to build a case that supports your claim of cause and effect. In other words, this pattern forces you to make and support an inference that one event caused or will cause another. The fact that one event followed another (the chronological ordering discussed earlier) does not prove that one event caused the other.

To select the appropriate method for ordering your message, you should analyze the situation, identify your audience's expectations and your purposes for communicating, and then select the approach that best suits that particular situation.

Include Topic Sentences A crucial element in making written messages easy to skim is to include an accurate topic sentence for each and every paragraph. Ideally, in business messages, each paragraph should *begin* with an accurate topic sentence or transitional phrase that ideally mentions one of the subtopics referred to in the introduction. This strategy makes your messages more coherent because you are providing the connections between your ideas, announcing the progression of your ideas, and reminding your audience of your topic and its subtopics. This strategy also makes written messages easier to skim; if you have announced the subtopics in your introduction, your reader may decide that he or she only wants to read information about one of them. In that case, your reader will attempt to skim the paragraphs of your message to locate that information.

In written messages that your reader may skim, you should focus the content of each paragraph narrowly on the subtopic announced in the topic sentence. Otherwise, if paragraphs cover more than one topic, your reader may be unable to quickly locate the information that he or she is looking for, or your reader may become confused about the relationship of the ideas covered in a paragraph. In either case, you have created a written message that is not audience-centered.

Developing good organization at the paragraph level usually occurs after you have organized your overall message. Although organization at the paragraph level is particularly important for written messages, it also should be considered when formulating oral presentations, since these are planned in advance and often in great detail, unlike other types of oral communication.

At the paragraph level, you should ensure that each paragraph begins with an accurate topic sentence that announces the topic in such a way as to remind the reader or listener of the subtopics you provided in the overview that is part of the introduction of the message. You should then review each paragraph to ensure that its contents are narrowly focused on the topic announced in the beginning sentence.

Ensure Paragraph Coherence

Ensure Paragraph Coherence   Another issue to consider at the paragraph level is **coherence.** Coherence refers to the logical flow of ideas throughout and within a paragraph. In other words, each sentence should clearly lead to the next, and clear connections should be provided between each point or each sentence. An easy way to establish coherence is to consistently end each sentence with the topic that will be discussed in the sentence that will follow. The example below indicates how sentences can be constructed to provide coherence within a paragraph.

> *John is an avid* golfer. *He loves* golf *so much that he has purchased a miniature golf game that he has set up in his* office. *As I entered his* office *last week, he almost put my eye out with a wild, flying* golf *ball!*

In the example, the first sentence ends and the second begins with a reference to golfing, while the second sentence ends and the third begins with a reference to "office." The final sentence also ends with the topic stated in the first and second sentences, golf. This repetition provides coherence between each sentence, in that the topic is clearly carried over from one sentence to the next and the entire passage is clearly focused on a single, primary topic, golf. In contrast, writing that is not coherent is often described as choppy or as lacking flow.

Provide Transitions and Forecasting

Provide Transitions and Forecasting   In the flex-time scheduling example discussed earlier, the topic sentence of the first sentence of the body of the message might read, "First, I will explain the need to adopt a policy allowing flex-time scheduling." This statement also serves as a **transition** to the first paragraph and subtopic.

Transitions assist your audience to move from one topic to another through your use of words and phrases that link the ideas you are developing. In oral presentations, a transition should clearly and thoroughly link the topic you are

Coherence

Coherence is the logical flow of ideas throughout a paragraph.

Transition

Transitions are elements that assist the audience in moving from one topic to another through words and phrases that link the ideas the writer or speaker is developing.

moving from to the one you are moving to. For example, if the message in the example above were delivered orally, you might state as a transition the following: "Now that I have explained why we should adopt a policy allowing flex-time scheduling, I will tell you about some of the benefits such a change would provide to the company and its employees."

In oral presentations, it is particularly important to fully link the topic you have just discussed to the one you are about to discuss. Remember, we tend to be poor listeners. Your intention in restating the topic you have just covered is to remind those listeners who may tune out for a moment what you are covering and to indicate where you are in the overall structure of your presentation. Since we recall only 50 percent of a message immediately after we hear it, an audience may have forgotten all the topics announced in the introduction once the speaker transitions into the body of the speech.

It is important to recognize that in business messages a little repetition is not a bad thing. Again, because businesspeople are often faced with time pressures and, in oral situations, we are poor listeners, it is often necessary to restate information briefly, yet in a slightly different manner to ensure that our audience receives our message successfully. Repetition is also helpful because for many types of information, repetition is necessary for retention. In other words, to move information from our short-term memory to long-term recall, it may need to be repeated. Repetition is not the same as redundancy, however. Redundancy is saying the same thing in the same way without adding anything new or moving the message forward through the progression of its ideas or toward its intent.

Forecasting

Forecasting elements are those that tell the audience what the reader or speaker will cover next.

Forecasting, like transitions, tells your audience what you will cover next. Bulleted lists, summaries, and preview statements or overviews are also effective forecasting devices. (Bulleted lists are covered in more detail in Chapter 8: Visual Impression.)

Consider the Use of Headings

In written messages, you might consider the use of headings to provide signposts to the topics being addressed. (Headings are covered in more detail in Chapter 8.) However, it is important to recognize that headings do not do *all* the work of transitioning between paragraphs or sections of a written text. That is because some people read differently: some people read headings, some people don't. That means that even if you use headings as signposts for your reader, you should also ensure that you have included accurate topic sentences in case the reader skips or quickly skims the headings.

The End

As stated above, the conclusion is one of the most important parts of a message, since your audience will be more likely to remember it. Consequently, you should take care to ensure that the conclusion is in fact memorable and focuses upon the final message that you want your audience to take away.

There are three basic types of conclusions: goodwill, summary, and sales. Goodwill conclusions are used for short, routine messages in which another type of conclusion might be inappropriate or for messages sent simply for goodwill purposes. Summary conclusions are typically used for more complex, informative messages, while sales conclusions are used for persuasive messages. Each of these is discussed below.

Goodwill Conclusions   If you are sending a goodwill message or even if you are conveying a short routine message, such as an e-mail, you will probably want to close with a few simple sentences or statements aimed at maintaining your relationship with your reader. This type of conclusion is called a goodwill close and might sound something like this, "I look forward to meeting you Tuesday to further discuss the proposed flex-time plan." A goodwill close should avoid sounding generic, since your purpose is to maintain your relationship with your audience. Therefore, your close should be as specific to the situation and the person you are communicating with as possible, as in the example above. A goodwill close provides you an opportunity to distinguish yourself as a person who truly recognizes and appreciates others. Because we often feel like little more than a number in our busy, impersonal society, the ability to make others feel like special individuals can be a welcome, appreciated talent.

Summary Conclusions for Informative Messages   If you are conveying an informative message, you should create a summary conclusion in which you restate the subtopics of your message in a slightly different manner. You have probably all heard the old saw: "Tell 'em what you're going to tell, then tell 'em, then tell 'em what you just told 'em." This is the organizational formula for an informative message and is intended to ensure that readers who skim or who are not listening well get your message through repetition. As discussed earlier, repetition is not the same as redundancy, however; when you repeat information, you should do so in a slightly different manner. Sometimes stating information differently can also help your reader or listener with comprehension. The first time we hear or read something, its meaning may not be completely clear. But if additional explanation is provided or if the message is stated again in a slightly different way, the chances improve that the meaning will be understood.

Sales Conclusions for Persuasive Messages   If you are conveying a persuasive message, your conclusion should focus on restating the benefits your readers or listeners will receive from adopting your proposal. This type of conclusion is considered a sales conclusion. In some persuasive situations, it may also be appropriate to conclude with a **call to action.** You use a call to action when you want your audience to take the next step in your proposal. In the example

Call to action

A call to action is a conclusion to a persuasive message that is intended to convince the reader to fully consider the writer's or speaker's proposal and, ideally, to commit to a decision or to take the next step.

provided above, a call to action might be "Let's meet later this week to discuss the details of my proposal. I will call you tomorrow to discuss a day and time that is convenient for you." In this example, you are attempting to get the reader to fully consider your proposal and ideally to commit to a decision.

Calls to action are generally not as effective, however, if you, as the communicator, are not the person charged with following through. For example, in the example above, you might write: "Let's meet later this week to discuss the details of my proposal. Please call me to let me know a convenient time for you." In this case, you have provided the reader an opportunity to "drop the ball." If he or she does not call to set up an appointment, your proposal is dead unless, after a week passes without a call, you follow up to schedule the meeting.

In cases of application letters, a similar statement might be interpreted as a lack of interest in the position or as a lack of initiative on the part of the applicant. To avoid these situations, you should take responsibility for attempting to ensure that the discussion continues in a timely manner.

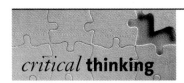

critical **thinking**

Do you generally provide clear beginnings, middles, and ends in your messages? If so, what are the results? If not, what strategies might you employ to produce these three parts of a message consistently?

ORGANIZING PERSUASIVE MESSAGES

Various models are available for organizing persuasive messages, since persuasion can be a more difficult communication purpose to achieve and thus may require more preparation and strategy formulation.

Broadly speaking, two persuasive situations exist: one in which you believe your audience is more or less receptive to your ideas or proposal and one in which you believe your audience is resistant or even hostile to you, your organization, or your ideas. In the former case, your audience may be so receptive that you simply need to request their agreement and you will receive it. In other cases, it might be helpful to consider the use of one of the models for persuasive messages.

AIDA approach

The AIDA approach is a popular model for organizing persuasive messages. AIDA is the acronym for attention, interest, desire, and action.

One popular model for organizing persuasive messages is called the **AIDA approach.** AIDA is an acronym that stands for attention, interest, desire, and action. The AIDA approach can be adjusted to meet the needs of both types of audiences in persuasive situations, those who are more or less receptive and those who are resistant or even hostile. However, it is more difficult to use for resistant or hostile audiences if you are a less experienced persuader. For that reason, a more detailed discussion of an organizational strategy for dealing with resistant and hostile audiences is also provided in this section.

Using the AIDA Approach

Each of the steps in the AIDA approach is discussed below.

1. **Attention.** The first step is to gain the audience's attention and interest, so you should begin every persuasive message with a brief statement that is personalized, audience-centered, and relevant to the situation and the audience. Your audience probably wants to know "what's in this message for me?" so you might call attention to the benefits it will receive.

2. **Interest.** In the second step, you should attempt to heighten the audience's interest in your topic or proposal. You can do this by explaining in more detail why your message is relevant to your audience. In this section, you might explain why current practices are not the best, if appropriate, or in other situations, provide examples, data, testimony, or other kinds of evidence to show your audience what life would be like if it adopts your proposal.

3. **Desire.** In the third step, you should provide evidence to prove the claims made earlier in your message. In product-related persuasion, you might provide evidence of the benefits your audience will receive.

   According to Hugh Rank (1982), persuaders can use four kinds of desire-stimulating tactics: protection, acquisition, relief, or prevention. First, they can promise the audience security or protection by showing that their advice will allow the audience to "keep a good" it may already have. Such a tactic might be used for a product intended to maintain good health, for example. Second, persuaders can show how an audience might acquire a good, such as a secure future through investment in their retirement products. Finally, persuaders can use tactics related to a bad or uncomfortable symptom or feeling. They can show how a product will provide relief from such a situation or how it will help the audience avoid it. Such a tactic might be used for deodorant, bad breath, or dandruff products.

4. **Action.** In the fourth step, you should suggest a specific action the audience can take and make it easy. You might also restate how the audience will benefit by acting as you wish. This last stage is similar to the issues discussed earlier in the section, "Sales Conclusions for Persuasive Messages."

Dealing with Difficult Audiences

As discussed earlier in this chapter, attempting to persuade a resistant or hostile audience requires a somewhat less direct approach. This is because such an audience may have already made up its mind about you, your organization, or your ideas. Even though you, your organization, and your ideas are separate from one another, they are associated, and some audiences will make this association. In this situation, you need to use a communication that will best help to ensure that your audience is open to hearing or reading and considering your persuasive message. For this reason, you may not want to announce your specific solution or proposal at the beginning of the message, because your audience already has an opinion about it and will stop listening to your message. That is why the ordering of a message to a resistant or hostile audience is important if you are to get the opportunity to persuade it. In general, you should use the general-to-particular ordering discussed earlier in this chapter.

The steps in persuading a resistant or hostile audience are explained below.

1. As was discussed earlier, you should open your message with a statement of common ground to defuse any differences that may exist between you and your audience. This statement should be followed with an indirect statement of purpose that generally explains your idea. You should also provide an overview of the contents of the body of your message.

2. The body of your message should begin by explaining the need for your proposed idea. Your goal is to show in a persuasive manner that there is a need for change of the type you are proposing.

3. After demonstrating the need for change, you must eliminate your audience's objections to your proposal. Your audience's objections might center upon several issues. In fact, you may have already addressed one objection: your belief in the need for change. Another objection your audience might have is that it favors another approach or solution. In this case, you must consider all the alternatives, discussing their benefits and disadvantages. In this section of your argument, you are working toward showing that of all the alternatives, your proposed solution is clearly best. You must do so in an objective way, however, to reduce the potential for judgments of bias. Your intent is to show that you are a reasonable, knowledgeable, and objective person who is systematically, yet thoroughly exploring the various options and the relevant issues.

4. After you tactfully eliminate your audience's objections through your careful analysis, you announce your specific solution and emphasize why it is the best of all possible choices. The strategy in this situation is to eliminate your audience's objections before announcing your idea, since to announce it earlier might affect their receptivity to your idea. In other words, you are attempting to keep them open to your message so that you have an opportunity to persuade them.

5. An additional step, if appropriate, might include a plan for implementation of your proposed solution. The easier the change is to make, the more attractive it may be to your audience.

When using this approach to persuasion, however, it is important to avoid deception or misleading statements. You can accomplish this by being honest and by using the general-to-particular organizational pattern explained earlier in this chapter.

The content of a persuasive message, including the use of evidence, is discussed in further detail in Chapter 6: Content.

Responsible Communication

According to Norman E. Bowie (2004), two issues led to the recent corporate scandals involving Enron, WorldCom, and Arthur Andersen: conflicts of interest and asymmetrical information. This exercise will focus on the latter, abuse of asymmetrical information.

Abuse of asymmetrical information exists "when one person has information that another person does not and does not share that information with the other when the other person has a legal and/or moral right to the information" (Bowie, 2004, p. 63). According to Bowie, the ethical violations by Enron were primarily abuse of information asymmetry violations. For example, in the Enron building, there existed a separate floor that was used to create the appearance that the company was doing energy trades when investors were in the building. But no such trades were taking place, and the floor was not usually used for such purposes. Thus Enron was able to deceive stockholders, investors, and even employees by withholding information from them and misleading them through manipulation of information (Bowie, 2004, p. 63).

The Sarbanes-Oxley Act of 2002 attempted to eliminate some of these abuses, although it is primarily limited to addressing the required auditing of publicly held firms. For example, it prohibits company officers and directors from misleading, manipulating, or coercing independent or certified accountants, such as Arthur Andersen in the Enron case. In addition, the CEO must attest to the accuracy of the financial statements. The act aims to provide the investing public with more and better information and to increase penalties for those who mislead. In other words, the act is intended to improve the *transparency* of publicly traded organizations.

Questions for Thought

1. **What are the ethical issues involved in reporting information accurately to the various stakeholders of an organization (shareholders, employees, customers, suppliers)?**

2. **What would you do if you were pressured by management to withhold information from others in such a way that it might be perceived as an act of deception or manipulation?**

- Learning to organize a message well is not just an academic exercise. It can have real effects on your career, your credibility, and your relationship with others. It can also affect how successful you are at conveying your message. Fortunately, good organization can be achieved by anyone willing to spend a few moments identifying the main issues he or she wishes to address, gathering information if necessary, and then creating a message that provides a clear, well-organized beginning, middle, and end.

- In order to achieve this goal, messages should be logically organized, unified, and complete so your audiences can readily and fully comprehend your intended purposes and meaning. A **logical structure** of information should be evident from the beginning and carried through to the end. The purpose or controlling idea should be logically developed, with each section of the message moving clearly to the next.

- The **introduction** should provide the overall purpose of the message and preview its organization and contents. It should be clear to your audience why it is important for it to read or listen to your message. For oral presentations, introductions should include an attention-getting statement intended to interest your audience in your message.

- **Coherence** refers to the logical flow of ideas both throughout the message and within its subsections or paragraphs. You should provide a topic sentence for each paragraph, each paragraph should develop one main point, each sentence should clearly lead to the next, and clear connections should be provided between each point or sentence. Presenting known prior to new information can help make connections.

- **Transitions** assist your audience to move from one topic to another through your use of words and phrases that link the ideas you are developing. In written messages, headings may provide a signpost as to the topic being addressed, but they do not do *all* the work of transitioning between paragraphs or sections of a written text. In oral presentations, transitions are particularly important for creating a coherent message and to provide a road map of your talk to your audience.

- **Forecasting,** like transitions, tells your audience what you will cover next. Bulleted lists, summaries, and preview statements are effective forecasting devices.

- The **conclusion** is important for providing your audience a sense of closure. Three common types of conclusion are goodwill, summary, and sales or call to action. Goodwill conclusions are often included in short messages, such as e-mails, letters, or memos; summaries are used for more complex messages that cover several points; and sales conclusions are used to motivate audiences to act. Conclusions should be simple, direct, and energetic.

- Because persuasion can be the most time-consuming and challenging purpose of business communication to achieve, organizational strategies have been created to make this task easier. Using the AIDA approach, the writer or speaker must first get the audience's attention; second, heighten its interests in the proposed idea; third, increase the desirability of the proposal by discussing its benefits; and finally, encourage the audience to take action.

- Resistant and hostile audiences may require the use of an organizational strategy aimed at keeping them open to hearing your proposal.

Using the general-to-particular organizational pattern helps because it provides the writer or speaker the opportunity to eliminate the audience's objections and to show why the proposed idea is the best.

Key Terms

AIDA approach, 136
Analysis, 127
Call to action, 135
Coherence, 133

Forecasting, 134
Indirect opening, 130
Transition, 133

Discussion Questions

1. How do the reading practices of academic audiences, such as instructors, differ from those of businesspeople? What are the factors that lead to these differences?

2. What strategies have you used to ensure that your messages are logically organized? What new strategies might you incorporate into your message creation process to ensure well-organized messages?

3. Do you think that using the indirect approach to organizing a message is manipulative or unethical?

4. What are some of the challenges you have encountered while attempting to persuade? How might the AIDA approach be used to better deal with these situations?

5. What are the critical elements that should be incorporated into an oral presentation to better ensure that an audience understands and can follow the logical progression of the message?

Applications

1. Create a formal outline for a research paper on one of the following topics:

   ■ Employee Privacy Rights in the Workplace

   ■ Controversial Television Advertising

   ■ Performance-Enhancing Drugs in Sports

   ■ Outsourcing Jobs to Foreign Countries

2. Using the Presentation Planner provided on page 128, create an outline for a presentation to accompany the written message that you planned in the previous exercise. Make sure to create a complete, relevant, and effective attention getter, include complete transitions between the main points, and wrap up with a memorable conclusion.

3. Revise the following message so that it is more logically ordered. You may also discover that some of the content is irrelevant and thus can be eliminated, and that the message also is missing some critical information needed to fulfill the customer's request.

   Mark Bellows
   Director of Customer Service
   GEEWHIZ Software, Inc.
   8403 Kentucky Avenue
   Cincinnati, OH 55003

   Dear Mr. Bellows:

   I recently purchased your new accounting software at Big Box Office Products. When I got the product home, I was unable to install the product on my Apple brand computer. I am a small business owner and think that your product will be very helpful to me in improving my productivity and potentially my company's profits.

I returned the product to Big Box Office Products to receive a refund or to exchange the product for one that might work on my computer. The manager told me that he could not make the exchange but that I should contact you, the maker, with my request.

Can you help me? I have enclosed the product with my letter.

Sincerely,

Sheila Woods
902 Oak Street
St. Louis, MI 60042

4. Using the AIDA approach, create a message to persuade your boss to approve your plan to hire two new people.

5. Using the steps to formulate a message to a reluctant or hostile audience, create a message to persuade a customer to consider the purchase of a new service or product your company is offering. Assume that the customer has previously had a bad experience with your company that involved the late delivery of your product or service, which resulted in a small financial loss for the customer. Also assume that the customer is currently pleased with the services he or she is receiving from one of your competitors.

 INFOTRAC ACTIVITIES

1. Using InfoTrac College Edition, type the word "brainstorming" in the keyword search engine. Visit some of the Web sites that are found to learn more about the use of brainstorming as a method for identifying topics that might potentially be covered in complex messages.

2. Using InfoTrac College Edition, type the word "transparency" in the keyword search engine. Visit some of the Web sites that are found to learn more about the issues involved in reporting information accurately.

Case Analysis

At the beginning of 2005, Blockbuster Inc., the world's leading rental chain of movies and video games, launched a major marketing campaign that put an end to rental late fees in order to gain a larger share of the market. However, the details of this new policy resulted in unforeseen complications for Blockbuster in the way of a consumer protection lawsuit brought by the State of New Jersey. The prosecutors claimed that Blockbuster's "No More Late Fees" policy was misleading to customers. The problem was that Blockbuster and its employees failed to inform their members about a charge that would be applied to their accounts if the rental was not returned within seven days after the due date.

According to State Attorney General Peter C. Harvey, New Jersey investigators "found that employees gave misleading or erroneous information on the policy" (Gold, 2005). Essentially, Blockbuster failed to communicate to customers that fees as large as $70 for out-of-print movies could be charged to their credit cards if videos or games are more than a week past due. In other words, customers would be charged the retail value of the item if they returned it after the seven-day grace period.

In order to learn about the policy, customers had to seek information about it on Blockbuster's Web site or ask an employee to fully explain the policy upon checkout.

The lack of communication between Blockbuster and its customers led to the misunderstanding and confusion. Tom Dougherty, managing director and senior strategist at Stealing Share, a brand development firm, says: "Consumers would want to go elsewhere because no one wants to feel like they are a sucker. Blockbuster now looks like a greedy business. And, it looks like a business that assumes that their customers are stupid and naïve" (MSNBC, 2005).

Discussion

1. Is Blockbuster's approach to communicating about its "No More Late Fees" program an example of the indirect communication approach? Why or why not?

2. What approach should Blockbuster have taken to communicate the information about its program to customers? Create an outline of the message that Blockbuster should have sent to avoid the confusion experienced by customers.

3. Now draft the message that Blockbuster should send in its ads and promotional materials to inform customers about its "No More Late Fees" program.

GLOBAL MEDIA VENTURES, INC.: OBJECTIVITY IN NEWS COVERAGE

Gina Jeffords is vice president of GMV's television division, which owns stations across the United States. Recently, the news media has come under fire for a perceived increase in bias of news coverage, particularly concerning politics. Some stations openly tout their conservative perspective, while others have been charged with promoting a more "liberal" view.

Ms. Jeffords started her career as a reporter trained in the belief that news should report the facts without the political spin. One way to provide such coverage is to present a balanced view, providing multiple perspectives of the situations being addressed. Coming from such a background, she has strong opinions about how news should be delivered. She is particularly concerned about reports of bias in the news being broadcast by GMV's own television stations across the country. She intends to craft a message to those stations, persuading them of the wisdom of balanced reporting. She hopes that this "softer" approach might be effective in sending the message to stations of her management philosophy regarding delivery of the news.

discussion...

1. How might Ms. Jeffords persuade television station managers of the importance of providing balanced news coverage? What claims might she make? What evidence might she use to support these claims?

2. What are the biggest challenges that Ms. Jeffords faces in persuading her audience to consider and implement her news philosophy? How might she overcome these challenges?

After studying this chapter, you will be able to

Determine the contents of an informative message.

Create a negative or "bad news" message.

Produce a persuasive message, using the three types of appeals.

Explain the challenges of creating logical yet ethical persuasive messages.

Content has to do with what you say or write. The ideas and information you include are important to the overall effectiveness of your message; they must also be presented clearly, purposefully, and adequately in order to "state your case" convincingly. Content should be logical, and thus it reflects on your reasoning abilities or how well you present claims and establish their merit with supporting evidence. Content thus should also be focused; the content of your message should maintain a clear and consistent direction and goal. All information should support clearly related topics that are guided by a central purpose.

Relevance of supportive information

Relevance of supportive information refers to the quality of the evidence or information provided and how appropriate it is for supporting and explaining the topic or subtopic.

Sufficient information

Sufficient information refers to the quantity of the information, or whether the writer or speaker has provided enough supporting evidence.

The information that you provide should support and explain your message topic and subtopics. This information should be both relevant and sufficient. **Relevance of supportive information** addresses the quality of the evidence or information you provide or how applicable and appropriate it is for supporting and explaining the related topic or subtopic. **Sufficient information** addresses the quantity of the information or evidence or whether you have provided enough supporting evidence or information given the position and needs of your audience(s). The amount and type of information or content that you provide is dependent upon your business communication purposes and your audience's interests, needs, and perspective.

This chapter will discuss how to select sufficient and relevant information to meet your business communication purposes and your audience's needs and interests. It will address how the purposes of your communication and your audience's interests and needs should determine the content to include in a message. These considerations are the basis of business communication strategy formulation.

CONTENT OF AN INFORMATIVE MESSAGE

To prepare for the delivery of a message intended to inform an audience, you need to begin by asking yourself, "What does my audience already know about the subject?"

If your topic is one of which your audience has a day-to-day working knowledge, meaning it is an expert audience, you may be able to eliminate background information and explanation to some degree. At the language level, you may be able to use acronyms rather than proper names, since your audience will be familiar with their meanings.

However, if your audience knows little about your topic—it is a non-expert audience—or it has not had exposure to it for a period of time, you may need to provide a discussion of the background of the topic you wish to discuss. You may need to define terminology and explain concepts. If the topic is somewhat complex or abstract, you may also need to provide examples in order to ensure clarity of understanding.

In an informative situation, giving some thought to your audience's knowledge about the subject should enable you to provide the information it needs and to achieve your communication purpose.

critical **thinking**

What are some of the common messages you send with the intent to inform? What considerations must you make to ensure that you achieve that goal? How do your audience, its characteristics, its needs, and its concerns affect the content of your informative messages?

CONTENT OF A NEGATIVE OR "BAD NEWS" MESSAGE

One particular type of informative situation may require you to give some additional thought to the approach and content you use in your message. This type of message is the negative or what is sometimes referred to as the "bad news" message. For example, you might need to tell a client that you cannot grant a request, you may need to inform a job applicant that he or she was not selected for a position, or you may need to tell employees that they will not be receiving raises this year.

These situations may require extra care because you do not wish to damage your relationship with your audience. Much of your ability to maintain your relationship with your audience in a negative message situation depends upon the content you provide. Your ability to maintain your relationship also depends upon the tone of your message. This aspect of messages will be covered in Chapter 7: Verbal, Vocal, and Nonverbal Expression.

In situations where you must deliver bad news, the first issue you should consider is whether you can reframe the message. In other words, can you identify some positive aspect of the situation on which you can focus? If so, you must take care that such a focus is not presented in such a way as to be misleading. If a message is reframed so that it glosses or misrepresents the negative information, you may damage your credibility and the relationship you have with your audience.

Let's take a look at some examples that will help to clarify the handling of this communication situation. In the first case mentioned on the previous page in which you need to tell a client that you cannot grant a request, you can soften the message by telling the client what you, he, or she might do. For example, if you are telling a customer that you cannot grant his or her request for a credit card from your bank, you might:

- Tell the customer that you still want his or her business.

- Tell the customer what he or she needs to do in order to receive a credit card.

- Ask the customer to reapply once he or she has completed these steps.

Figure 6-1 below provides an example that illustrates the application of these concepts.

FIGURE 6-1. *Example of message refusing a credit card application.*

International Credit Cards
1800 Olney Avenue
Philadelphia, PA 19140
215-555-7800

April 8, 2006

Henry Louis
2407 Kearney St.
Kansas City, KS 68807

Dear Mr. Louis:

Thank you for choosing International Credit Cards for your credit needs. After checking your credit rating with the three national credit-reporting firms, we are unable to fulfill your request for an International Credit Card at this time.

We are eager to fulfill your credit needs and encourage you to obtain your credit report so that you can discover whether errors regarding your credit history are affecting your credit status. You can obtain your credit report via the Internet at creditrating.com.

Once your credit rating has improved, please reapply for your International Credit Card. International Credit provides many benefits to its clients, including a competitive interest rate and special offers for discounts at the best hotels and popular rental car companies.

Sincerely,

Joann Pleasant
Customer Service Manager

© DIGITAL VISION/ GETTY IMAGES

When attempting to persuade others, we should select information aimed at addressing their needs and expectations and answering their questions and concerns.

This information provided in the letter shown in Figure 6-1 sends the message that the company values the customer and wants to help the customer achieve his or her objective. Since you should be concerned that your bad news message may negatively affect your relationship with the customer, you must send the message that you do not wish damage to occur and are willing to take the steps necessary to maintain your relationship, to the highest degree possible.

The "bad news" portion of the message shown in Figure 6-1 also illustrates the importance of downplaying the negative aspects of the message. The bad news is treated immediately and concisely. In other words, the letter does not emphasize the bad news, but attempts to focus the message on the potential for a future relationship with the customer that will benefit both parties.

A similar strategy might be used for the second situation mentioned at the beginning of this section: you must communicate to a job applicant that he or she was not selected to fill a position. Textbook writers have many opinions upon the appropriate way to handle this situation. This may be because such a situation is highly dependent upon company practices, the qualifications of the particular applicant, and legal considerations.

Whenever hiring or dismissing an employee, special care needs to be taken so that you do not communicate a message that may be used in a legal action against your company. That means that when you write a letter that delivers the bad news that an applicant was not selected, you must not make any kind of promise to employ the applicant later or provide specifics about the reason that person was not hired that might be considered illegal.

However, in such a situation you may be able to say, without risk of legal action, why the person was not selected. In this case, you would begin the message by stating something positive about the person and then briefly say why he or she was not selected. Many letters contain phrases, such as the following: "Although your résumé contained many attractive qualifications, we received several applications that better addressed our needs for this particular position." Essentially, you are saying that although the applicant has some valued skills and experiences, others were better qualified. Your goal is to make the person feel valued, even though he or she did not get the position.

You might, depending upon the situation, suggest that the person apply for a different position within your company that better suits his or her qualifications, or you might communicate your company's policy for handling job applicant files. Some letters close with a goodwill conclusion that wishes the applicant success in his or her job hunt. However, even this detail must be handled carefully so that it does not sound flippant or undercut the seriousness of the situation.

Your goal in such a letter is to clearly state that the applicant did not get the job, skirt any statements that might get you into legal trouble, and to attempt to communicate that you wish to treat the person as an individual with unique qualifications and consideration for the disappointment often involved in the job application process. In contrast, generic letters send the message that your company views and treats people like undifferentiated, easily replaceable cogs. If you can write bad news letters to job applicants that do not sound generic, you can send the message that your company values people, even if the recipient did not get the job. This message is intended to distinguish your company in a positive way from its competitors in the employment market. In Figure 6-2 below, you will find an example of a letter that delivers the "bad news" that an applicant was not selected for a position.

FIGURE 6-2. *Example of a letter delivering the bad news that an applicant was not chosen for a position.*

Johnson PC Corp.
3376 Forbes Street
St. Louis, MO 63166
340-833-5567

August 4, 2006

Katherine Grassey
534 De Paso Street
El Paso, TX 75431

Dear Ms. Grassey:

Thank you for your interest in contributing your skills and expertise to Johnson PC Corp. Your application listed many valuable attributes and skills. Unfortunately, hundreds of applicants applied for the position, and even though it was a difficult decision to make, we selected a person who will bring to us 12 years of marketing experience in the personal computing industry.

We will keep your application on file for one year in case other marketing positions become available at Johnson PC. We encourage you to remain abreast of the job opportunities within our company, so that you can actively follow up in case another marketing position becomes available.

In the meantime, we wish you the best in your job search.

Sincerely,

Francis Toomey
Human Resources Specialist

In the final situation mentioned at the opening of this section—you must inform employees that they will not be receiving raises this year—you must explain very clearly why this decision was made. If you can honestly state that the decision was made with some consideration of benefits for the employee in the future, you should include this information as well. For example, the decision might have been made because the company's profits have fallen dramatically. In order to keep the company financially solvent, cuts had to be made. Several options were considered in making this decision: whether to lay off employees or reduce expenses. The latter option was chosen. However, as part of that expense reduction plan, one of the cuts will be made in employee compensation for the next year.

Such a message should also discuss plans for improving profits so that this measure—no employee raises—will not carry over into the future.

Your goal in providing this information is multifold. First of all, you want to send the message that management is being forthright with employees. This message helps management to maintain credibility with employees. Secondly, you want to send the message that, in making the decision, management considered employee needs. This message also helps management to maintain credibility as well as its relationship with employees, since it says that management values its employees and makes decisions that consider their needs (to be employed, in this case). However, employees are not going to be pleased that they will not be receiving raises, so to maintain goodwill, the message needs to contain information about the steps that will be taken to avoid a similar situation in the future.

To summarize, negative or bad news messages often require some time, thought, and strategic planning about the content you provide to the audience. Because negative messages hold a high probability of damaging your relationship with your audience, you should take care in deciding what information to provide to best ensure the continuation of a positive relationship.

CONTENT OF A PERSUASIVE MESSAGE

In business situations, we are almost always persuading or attempting to influence others. We are almost always attempting to sell ourselves, our ideas, our company's products or services, or our company and its reputation to others. Included in these types of messages are job application letters and résumés, since you are attempting to show that you offer better qualifications and experience than your competitors for the position.

Even if we are just informing our audience, we are attempting to persuade it that we are credible and knowledgeable and that we value our relationship with it. As this latter sentence implies, in order to be successful at persuasion, you must almost always pay attention to the third and fourth purposes of communication, establishing and maintaining goodwill and credibility. If we do not have a credible, likeable persona or image, it will be difficult for us to persuade an audience to accept our ideas.

The information you provide in persuasive situations is totally dependent upon your audience's perspective or view of your proposal. For example, if you believe that your audience is very receptive to your idea, you might simply be able to ask it to accept your proposal with minimal information provided. However, the less receptive your audience is to your proposal, the more information you may need to provide and the more time you might need to take to formulate a strategy for its presentation. In order to determine the information you will need to provide in order to best ensure your success at persuasion, you should ask yourself and answer the following questions:

1. **How will my audience initially react to my proposal**?

   A second question that may help to clarify the issues involved in the first is "What feelings or fears might my proposal elicit in my audience?"

   Both these questions highlight the importance of knowing your audience in achieving your business communication goals. For example, if you unwittingly make a proposal that brings up a number of negative emotions and reactions in your audience, you will most likely fail in your goal of persuasion because your message will not have taken into account this potential reaction by your audience. Not only may you fail at your goal of persuasion, you might also damage your credibility and relationship with that audience.

2. **How does my audience feel about me, my company, or my product or service?**

   You may have had past encounters with your audience that did not go as well as they might. These events may have left your audience feeling reluctant to communicate with you. If this is the case, what can you say to help overcome this reluctance?

   Likewise, your audience may have had past dealings with your company. Based upon those dealings, what does your audience think or how does it feel about your company? Perhaps your audience has not had past dealings with your company, but your organization or industry has recently received negative publicity in the news. If this is the case, what information must you provide to help overcome the effects of this negative exposure?

   Similarly, your audience may have purchased your product or service in the past, or one like it. If so, what was your audience's experience with that product or service? If it was not as positive as it could have been, what information must you provide to overcome this perception?

3. **What are your audience's needs? In what ways does your idea or proposal fulfill those needs?**

   If you can identify your audience's needs, you then can tailor the content of your message to explain how your proposed idea—or, in the case of customers, your product or service—meets those needs. Your audience will be more interested in the information you present if it is narrowly focused on explaining how your proposal meets its needs. This strategy also shows that you are interested in your audience, which helps you to convey goodwill.

A job application letter is an example of a document that must be narrowly focused on addressing the audience's needs in order to ensure you achieve your message intent. An application letter is intended to show that you are well qualified for the job. In order to accomplish this task, you must know what the audience's needs are. This information is generally easy to find; it is often provided in the description of the job or in the advertisement or job notice. A well-written application letter would show that you know what the audience's needs are (the qualifications for which it is looking) and that you indeed meet those needs.

4. **What benefits does your proposal provide to your audience?**

The answer to this question may be similar to that of the previous one. However, in asking this question, you may find yourself placed in the role of educating your audience about your proposal. For example, your audience may have voiced its needs, but it may not have identified all the potential benefits your idea will provide. For example, your audience may have expressed a need for a new photocopier; however, it may be unaware that in addition to the features that the copier you are selling provides, your product will also save your audience money. This savings might come from the fact that your copier uses less ink, so the costs for cartridges will be lower, since fewer are needed. By giving some thought to all the benefits that your proposal might deliver to your audience, you have the potential to make your idea more persuasive.

As mentioned above, a job application letter is a persuasive or sales document. In such a letter, your goal is to show that you are well qualified for the job. An excellent letter would go the extra step to show how your qualifications will specifically benefit the potential employer. This extra step is one strategy for successfully differentiating yourself from your competitors for the job.

Generally, the type of benefit that is most persuasive to a business audience has to do with money: making it or saving it in some way. That does not mean that you ignore the other types of benefits one might accrue, such as the satisfaction one might feel from a job well done. However, this type of benefit is generally less persuasive than those that save or make money in some way. Typically, you would use other types of benefits, such as satisfaction, pleasure, and so on, as additional information to make your proposal more persuasive.

5. **What obstacles or objections must you overcome?**

Answering this question will not only help you identify what information you need to provide in your message, but also how much information. For example, if your audience is resistant to your proposal, you will probably need to provide more information to persuade it to accept your proposal. If your audience holds another position, you may need to provide information that shows that that view is not the best, and explain why. How you accomplish this goal has to do with the tone as well as the content of your message. (Tone is discussed in Chapter 7: Verbal, Vocal, and Nonverbal Expression.)

You must eliminate your audience's objections in order to set the stage for it to be open to hearing your proposal. If you do not eliminate your audience's objections or weaken the strength of its position through the quality of the information you provide, you will probably be faced with addressing those objections once you deliver your proposal, and you may find yourself back at step one in the process of persuasion.

If your audience is resistant, another strategy that may make your message more persuasive might be to supply information that shows that your proposal is easy to accept. For example, if you are attempting to persuade your department manager to change a procedure, you should also explain how to implement that procedure. Doing so makes the change easier for your manager to accept and implement and thus makes your message potentially more persuasive.

6. **Is this a sales proposal or competitive message? If so, what do my competitors offer? How might I distinguish myself or my ideas favorably from my competitors?**

Whenever you are competing with others for scarce resources—a job, a contract, a raise, a promotion, or a sale—you must consider how you compare to your competitors for those resources and how you can favorably distinguish yourself from them. You must therefore have some idea of what your competitors offer.

When you apply for a job, you are competing with dozens, perhaps hundreds of others. You should give some thought to the qualifications those competitors might bring to the situation, and then attempt to show that you are as well qualified, or more so, than they are. Reaching this objective depends upon the quality of the content or information about yourself that you are able to provide.

Once you have answered these questions, you should have a good idea about the amount and type of information you need to provide to successfully persuade your audience to accept your proposal.

As mentioned earlier, a common persuasive message is an application letter. A well-written application letter would focus on the audience's or employer's needs and concerns and show how the applicant would meet these needs and benefit the employer. Furthermore, a well-written application would provide concrete evidence to illustrate that the potential employee has the skills and abilities for which the employer is looking. An example of an application that is audience-centered and that provides the evidence an employer is looking for is provided in Figure 6-3 on the next page. The letter is in response to the following job advertisement:

Entry-Level Accounting Position

XYZ Accounting Consultants is an international company that provides accounting services to large corporate clients. XYZ Accounting Consultants is currently looking for applicants for its entry-level accounting position. The qualified applicant should have the following:

- A bachelor's degree in accounting.

- Entry-level accounting experience.

- Knowledge of basic accounting principles and practices.

- Excellent communication skills.

- Such personal characteristics as being hardworking, able to manage time efficiently, and dedicated to producing quality work.

Please send letters of application and resumes to the manager of our Los Angeles office, 345 Figueroa Street, Los Angeles, CA 90001

A job advertisement is often the best source for identifying what an employer is looking for in an applicant. A well-written application letter will use the same language as the advertisement to refer to the applicant's skills. Using the same language makes it easier for the employer to read the message, since he or she is looking for that information; it also shows that the applicant is knowledgeable about those qualifications and addresses them specifically.

critical **thinking**

Identify a time that you were unsuccessful at persuasion. Why were you unsuccessful? In retrospect, what could you have done to have improved your chances of success?

Basic Components of a Persuasive Message

Entire courses are devoted to the teaching and learning of persuasion. In fact, persuasion, or argumentation as it is called in the academy, is its own field of study. Subsequently, the study of persuasion involves a detailed history, content, and discussion that will not be reproduced here. However, it is helpful to know the basic components of a persuasive message. At the most foundational level,

JoAnn Dunn
123 Sepulveda Street
Los Angeles, CA 90001
(213) 741-4567
jdunn@midtown.edu

February 1, 2006

Maria Munoz, Manager
XYZ Accounting Consultants
345 Figueroa Street
Los Angeles, CA 90001

Dear Ms. Munoz:

I am responding to your ad for an entry-level accountant that was posted on JOBSTAR. I have all the attributes your company is looking for in a new employee; I am knowledgeable of accounting principles and practices, I have recent accounting experience, and I am a hard worker with excellent time management skills.

As a student at Midtown University, I have taken many accounting courses to help me prepare for a career in accounting. These courses include Financial Accounting, Tax Accounting, and Accounting and the Law. I did very well in these courses, earning an "A" grade for my work in each. This knowledge prepares me well to begin contributing to your company's goals immediately as an entry-level accountant.

I have had the additional opportunity to put this knowledge into practice during my internship last summer at Deloitte and Touche. I assisted an account executive to audit and prepare reports for three Fortune 500 companies. This experience also enabled me to practice and improve my writing and speaking skills, which will benefit you by enabling me to represent your company as a well-spoken and credible professional.

I also work hard and have excellent time management skills. Not only was I able to attend college full-time and maintain a 3.5 GPA, but I also worked full-time as a sales associate at Office Max to fund my education. These characteristics will enable me to be an efficient employee who doesn't stop until I get the job done while still maintaining quality work.

I would like to schedule an interview with you to discuss my qualifications further. I will call you next week to set up an appointment at your latest convenience.

Sincerely,

JoAnn Dunn

FIGURE 6-3.   *Example of an audience-focused application letter.*

Claim; Evidence

A claim is often general or abstract; on the other hand, evidence is more specific.

persuasion consists of two parts: a **claim** and the information or **evidence** that supports it. Another way to think about these two components is that a claim is often general or more abstract, while evidence is more specific. This way of thinking about evidence also helps us to understand why evidence is often necessary for the clarity of our message in addition to persuasiveness. Below, you will find examples of claims and supporting evidence.

Claim: Effective writing will save your business money.

Evidence: Studies indicate that employees waste one hour a day attempting to interpret or follow up on poorly written messages. This means that for each employee, a company loses one hour of pay a day because of poorly written messages. This hour could be used more productively for other activities, or the money that goes to pay that wasted wage could be invested in other resources.

Claim: You should buy our hybrid automobile, the Solare, because it will provide you with several benefits.

Evidence: The largest benefit you will receive from purchasing our hybrid automobile, the Solare, is the savings you will receive from less gasoline use and its purchase. The Solare is primarily fueled by hydrogen and requires gasoline only for sudden acceleration or unusual engine loads, such as driving up steep inclines. If most of your vehicle use is confined to city streets and you avoid rapid acceleration, you may rarely if ever require a stop at the gas station!

Classic scholars have brought to us another consideration to make when selecting information or evidence to provide in a persuasive message: the type of appeal which would be most effective for a particular persuasive situation. The different types of persuasive appeals are discussed in the following section.

Types of Persuasive Appeals

More than two thousands years ago, the Greek philosopher Aristotle (384–322 BC) proposed that evidence or the information you provide in a persuasive message could be divided into three broad categories: logical, ethical, and emotional. Although this schema is centuries old, it is still useful to us today.

Logos

Logos, or the logical appeal, consists of information such as facts or statistics.

A logical appeal, or **logos,** consists of such information as facts and statistics. It is a fact, for example, that mammals breathe oxygen. A fact is any information that is broadly accepted as true. Business audiences tend to be persuaded by logical evidence, particularly numbers, dollars, and statistics. They also often prefer that this information is presented in the form of graphs. Chapter 8: Visual Impression will discuss this aspect of business messages in more detail. Both of the examples of claims and evidence provided in the previous section largely rely upon the logical appeal for their persuasiveness.

Ethos

The ethical appeal, or *ethos*, refers to information that provides credibility to ourselves or to our position.

An ethical appeal, or **ethos,** does not refer to ethics as we normally think of the concept but rather to information that provides credibility for ourselves or to our position. One of the easiest ways to make an ethical argument is to cite authorities in the subject of discussion. Most of us have used this method when we have been asked to write a research paper in school. In the first example of a claim and its evidence in the previous section, the reference to "studies" is an ethical appeal, since it implies that experts were involved in the gathering of this information. This appeal might be stronger if the names of the experts involved in the studies were known to the audience. In this case, this information might carry greater weight or persuasiveness.

Another way to build credibility is to consider both sides of an issue; if you discuss both the pros and the cons, you will probably be considered fair-minded and thus

When it comes to persuasion, the early Greeks believed that there were two sides to every issue. Aristotle made such a belief part of his theory of effective communication. The confrontation of opposites is a fundamental process of reasoning. Unfortunately, some claim that the Greek ideal is a long way from the type of persuasion we find today. The typical ad, for example, is one-sided and often consists of little information but instead, exaggerated claims: "Lose weight fast." "Immediate relief." Even political campaign rhetoric is often simplistic and one-sided, ignoring the complexities of today's world. In fact, surveys show that a large percentage of the American public now picks its news media on the basis of how closely they represent their personal and political views, rather than on their ability to provide balanced coverage (Saltzman, 2004).

Still, the ideal of presenting the multiple perspectives of an issue persists today as the basic foundation of critical thinking and sound decision making. In addition, acknowledging the views of others can contribute to our credibility, since we may be perceived as being more objective and fair. It can also help us to convey goodwill to those members of our audience who may hold a view other than our own.

Questions for Thought

1. **What are your own views on the one-sided presentation of information? Do you believe such presentations can be called examples of "responsible communication"? Why or why not?**

2. **Why is it important to discuss all perspectives on an issue during the decision-making process?**

more credible (i.e., you are not biased and therefore one-sided in your argument). You can also establish your credibility by showing that you are experienced and knowledgeable in a particular relevant area. For example, if you are selling photocopiers, you might tell your audience that you have been in the photocopier business for 10 years. Such a statement indicates that you are knowledgeable about that industry, your product line, and probably your competition.

Another, perhaps more subtle, aspect of the ethical appeal is your professional image. Your professional image consists of your dress, mannerisms, quality of communication (oral and written), and relationships with your colleagues. Even though we may be highly competent or knowledgeable in a particular field, we may damage our credibility if we do not project a professional image to our audience. This aspect of business communication is discussed further in the next chapter, Chapter 7: Verbal, Vocal, and Nonverbal Expression.

Pathos

Pathos is an emotional appeal, an attempt to win over the audience by appealing to its emotions, often by telling a story or evoking a picture with which the audience can empathize.

The final type of evidence is the emotional appeal, or **pathos.** An emotional appeal does not work by simply writing or stating emotional words. An emotional appeal often depends on telling a story or evoking a picture or experience with which your audience can identify or empathize. For example, commercials that show pictures of starving children are intended to make us empathize with them so that we will contribute money to help lessen their plight.

communication IN YOUR WORLD

Each day, we are exposed to hundreds, perhaps thousands, of advertisements whose goal is persuasion. *Advertising Age* magazine estimates that the average American sees, reads, or hears more than 5,000 persuasive advertising messages each day. According to communication scholar Neil Postman (1981), by the time a young person in the United States reaches the age of 20, he or she will likely have seen about a million commercials, an average of 1,000 a week. Postman claims that because of such exposure, advertisements are powerful shapers of our values. Postman says,

This makes the TV commercial the most voluminous information source in the education of youth.... A commercial teaches a child three interesting things. The first is that all problems are resolvable. The second is that all problems are resolvable fast. And the third is that all problems are resolvable fast through the agency of some technology.

Postman's definition of technology includes drugs and cosmetics as well as actual machinery.

Discussion

1. Do you agree with Postman's claim that advertising is one of the primary sources of our values?

2. Do agree with Postman's assessment of the lessons learned from advertising? If so, what might be done to counter these messages?

Similarly, advertisements that show young people at the beach in an SUV are intended to make us identify with them. Advertisers want us to identify with the youthful fun we see and then associate that fun with the SUV. These feelings are expected to make us want to buy the SUV so that we can have the same experience.

An emotional appeal might be used in a professional setting to motivate employees or colleagues. For example, if you want your staff to increase their quarterly sales, you might hold a meeting at a lush resort that also involves group activities aimed at increasing camaraderie and overall good feelings toward the company and among the sales staff. Such an event might include an awards ceremony and closing speech intended to motivate employees to feel valued and do their best to reach company goals. Such an event is intended to play upon the emotions and identities of the participants in such a way as to persuade them to put in the necessary effort to achieve the company's objectives.

Different types of audiences are convinced by different types of evidence and by varying amounts. Generally, the more resistant an audience is to your idea, the more evidence you will need to present. More resistant audiences may also require the use of all three types of evidence in varying amounts. Sometimes the situation dictates, to some degree, the type of evidence required. For example, when we are at home in front of the television, we may want to relax and be entertained. That's why so many commercials rely upon the emotional appeal;

they work subtly on our feelings rather than requiring a lot of mental work. After a long day at work, we may be less receptive to a half-hour-long, fact-filled discussion of the benefits and disadvantages of buying a particular product, although that sort of discussion is generally expected in the workplace.

critical **thinking**

What are the key elements of persuasion as a strategy? Should you state the opposing view when you write a persuasive message?

Quality of Evidence

Not all evidence is relevant or of high quality. Evidence can be used, intentionally or unintentionally, to mislead an audience. However, evidence can also be tested for its validity. The three primary tests of evidence and its quality are provided in Table 6-1 below.

TESTS OF EVIDENCE

- *Statistics.* Tests for quality of statistical evidence include:

    1. Is the sample from which the statistics are drawn a representative one?

    2. Is a single instance used as an example of *all* instances?

- *Testimony.* Tests for quality of testimonial evidence include:

    1. Is the person an authority on the subject, and if so, how reliable is he or she?

    2. Was the person giving the testimonial close enough to witness the event?

    3. Is it possible that the person giving the testimony is biased?

- *Comparison and Analogies.* (The fallacy of faulty comparison or faulty analogy.) Tests for the quality of a comparison or analogy include:

    1. Do both items or activities have the same resources or authority?

    2. Are both items or activities governed by the same rules?

    3. Do both activities occur during the same time period?

    4. Are both items or activities measured in the same way?

TABLE 6-1. *Tests of evidence.*

Misuse of statistics commonly occurs when one instance is used to represent all cases. For example, the statement that "Intel saved $10 million by outsourcing the production of its microprocessors to India" would be misused if it was used to support the claim, "All companies will save millions of dollars by outsourcing their manufacturing and services to foreign countries." One company's experience does not represent that of all companies, since organizations have varying resources, produce different products with differing requirements, provide various services, have differing resources and needs, and so on.

Similarly, testimonial evidence can be used to present a biased opinion. For example, if the testimony of a U.S. Commerce Department official is used to support outsourcing, the testimony might be considered biased, since presumably such a person would lean toward supporting pro-business interests and positions and would thus ignore or downplay social or ethical considerations.

Finally, analogies can be faulty. For example, the analogy "Outsourcing is like farming, because most farm labor in the U.S. is now provided by migrant workers from Mexico," is faulty. One reason is that not all outsourced jobs can be performed by relatively unskilled workers, so there may be other costs of outsourcing that do not occur in the farm labor situation. Furthermore, the pay scales of U.S. farm workers may not match those of workers in other countries in relation to the cost of living of both countries. Finally, it might be argued that many migrant workers from Mexico provide U.S. farm labor because U.S. citizens are unwilling to do that work. However, U.S. jobs might be outsourced even though a workforce exists that is willing to perform those particular jobs. In summary, the conditions and details of the two situations may not match in ways that make the comparison dissimilar.

CHALLENGES TO ETHICAL, LOGICAL PERSUASION

One of the problems of constructing and analyzing persuasive messages is dealing with the amount of information with which we are bombarded each day. More information has been produced in the last 30 years than in the previous five thousand. A single edition of *The New York Times* contains more information than the average person was likely to be exposed to in an entire lifetime in 17th-century England (Wurman, 1989). In fact, more information is generated worldwide in a 24-hour period than you could process and absorb in all your years on earth. With the increasing use of the Internet, we are approaching a point in which more information will be generated in one hour than could be processed and absorbed in your lifetime (Davidson, 1996).

The corresponding overload of information affects our ability to gather, analyze, and identify the data necessary to evaluate persuasive messages as well as our ability to create effective ones. This problem calls for a strategy to deal with the barrage of information we experience on a daily basis. It also requires that we become aware of the subconscious methods we use to process information that may lead us to faulty decisions. Finally, it requires that we become aware of the ways in which information can be used to lead us to faulty conclusions. This section will discuss each of these issues in further detail.

Thinking Styles

In general, you can process information in one of two ways: you can absorb it like a sponge or filter it. Perhaps the more common way of processing information is absorbing it. This process is passive and requires little thinking. Although the advantage of this process is that it enables you to absorb a lot of information, the disadvantage is that it provides you with no method to decide whether information is valid or useful.

In contrast, the filter method provides you a way of processing information more actively, effectively giving you a choice in what you absorb and what you ignore. Using the filter model essentially requires that you ask questions about the material being presented. Your mission is to critically evaluate the material and formulate personal conclusions based upon that evaluation.

Browne and Keeley (1981) suggest a list of the critical questions to ask when evaluating information:

1. What are the issues and the conclusion?

2. What are the reasons that are given?

3. What words or phrases are ambiguous?

4. What are the value conflicts and assumptions?

5. What are the assumptions about the definitions and descriptions being used?

6. Are the samples representative and the measurements sound?

7. Are there flaws in the use of statistical information?

8. Are the causal explanations adequately supported with quality evidence?

9. Are there any errors in reasoning?

10. What significant information is omitted?

11. What alternative conclusions are consistent with the evidence presented?

12. What are your value preferences in this controversy?

When asking and answering these questions in your evaluation of information, it is also helpful to recognize that for many contemporary issues, no single correct answer exists. Because our world is a complex place, many points of views and perspectives have valid points. Depending upon the broader goal or a person's value system, choosing the best solution can be a difficult process.

Secondly, you should also try to put your emotions aside when evaluating information. Emotions can get in the way of our ability to be open to all the relevant information and to weigh that information as objectively and thoroughly as it deserves.

Finally, it is important to ask "Who cares?" Since we are human beings, we often have personal interests at stake in the arguments that we make. Therefore, it is useful to ask yourself who will benefit from this proposal? Is the information that is presented colored by that perspective? Is this a one-sided argument? If so, what is the other side of the issue?

Learning how to evaluate information critically can help you to gather better information upon which to make decisions that may affect your career and your life.

Perceptual Mindsets

Another challenge to evaluating information effectively and marshalling it to produce effective persuasive messages is our **perceptual mindsets.** Perceptual mindsets are our psychological and cognitive predispositions to see the world in a particular way (Rothwell, 1998, p. 183). These biases, preconceptions, and assumptions get in the way of our ability to make effective decisions and to solve problems. Because of our mindsets, we are prepared to receive only certain messages and to ignore others. To put it bluntly, we are conditioned to view the world narrowly.

Our mindsets are affected by several practices that limit our ability to consider information thoroughly and objectively. These include confirmation bias, false dichotomies, and inferential errors.

Confirmation Bias   **Confirmation bias** is a tendency to distort information that contradicts our currently held beliefs and attitudes (Hunt, 1982). Confirmation bias exhibits itself in group communication situations as well as affects our individual decision making.

In groups, research indicates a strong tendency among members to "show interest in facts and opinions that support their initially preferred policy and take up time in their meetings to discuss them, but they tend to ignore facts and opinions that do not support their initially preferred policy" (Janus, 1982, p. 10).

For individuals, confirmation bias can also distort evidence that disconfirms our viewpoints and perceptions. This process is called self-confirmation (Postman, 1976). Women, for example, often have to deal with self-confirming beliefs of supervisors and colleagues (Haslett et al, 1992). In other words, they may believe that they must conform to stereotypes by acting in accommodating, unassertive ways, and they may have more difficulty being taken seriously by others and thus receiving promotions and raises. However, refusing to accept these stereotypes may also have negative consequences. In some cases, assertive women may be judged as too aggressive and uncooperative, and thus be deemed undeserving of promotion or advancement.

To combat confirmation bias, Rothwell (1998, p. 186) suggests that you:

1. Actively seek out disconfirming information and evidence.

2. Vigorously present and argue disconfirming evidence to others or the group.

3. Play devil's advocate.

4. Gather allies to challenge confirmation bias.

Perceptual mindsets

Perceptual mindsets are our cognitive and psychological predispositions to see the world in a certain way.

Confirmation bias

Confirmation bias is a tendency to distort information that contradicts the beliefs and attitudes we currently hold.

False dichotomy

A false dichotomy is a dichotomy that is not jointly exhaustive (i.e., there are other alternatives), or that is not mutually exclusive (i.e., the alternatives overlap). A false dichotomy may be the product of either/or thinking.

Inferences

An inference is a conclusion about the unknown based upon the known.

Correlation

A correlation is a consistent relationship between two or more variables.

False Dichotomies   Dichotomous, either/or thinking is the tendency to see the world in terms of black and white or opposites. Either/or thinking often leads us to describe situations in the language of extremes. Such thinking is typically false because there are more than two possibilities in our complex world. In these cases, we have created a **false dichotomy.**

The bell-shaped curve is an obvious challenge to such extreme views. If specific information was gathered from a random group of individuals, the data would tend to bunch up in the middle. Either/or thinking focuses on the few individuals or situations that lie at the extreme ends of the spectrum and ignore the more numerous cases in the middle (DeVito, 1989). Such thinking often leads to poor decisions, since it ignores the bulk of the most valid information available on the subject.

To avoid the pitfalls of false dichotomies, Rothwell (1998, p. 188) suggests that you

1. Be suspicious of absolutes. Look for alternatives to the one or two suggestions recommended.

2. Employ the language of qualification. Speak in terms of degrees by using such terms as sometimes, rarely, occasionally, mostly, usually, and moderately.

Inferential Errors   **Inferences** are conclusions about the unknown based on the known. We draw inferences from previous experiences, factual data, and predispositions. Because of this tendency, inferences are guesses varying from educated to uneducated.

Making inferences is not necessarily a negative practice. In fact, the human thinking process is inferential. We could not function on a daily basis without making inferences. However, the principal problem with inferences is that we are often unaware that we are making them and thus rarely question their accuracy.

The two general sources of inferential errors are a faulty information base or misinformation, and a seriously limited information base (Rothwell, 1998, p. 194). However, more specific sources of inferential errors exist. These are vividness, unrepresentativeness, and correlation.

Vividness. Graphic, outrageous, shocking, controversial, and dramatic events draw our attention and tend to stick in our minds. We tend to overvalue vivid, concrete information and undervalue abstract, statistical information, which tends to be dry and lifeless in the sense that it often leaves representations of people and real consequences to their lives out of the equation.

Unrepresentativeness. When we make a judgment, we tend to assess its accuracy based upon our knowledge of information in a general category. However, if the information is not representative or does not agree with that general information, our inference will be incorrect.

Correlation. A **correlation** is a consistent relationship between two or more variables. An example of a positive correlation is that as you grow older, your ears grow larger. In this case, a correlation exists between age and ear size. In contrast, a common correlation is that the death penalty decreases the instance of crime. However, no significant evidence exists that this is the case. In fact, Stephen Jay Gould (1981) finds that "the vast majority of correlations in our world are, without a doubt, noncausal" (p. 241).

To avoid the problems associated with inferential errors, Rothwell (1998, p. 202) recommends that we ask the following questions:

1. Is the evidence sufficient to draw the inference?

2. Is the evidence the best available?

3. Is the evidence recent?

4. Is the evidence relevant to the inference? Does it really prove the claim?

5. Is the evidence one-sided? In there contradictory information?

6. Can you verify the facts? How do you know that what is said is actually true?

7. Are the sources of the information reliable?

8. Are the sources of the information authorities? Are the authorities trustworthy or biased?

9. Is the statistical sample representative of the whole? Is the sample size adequate?

10. Is the example typical or is it an exception?

11. Is the relationship only a correlation, or is it causal?

Persuasive Fallacies

The persuasiveness of a claim may be undermined by what is referred to as a **fallacy.** A fallacy is the deceptive appearance of a false or mistaken idea. It is an often plausible argument that uses a false or invalid reference. Even though the common fallacies that appear in persuasion have been identified for hundreds of years, they still occur frequently in political campaigns, advertisements, and personal and professional communication. Fallacies can occur in the use of each type of appeal discussed earlier; there are logical, ethical, and emotional fallacies. Some of the most common fallacies are listed and briefly explained in the table below.

Fallacy

A fallacy is the deceptive appearance of a false or mistaken idea, an often plausible argument that uses a false or invalid reference.

TABLE 6-2 *Logical Fallacies*

Logical Fallacies

- Hasty generalization or stereotyping: Leaping to a conclusion without evidence (similar to slogans or platitudes). Example "Lawyers are dishonest."

- Faulty cause-and-effect relationships: Attributing a cause to an event without really investigating the event. Example: "Outsourcing makes nations freer."

Continued on next page.

- Evading the question: Moving away from the issue and talking about a related one. Example, in the case of outsourcing: "Globalization makes the world freer."

- Begging the question: Assuming as a basic premise something that needs to be proven. Example: Any claim that your reader might dispute.

- Either/or reasoning: Limiting the reader's choices artificially. In some situations, there are more than two alternatives. Either/or reasoning is also called black-and-white thinking and is usually regarded as simplistic.

- Straw man: Setting up an artificial opposition that is easy to refute. Example: Going to war or the death of democracy.

- Stacked evidence: Stacking evidence to represent only one side of an issue that clearly has two sides, thus giving a distorted impression of the issue. This approach won't work if you are talking to a knowledgeable audience.

- Equivocation: Using vague language to mislead an audience. Examples: Rights, freedom, law, justice, real. When you use such language, make sure you define what you mean and stick to that meaning.

Ethical Fallacies

- Ad hominem: Attacking a person's character rather than a person's ideas.

- Guilt by association: Suggesting a person's character can be judged by the character of his or her associates.

- Using authority instead of evidence.

Emotional Fallacies

- The Bandwagon appeal: Arguing that everyone is doing something so you should, too.

- Slippery slope: Using scare tactics to suggest that if we allow one thing to happen, we are on the slippery slope to disaster.

- Creating false needs: Creating a false or heightened sense of need. Example: Marketers who say, "You have the next five minutes to send in your order."

TABLE 6-2 *Continued*

It is important to analyze the quality and relevance of the information that is available in determining whether a persuasive message is ethical or logical, and in constructing your own persuasive messages to ensure their success. The abundance of information available today makes this a daunting task, but becoming aware of the common errors in information use and using the tools that are available to analyze information can help you to achieve these goals.

CONTENT OF ORAL PRESENTATIONS

Although many of the rules about content thus far discussed apply to both written and oral presentations, the latter channel of communication deserves some additional discussion.

Because an oral presentation is a different channel of communication than writing, it has different advantages and disadvantages and thus is best used in particular communication situations.

Much of an oral presentation's success depends upon the delivery techniques that are used. (These aspects are discussed in more detail in Chapter 7: Verbal, Vocal, and Nonverbal Expression.) What this means is that the success of an oral presentation depends upon the speaker's ability to gain the audience's attention and maintain it.

Organization is also an important part of maintaining an audience's attention: if an audience becomes confused or lost about the direction or topic of the presentation, it will probably stop listening.

The content you select for an oral presentation also should be considered. For the delivery of complex, detailed information, the written channel of communication is best. That is because if the reader becomes confused or lost, he or she can reread the written message to clear up that confusion.

However, in an oral presentation, the audience member probably does not have the opportunity to review what has been said. If he or she becomes lost or confused, the audience member will probably remain so. What this means in terms of content selection for an oral presentation is that you should avoid delivering much detailed information.

Instead, an oral presentation should focus on delivering "the big picture" or the overarching framework of your idea, supplemented with vivid and memorable evidence or examples that are intended to make your message concrete and engaging. Sometimes an oral presentation is intended to introduce the main topics of your message, which is then supplemented by a written report to fill in the details.

critical **thinking**

What are some typical uses for the persuasive strategy when writing in the workplace? What are some dangers to watch out for when writing a persuasive message?

In summary, an oral presentation is generally not the appropriate channel to provide detailed, complex information, because it may bore your audience—who may subsequently stop listening—or it may confuse your audience. If you have detailed, complex information to deliver, you should typically use a written message to do so, although you might decide to supplement that written material with an oral presentation intended to highlight the main points of your message and to bring them to life for your audience.

- Content is the substance of what you say or write. The ideas and information you include are important to the overall effectiveness of your message; they must also be presented clearly, purposefully, and adequately in order to "state your case" convincingly. Content should be logical, and thus it reflects upon your reasoning abilities or how well you present claims and establish their merit with supporting evidence. Content thus should also be focused; the content of your message should maintain a clear and consistent direction and goal. All information should support clearly related topics that are guided by a central purpose.

- The purposes of your message and your audience's needs, expectations, and concerns should guide the selection of the content of your message. For informative messages, you should identify the information that your audience needs to clearly understand your message. For "bad news" messages, the content of your message should attempt to downplay the negative information you must convey and to maintain your relationship with your audience.

- In persuasive messages, the information that you provide should support and explain your message's topic and subtopics. This information should be both relevant and sufficient. **Relevance of supportive information** addresses the quality of the evidence or information you provide, or how applicable and appropriate it is for supporting and explaining the related topic or subtopic. **Sufficient information** addresses the quantity of the information or evidence, or whether you have provided enough supporting evidence or information given the position and needs of your audience(s).

- Evidence can be broken down into three categories: emotional, logical, and ethical. Analyzing the situation and your audience's interests and preferences can help you to choose the appeal or combination of appeals that will help you to achieve your persuasive goals.

- However, you should be aware of the challenges of creating logical yet ethical persuasive messages. To deal effectively with these challenges, we need to become more aware of the subconscious processes we use to process information, which may lead us to faulty decisions. We can learn techniques to process the information we receive more critically to reach more effective decisions. We can also become more aware of the ways in which information can be used to lead us to faulty conclusions. Learning the skills and processes of critical thinking can help us to make better decisions and to produce more effective persuasive messages.

KEY TERMS

Discussion Questions

1. What is the difference between a logical appeal and an emotional one? Give examples of each and explain how they differ in their effects.

2. Which types of evidence would be most persuasive to a business audience? Give examples.

3. What is an ad hominem fallacy? Give an example. How has the ad hominem been used in recent elections?

4. What are some ways that evidence, such as statistics and testimony, can be misused? Give examples.

5. What are some examples of black-and-white or dichotomous thinking from recent news reports or opinion columns you have seen or read? What other possibilities might exist to broaden the views or options presented in these reports?

Applications

1. You are a sales representative for the pharmaceutical company, Dermacor Inc., which specializes in the development of skin care products sold through dermatologists' offices. You recently organized a luncheon for a dozen dermatologists in your city to promote your new product, Revitalique. As part of that event, you flew in recognized cosmetic dermatologist Vince LaRoche, who has received national media exposure for his techniques, to deliver a talk on his skin care philosophy. Write two goodwill thank-you letters: one to Dr. LaRoche and another that can be delivered to the dermatologists who attended your event.

2. You are a customer service representative for Real Estate Success, a company that organizes and holds seminars across the United States. These seminars are intended to help educate "regular" people on how to become financially independent through the purchase, resale, and rental of single-family homes and multi-unit apartment buildings. In addition to the seminars, the company sells videotapes and audio recordings of its founder, Lex Andreason, espousing his sales methods and techniques. With the increasing values of real estate, Lex's seminars and tapes have become so popular that your production has not kept up with demand. To make matters worse, you advertise "same-day" shipping in your promotional materials. You have just received approximately 50 orders for the two-volume videotape set that sells for $95. Write a "bad news" letter that you can send to these customers, explaining the situation.

3. You work in the information services department of MicroFast Systems, Inc., a maker of computer connectivity products. Your job, along with the other members of your department, is to provide computer support to the employees of MicroFast Systems. Several years ago, MicroFast was purchased by a computer products giant, International Connectivity Solutions (ICS). Because your company had an excellent reputation for its customer service and extensive and positive brand recognition, ICS chose to leave your division with its well-respected name.

Coincidentally, perhaps, MicroFast Systems uses the same product as its parent company for electronic collaboration among project development teams, TeamMAX. TeamMAX was created by another company that ICS now owns, but it is not the only product of its kind on the market. Because of lingering bitter feelings about the company takeover, there is a move among the employees of your department to switch to a newer collaboration product, Virtual Team. Write a persuasive letter to your supervisor, Joan Morrow, to persuade her to stay with the TeamMAX product.

4. Using the situation described in Application #3, create a persuasive presentation for your boss and

the management team of MicroFast Systems. In selecting the content of your presentation, focus on the benefits that you must communicate to the management team and how you can convey those benefits in a clear, vivid, and memorable way.

5. Select an editorial or opinion piece from a newspaper or magazine and write a brief essay, analyzing the arguments made in the article. What type of proof was most dominant? Was it the most effective type of proof to use for this topic? Why or why not? Did the article contain fallacies? If so, which ones? Based upon this analysis, how effective was the writer at persuasion?

InfoTrac Activities

1. Using InfoTrac College Edition, type the word "persuasion" in the keyword search engine. Select the persuasion/rhetoric periodicals option and explore the articles you find there as well as related subjects.

2. Using InfoTrac College Edition, type the word "evidence" in the keyword search engine and read some of the references listed to discover how many kinds of evidence exist.

Case Analysis

McNeil Nutritionals, LLC, is a leading global marketing firm whose line of innovative products includes Lactaid, Viactiv, Benecol, and Splenda No Calorie Sweetener. As a subsidiary of pharmaceutical and healthcare conglomerate Johnson and Johnson, McNeil is committed to offering its consumers healthy options that are based on sound science, have solid relevant benefits, and deliver exceptional taste, according to company materials. The company's mission is to give people the ability to actively manage their own health through scientifically credible, nutritional approaches.

In December 2004, Merisant, the maker of NutraSweet and Equal, along with the Sugar Association, an industry trade group, filed separate suits against McNeil, claiming that Splenda's current marketing campaign is deceptive (Gogoi, p. 1). These competitors charge that Splenda's current marketing slogan, "Made from sugar so it tastes like sugar," is misleading the general public to think that Splenda is a natural sweetener when it is not. With the lawsuit filing, Splenda's competitors began a campaign against the product, which was aimed at telling the public through Web sites and other media channels that the artificial sweetener could be a potential health hazard. One Web site developed by Merisant,

http://truthaboutsplenda.com, contains hundreds of articles, each containing commentary from physicians who claim there is sufficient evidence that proves Splenda is unsafe.

McNeil claimed that this campaign is one-sided and misleading. In response, McNeil countersued the Sugar Association and other defendants to stop them from making false and misleading claims about Splenda.

Discussion

1. Do you believe that the slogan "Made from sugar so it tastes like sugar" supports the charges of the Sugar Association and Merisant that it is misleading because it contains the claim that the product is all natural?

2. Using the Internet and databases, such as InfoTrac College Edition, research both sides of the issue of the marketing of Splenda. What is the evidence provided to support the Sugar Association's and Merisant's claims? What kinds of appeals are used? What is the evidence provided to support McNeil's charge that their claims are false and misleading? What kinds of appeals are used?

After looking at the evidence, which position is more persuasive? Why?

Verbal, Vocal, and Nonverbal Expression

GLOBAL MEDIA VENTURES, INC.: DEALING WITH THE PRESS

After a stressful two-month trial that received an enormous amount of press coverage, James Cooke, president of GMV's publishing division, has been found guilty of sexual discrimination and harassment. Kathryn Colter, Chief Executive Officer of GMV, received the news late yesterday afternoon. Working with GMV's corporate communications department, Colter has since been preparing for a press conference later today. Colter will be unable to speak about the specifics of the lawsuit, since the penalty has yet to be announced. In addition, she anticipates that Cooke will appeal the decision. Regardless, she believes that the company must make some kind of statement and be willing to answer some of the press's questions.

Colter sits down to draft the message she and corporate communications staff have discussed. She also must plan for the question-and-answer session that will follow. The draft will be reviewed and revised by corporate communications before this afternoon's press conference, and Colter still must practice delivering her message.

discussion...

1. What are the primary purposes of Colter's statement? Why?

2. What should be the content of Colter's message? Why?

3. What questions should she anticipate from members of the press? How should she answer these? What should she do if she is asked a question about the lawsuit?

4. When practicing her speech, what nonverbal communication behaviors should she avoid? How can she use her voice and her body to better accomplish her purposes?

Convey the appropriate style and tone in your written messages.

Achieve the appropriate vocal delivery in your oral messages.

Be more aware of your nonverbal communication and better able to align it with the oral message you wish to express.

Prepare for an oral presentation.

Reduce speech apprehension.

Handle question-and-answer sessions.

Prepare for and perform employment interviews.

Practice effective listening techniques.

The style and tone of both verbal, vocal, and nonverbal messages can help you achieve your business communication purposes, including the establishment of credibility and goodwill, or a positive relationship with your audience. When formulating an effective business communication strategy, you should therefore give some consideration to the style and tone of your verbal, vocal, and nonverbal messages in addition to the other elements that have been discussed in this book. This rule applies to messages that are delivered in writing as well as those that are delivered orally.

In addition, this chapter discusses several common situations in a professional environment in which oral communication skills are used, including business presentations and employment interviews. The chapter closes with a discussion of effective listening. While it is important to understand and be able to practice the skills associated with effective oral communication, it may be even more important to improve our ability to listen to and actively engage with others if we are to achieve our goal of effective communication.

VERBAL EXPRESSION IN WRITING

A communicator selects the style and tone, or verbal expression of a message, depending on the purposes of that message, the audience's needs and expectations, the communicator's relationship with the audience, and an organization's culture.

Style

Style refers to the level of formality in written communications.

Style is the level of formality of your written communication. Business communication typically should use business style, which is less formal than traditional academic writing and more formal than a conversation. Business style is friendly and personal (you may refer to your audience by name and to its specific circumstances), yet correct.

This means that written business messages should use:

- Short, simple, precise words, yet avoid slang.

- Short yet complete sentences and short paragraphs.

- Standard English.

- First- and second-person pronouns.

Using first- and second-person pronouns, such as "I," "we," and "you" helps you to achieve a friendly and personal style, which can aid you in conveying goodwill. Using "you" as the predominant pronoun in your writing also subtly sends the message that you are interested in your audience and meeting its needs, concerns, and interests. Some examples of the "you" focus are provided below.

EXAMPLES OF "YOU" FOCUS

The benefits you will receive from the Solare hybrid-fuel vehicle include lower fuel bills, a quieter ride, and the satisfaction that you are doing your part to protect the environment.

In this package, you will find the information you requested to put you on the path to a more secure financial future.

However, there are instances when you should not use "you" as the predominant pronoun in your writing, and that is in cases where it might sound as if you are blaming your audience. In these cases, you should communicate as impersonally as possible, focusing on the solution rather than the problem and its cause. Not only does this approach avoid blaming and the subsequent potential for alienating your audience and blocking effective communication, but it also sends the positive message that you are a solution-oriented person. Examples of the improper use of "you" focus are provided below.

EXAMPLES OF IMPROPER USE OF "YOU" FOCUS

How can you justify these departmental expenditures?

You improperly filled out the form for supplies, and now our department will have no copier paper for another week.

If these statements were aimed at you, how would you feel? You might become defensive. That is because the problem has become personal; in effect, "you" are the problem and the intent of such a message is to find fault rather than solutions.

Tone

Tone is the implied attitude of the communicator toward his or her audience. Just as tone of voice can convey the speaker's attitude about his or her audience or a situation, attitude can also be conveyed in writing. When considering tone, you should think about language choices, level of formality or familiarity, the power relationship between you and your audience, and your use of humor or sarcasm. In other words, appropriate tone depends upon who you are, who your audience is, your relationship, and the situation. Consideration of the corporate culture and the context of the situation may also be helpful in determining the appropriate tone of a message.

This assessment leads to another general principle of business communication: you should focus on the positive whenever possible. In the examples of the improper use of "you" above, how might you rephrase or reframe the statements to have a more positive tone, one that avoids blaming?

Generally, such statements can be rephrased by removing the personal pronouns, writing the sentence in passive voice, or taking responsibility for the situation yourself. Sometimes, the situation can be reframed as an opportunity to implement better procedures to avoid such problems in the future, or what might be considered as a "problem-solving orientation." Below, the two examples provided above have been rephrased to create a more positive communication situation.

EXAMPLES OF NEUTRAL TONE AND PROBLEM-SOLVING ORIENTATION

I am concerned that some of the money that was spent in the department might have gone to more productive uses. We need to review the department expenditures, identify ways to better spend our funds, and perhaps implement policies to ensure that this objective is consistently reached in the future.

Because of a mistake that was made in the ordering of supplies last week, we will not have copier paper for another five days. To ensure that this situation does not recur, I have attached instructions for properly ordering supplies to this e-mail message.

As mentioned above, effective business communication should be positive in tone whenever possible. In the worse-case scenario, it should be neutral. Business messages should *never* be negative in tone, since such a tone will likely have adverse effects upon your relationship with your audience, and potentially your credibility.

Some people confuse a negative tone, however, with the ability to analyze and identify problems and to promote positive change. What this means is that being able to identify areas for improvement in an organization and to communicate steps to achieve that improvement—being a critical thinker and problem solver—is not the same as being negative. However, some people are extremely sensitive to any communication that might be considered critical—this is because we often have a tendency to take such criticism personally—so it is generally useful to phrase such suggestions as positively as possible and to downplay any critical aspects. In some cases, depending upon your audience and its attitude and personality, you may want to avoid any mention of the problems that are being experienced and focus your message solely on your ideas for improvement and their benefits. However, you may run the risk that some individuals will still interpret such messages as personal criticism, even though the intended message is not about them at all. In such cases, working to establishing a trusting relationship with these individuals may lessen their defensiveness.

More generally, it is critically important to avoid communicating negative emotions in a business situation. In other words, you should not send messages that sound angry, frustrated, or hostile, because they have the potential to negatively affect your credibility as well as your relationship with your audience. This is because businesspeople are generally expected to be reasonable and make objective decisions based upon good information. Consequently, expressing excess negative emotions can make you appear to be irrational or unreasonable and lacking in judgment and self-control.

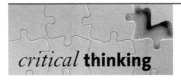

critical **thinking**

Have you read e-mail or other written messages that conveyed a negative tone? What was your reaction? Did the tone of the message affect the writer's credibility? Did the tone affect your relationship with the writer?

None of these qualities is generally considered desirable in a professional work environment, although corporate cultures do exist in which this sort of behavior is not unusual. In such cultures, the power that is exercised may tend to be coercive in nature. John R. P. French & Bertram Raven (1959) have identified the six key **power bases** that arise in groups and organizations. The table on the next page shows the six key power bases as described by French and Bertram.

Of the bases of power, the first three are typically conferred upon an individual by an institution or organization. For example, supervisors typically have the power to reward employees for their work or to punish them. Because of their position, they have the legitimate right to require obedience, as do police officers.

For those of us who have not been conferred power by the organization of which we are a part, the forms of power we may exercise are generally limited to the last

TABLE 7-1. *French and Raven's six bases of power.*

FRENCH AND RAVEN'S SIX BASES OF POWER

Base	Definition
Reward power	The capability of controlling the distribution of rewards given or offered the target.
Coercive power	The capacity to threaten and punish those who do not comply with requests or demands.
Legitimate power	Authority that derives from the power holder's legitimate right to require and demand obedience.
Referent power	Influence based on the target's identification with, attraction to, or respect for the power holder.
Expert power	Influence based on the target's belief that the power holder possesses superior skills and abilities.
Informational power	Influence based on the potential use of informational resources, including rational argument, persuasion, or factual data.

three discussed in the table: referent, expert, and informational power. In other words, our ability to influence may depend upon our relationship with our audience (attraction and respect), our knowledge and expertise, and our ability to communicate logically, persuasively, and well. As you probably recognize by now, all these aspects are part of the business communication purposes of conveying goodwill and establishing credibility.

VOCAL DELIVERY IN ORAL MESSAGES

When delivering an oral message, additional aspects of verbal expression should be considered. These aspects have to do with the vocal delivery of the message.

Your voice plays an important role in the meanings listeners find in your words. By varying the volume, rate of delivery, pitch, or inflection of your voice and message delivery, you can easily change the meaning of your words. In oral presentations, your vocal delivery can also enhance your message by making it more lively, interesting, and convincing to your audience. Vocal delivery can also affect your relationship with the audience and your credibility. As discussed in Chapter 2: Purposes, you are better able to establish a relationship with your audience if you are considered likeable. Your vocal delivery, as well as the content of your speech, helps to achieve this goal. It is also important to appear confident, since if you lack this characteristic, your credibility may also be undermined. That is, we are less likely to believe people who lack confidence in themselves and their ideas.

Norms of vocal delivery differ by culture. For example, Arabs speak loudly because they believe doing so is a sign of strength. In contrast, people from the Philippines tend to speak softly, believing this is a sign of good breeding and

communication 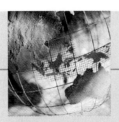 IN YOUR WORLD

The invention of the Internet has provided new channels of communication for organizations and individuals. One of the latest uses of the Internet is personal Web sites, or blogs. Blogs are often used by their owners to muse about their likes and dislikes, including their family members, friends, and coworkers. About 27 percent of online U.S. adults read blogs, and 7 percent write them, according to The Pew Internet and American Life Project (Jesdanun, 2005).

However, blogs can get you fired if they contain information or language that can put your employer in a bad light. That's what happened to former Google employee Mark Jen, who speculated online about his employer's finances and talked about life at the company (Jesdanun, 2005).

Web designer Heather Armstrong was fired for her posts that included "Comments Heard In, Around, and Consequent to the Company Christmas Party Last Evening" (Jesdanun, 2005). Cameron Barrett lost a job at a small marketing firm after coworkers stumbled upon some "experimental" short stories from his creative writing class on his Web site (Jesdanun, 2005). And flight attendant Ellen Simonetti was canned for posting suggestive photographs of herself in uniform on her blog (Jesdanun, 2005).

However, some companies encourage personal, unofficial blogs and have policies defining what employees can and cannot post. Such companies believe there can be value in engaging customers through blogs that contain appropriate content. Sun Microsystems Inc., for example, encourages blogging but warns bloggers not to reveal secrets or make financial disclosures that might violate securities law. Only in rare cases are employees "unofficially asked to soften some wording," says Tim Bray, chief architect of Sun's policy (Jesdanun, 2005, p. C6).

Discussion

Have you read blogs that revealed the name of the writer's employer and contained unflattering information about that employer? What kinds of information or language do you think should be avoided on blogs?

---

education. Rate of delivery also differs among cultures: Arabs and Italians speak faster than people of the United States.

The elements of vocal delivery are described below.

- The **volume** of your speech must be loud enough to be heard but not so loud as to be overwhelming. When speaking before a group, you generally need to speak louder than you do in general conversation.

- The **rate of delivery** refers to the speed at which you speak. For a speech to be effective, you should vary the rate of delivery to reflect the changes in the content of the material being presented or its desired effect. Serious material calls for a slower, more deliberate rate, while lighter topics need a faster pace. Beginning speakers, because of their anxiety, have a tendency to speed up their presentations and run their words together, making it difficult to understand their message. An audience will thus interpret rapid delivery as a sign of

Volume

Volume is the relative sound level of speech; it must be loud enough to be heard, but not so loud as to be overwhelming.

Rate of delivery

The rate of delivery is the speed at which one speaks.

anxiousness or lack of confidence. It is therefore important to focus your efforts on slowing delivery so that your credibility is not undermined if you are struggling with speech apprehension.

Pitch

Pitch is the sound quality of the speaker's voice, ranging from low and deep to high and squeaky.

- **Pitch** ranges from low and deep to high and squeaky. Optimum pitch is the level at which you can produce your strongest voice with minimal effort and also allow variation up and down the scale. Pitch is an issue that deserves some attention, since those with high, squeaky voices or breathy ones may be judged as being less competent, serious, and credible. Through practice and training, you can lower the pitch of your voice.

Vocal variety

Vocal variety refers to the varying use of the vocal aspects of volume, rate, and pitch.

- **Vocal variety** refers to the varying use of the vocal aspects of volume, rate, and pitch. Speaking in a monotone without such variations sends the message that the speaker is not interested in his or her topic or that he or she is nervous or lacks confidence. Making this kind of impression can undermine your credibility as well as make your message less engaging.

Articulate

To articulate is to pronounce all words clearly and fluently.

- Speakers should **articulate** words clearly. Clear articulation is important for two reasons: so that you are easy to understand and because poor articulation can negatively affect your credibility with your audience.

- *Pauses* should be used to emphasize important points and enhance the meanings of words and phrases. Beginning speakers often do not use pauses effectively because they feel uncomfortable with silence. This lack of comfort with silence also can lead to the problem discussed below: vocal distractions or disfluencies.

Disfluencies

Disfluencies or vocal distractions are such speaking errors as stammers, stutters, double starts, and excessive use of "filler" words such as "um" and "uh."

- Avoid *vocal distractions* or **disfluencies.** These include stammers, stutters, double starts, and other empty filler words, such as the excessive use of "uhs" and "ums". An excess of vocal distractions makes a speaker sound disorganized, nervous, and uncertain, leading to a potential loss in credibility. You can reduce vocal distractions in your delivery by focusing on them and practicing to eliminate them during day-to-day conversations.

Many of these aspects of vocal delivery can positively or negatively impact your credibility, so it is important to sensitize yourself to each of them and to identify those that you might work to improve. Mastering these aspects of vocal delivery can also help to make your speaking more engaging and even charismatic. However, vocal delivery is just one aspect of successful oral presentations. In the next section, another element, nonverbal expression or body language, is discussed.

critical **thinking**

How important is the quality of vocal delivery in a presentation? Have you witnessed presenters whose vocal delivery was lacking in one of the elements mentioned above? What was your reaction? Do you struggle with any of the elements of vocal delivery in your oral presentations?

NONVERBAL EXPRESSION IN ORAL MESSAGES

According to Burgoon and Saine (1973), nonverbal communication is defined as the "attributes or actions of humans, other than the use of words themselves, which have socially shared meaning, are intentionally sent or interpreted as intentional, are consciously sent or consciously received, and have the potential for feedback from the receiver."

Developing an awareness of your own nonverbal communication is important, because during face-to-face communication, most of the information that is provided comes in the form of nonverbal cues. In fact, nonverbal cues provide 93 percent of the meaning exchanged in face-to-face communication situations, including oral presentations and meetings. Of that percentage, 35 percent of the meaning comes from tone of voice, while 58 percent comes from gestures, facial expressions, and other physical cues.

What these statistics mean to the business communicator is that to be believable and credible, the way you think and talk about yourself and others must be consistent with the way you act in that regard. This notion is reflected in the adage "actions speak louder than words." Because of this belief, it is important to ensure **strategic alignment** between your oral messages and your nonverbal ones.

Strategic alignment

Strategic alignment is the practice of making oral messages consistent with the nonverbal messages the speaker is sending.

In nonverbal communication, communication channels are multiple and simultaneous. These channels include information that we receive from another person's facial expressions and eyes; body posture, movement, and appearance; the use of space; the use of time; touching; vocal cues (which were discussed in the previous section); and clothing and other artifacts.

Bodily Movement and Facial Expression

Kinesics

Kinesics is the study of posture, movement, gestures, and facial expressions.

The study of the first of these channels—posture, movement, gestures, and facial expression—is called **kinesics.** Like many aspects of communication, the meaning of body movements and facial expressions can differ by culture. While in the United States many people may sprawl when they are seated and slouch when they stand, such postures would be considered rude in Germany. While crossing the legs or feet is common in the United States, doing so is inappropriate in the Middle East, since showing the sole of your shoe or bottom of your foot to someone is considered rude.

Gestures have different meanings depending on the culture, too. In the United States, people generally gesture moderately, while Italians, Greeks, and some Latin Americans use more dramatic gestures when speaking. The Chinese and Japanese, in contrast, tend to keep their hands and arms close to their bodies when speaking.

Even the use of facial expressions differs by culture. In China, people rarely express emotion, while the Japanese may smile to show a variety of emotions, such as happiness, sadness, or even anger.

In the United States, Albert Mehrabian (1971) studied nonverbal communication by examining the concepts of liking, status, and responsiveness of people in communication situations. He found the following:

- **Liking** was often expressed by leaning forward, standing face-to-face and in close proximity, increased touching, relaxed posture, open arms and body, positive facial expression, and eye contact.

- **High status** is communicated nonverbally by bigger gestures, relaxed posture, and less eye contact.

- **Responsiveness** is exhibited nonverbally by moving toward the other person, using spontaneous gestures, shifting posture and position, and facial expressiveness. The face and body should provide positive feedback to the person or persons with whom you are communicating.

In other words, body language is a strong indicator of the extent to which communicators like one another and are interested in each others' views. In addition, it indicates the perceived status, or power relationship, between the communicators. Understanding the use and meaning of body language is helpful in all types of face-to-face communication situations, including job interviews. During a job interview, you can indicate your interest in the position by leaning forward in your chair, maintaining eye contact with the interviewer, using animated facial expressions and varying the volume, rate, and pitch of your voice.

All these nonverbal communication behaviors can be used when appropriate to increase your ability to establish credibility and a positive relationship with your audience in speaking situations, including presentations.

Bodily Appearance

Our body type and physical attractiveness also affect our ability to communicate with others because of their perceptions about these issues.

Somatotype

Somatotype, also known as body type, is a combination of a person's height, weight, and muscularity.

Body type, or **somatotype,** is comprised of a combination of height, weight, and muscularity. Tall people are generally more successful and are viewed more positively by others. Taller people are more likely to be hired in employment interviews, and they tend to have higher incomes (Hensley, 1992; Knapp & Hall, 1992). Regarding attractiveness, women generally find tall men more attractive than short ones; however, they view men of medium height as the most attractive and likeable. Those who are short, soft, and round are often judged negatively in terms of their personalities and their concern about self-presentation.

Particular physical characteristics are considered as universal aspects of attractiveness: bright eyes, symmetrical facial features, and a thin or medium build (Brody, 1994). Physical attractiveness generally leads to more social success in adulthood; attractive people receive higher initial credibility ratings than do those who are viewed as unattractive (Knapp & Hall, 1992; Widgery, 1974).

Proxemics

Proxemics is the study of human space, and revolves around the concepts of territoriality and personal space.

Territoriality

Territoriality is a person's need to establish and maintain certain spaces as one's own.

Personal space

Personal space is the distance between ourselves and others with which we feel comfortable.

Intimate distance

Intimate distance extends no farther than about 18 inches, is used to communicate affection, give comfort, and protect. Intimate distance is more common in private than in public.

Personal distance

Personal distance is the distance used by people in the United States for conversation and non-intimate exchanges. It ranges from about 18 to 48 inches.

Social distance

Social distance ranges from 4 to 8 feet and is the distance used for professional communication.

Public distance

Public distance, used for public speaking, exceeds 12 feet.

Chronemics

Chronemics is the study of how people organize and use time.

Physically attractive people are more likely to be hired and to receive higher salaries (Knapp & Hall, 1992; Schneider, 2001). However, these views may not hold for gender. Studies have shown that attractive females are sometimes judged as less competent than less attractive females (Kaplan, 1978).

Space

The study of human space, or **proxemics,** revolves around two concepts: territoriality and personal space. **Territoriality** refers to your need to establish and maintain certain spaces as your own. In a workplace environment, the walls of your cubicle or office often establish your territory. **Personal space** is the distance between you and others with which you feel comfortable. When someone invades your personal space, you often automatically move away from that person. But personal space preferences can differ among people. For example, large people usually prefer more space, as do men.

Similarly, personal space preferences differ by culture. People of the United States tend to need more space than those from Greece, Latin America, or the Middle East. The Japanese tend to prefer a greater distance than people of the United States in social situations.

Anthropologist Edward T. Hall (1966) defined four distances people use when they communicate. **Intimate distance** is used more in private than in public and extends about 18 inches. This distance is used to communicate affection, give comfort, and to protect. **Personal distance** ranges from 18 inches to 4 feet and is the distance used by those in the United States for conversation and non-intimate exchanges. **Social distance** ranges from 4 to 8 feet, and it is used for professional communication. The higher the status of the person, generally the greater the social distance he or she maintains. **Public distance** exceeds 12 feet and is used most often for public speaking.

Your relationship to other people is related to your use of space. You stand closer to friends and farther from enemies, strangers, authority figures, high-status people, physically challenged people, and people from different racial groups than your own. The effectiveness of communication, or the way you respond to others, can be affected by personal space violations.

Time

Values related to time, or **chronemics,** refers to the way that people organize and use time and the messages that are created because of our organization of time and use of it. Our use of time communicates several messages. Our urgency or casualness with the starting time of an event could be an indication of our personality, our status, or our culture. Highly structured, task-oriented people may arrive and leave on time, while relaxed, relation-oriented people may arrive and leave late. People with low status are expected to be on time, while those with higher status are granted more leeway in their arrival time. Being on time is more important in some cultures than others; for example, being on time is more important in North America than in South America, while people of Germany and Switzerland are even more time-conscious than people from the United States.

Touching

Haptics

Haptics is the study of touch and its relation to communication.

Haptics, or touch, communicates a great deal. What is appropriate and people's tendency to touch differs by gender and culture. Studies indicate that women value touch more than men, women are touched more than men, men touch others more than women do, and men may use touch to indicate power or dominance (Fisher, Rytting, & Hesslin, 1976; Jourard & Rubin, 1968; Henley, 1973–1974).

People from different countries also handle touch differently. Sidney Jourard (1968) determined the rates of touch per hour among adults of various cultures. Adults in Puerto Rico touched 180 times per hour; those in Paris touched about 110 times an hour; those in Gainesville, Florida touched two times per hour; and those in London touched once per hour.

Touch can be very powerful in its effects. When your intention is to communicate caring, concern, and affection, it is generally welcome and appreciated. When the right to touch is abused, it can result in distrust, anxiety, and even hostility.

Clothing and Other Artifacts

Your clothing and other adornments, such as jewelry, hairstyle, cosmetics, shoes, glasses, tattoos, and body piercings, communicate to others your age, gender, status, role, socioeconomic class, group memberships, personality, and relation to the opposite sex. Such cues also indicate the historical period, the time of day, and the climate. Clothing and other artifacts also communicate your self-concept or the type of person you believe you are (Fisher, 1975). Conforming to current styles has been correlated to a person's desire to be accepted and liked by others (Taylor & Compton, 1968).

Individuals believe that clothing is important in forming first impressions (Henricks, Kelley, & Eicher, 1968). Clothing has been shown to affect others' impression of our status and personality traits (Douty, 1963). For this reason, most advise that you should pay attention to dressing professionally in business situations, since it can affect your credibility, attractiveness, and perceived ability to fit within a professional culture. This rule can be particularly important when dealing with international audiences, because they tend to make assumptions about another person's education level, status, and income based upon dress alone (Gray, 1993). Therefore, those who are interested in careers in international business should follow Molloy's (1996) rules for business dress: clothing should be conservative, upper class, and traditional.

How important is another person's dress to you? Does it affect your response to that person or your judgment about him or her? Do you clearly understand the expectations regarding professional dress in the workplace?

NONVERBAL COMMUNICATION IN ORAL PRESENTATIONS

All the various aspects of nonverbal communication discussed above affect our ability to communicate in any interpersonal, or face-to-face, communication situation. They also are critically important to the effectiveness of our oral presentations. Your nonverbal communication in an oral presentation situation can help you to engage your audience and to convey goodwill. It can also help to reinforce your message.

For beginning speakers, it is important to pay attention to and identify the types of nonverbal signals you provide your audience, since they can have an immediate and immense impact on your credibility and perceived professionalism. As discussed above, your clothing leaves an immediate impression of you, your credibility, your professionalism, and sense of belonging within the group, so it is important that you select clothing that is appropriate for the situation. If you are uncertain what is appropriate for a particular situation, such as an employment interview, you should err on the side of formality and conservatism.

To develop a professional, credible persona, you must identify the particular nonverbal signals you may be sending that indicate you lack confidence or may be suffering from anxiety. ("Reducing Presentation Anxiety" is discussed in more detail on page 187.) Common indicators of a lack of confidence include:

- Poor eye contact.

- Rigidity or stiffness of the body and its movements.

- Crossed arms or hands jammed into pockets.

- Unintentional body movements.

Some nervous speakers look at the floor, for example. Another common cause of poor eye contact is the overuse or inappropriate use of notes. You should *not* use notes if you have a tendency to read them once you become nervous.

Standing stiffly with your arms locked behind your back or in any position also is often interpreted as a sign of fear by audiences. Ideally, you should stand with your hands hanging loosely at your sides so that you can more easily, naturally, and spontaneously gesture. Letting your hands hang loosely at your sides sends a second message to the audience: that you are open to it and its ideas. Placing your hands or arms across the front of the body may be interpreted as a sign of defensiveness or anxiety or as a cue that you are not open to your audience and its perspectives.

Unintentional body movements include playing with or tossing your hair or an article of clothing, twisting your body, swaying, pacing, and fidgeting your feet. All these actions can be considered signs of anxiety. Ideally, speakers stand solidly on the floor with their feet apart and only move their body to lean forward or to gesture naturally to emphasize their message. Moving intentionally around the room can help you to engage your audience, but beginning speakers should first master the ability to stand in one place without displaying other unintentional body movement before they move on to this step. If you begin moving around the room before you have learned to control your anxiety, your nervousness may be exhibited through pacing.

Each person typically displays anxiety in a unique way. It is helpful if you can enlist the help of others to observe you presenting and to provide you feedback on the body movements you are making that indicate your nervousness. Once you identify how you display your anxiety, you can focus your attention on eliminating that behavior.

An important goal of a business presentation is to make an immediate, positive, and confident impression of yourself with your audience. (This objective is true for all business communication situations.) To do so, you should smile confidently at your audience when your presentation begins and greet it warmly and sincerely, if appropriate for the message you are about to deliver. As the presentation continues, you should ensure that your body language is not telling your audience that you are unduly fearful, anxious, or nervous, because this knowledge can undermine your credibility. In professional presentation situations, you never want to "let them see you sweat."

A list of the specific nonverbal behaviors that generally enhance a professional presentation is provided below.

- Speakers should establish and maintain **direct eye contact** with their audience. A speaker who talks directly to the audience will be seen as more sincere and more engaged with the audience.

- An effective speaker should **stand up straight and use good posture** without becoming stiff. Good posture projects a confident, yet relaxed image.

- Speakers should use **natural gestures** to animate the presentation. Gestures should grow out of a response to your material and should appear natural and spontaneous, prompted by your feelings. If you are speaking to a large group that may have trouble seeing your gestures, you should make them larger than those you would use in normal conversation.

- Speakers should **move** around the presentation area or room to engage the audience and keep its attention. However, movement should be purposeful. Nervous pacing distracts the audience from your message.

- Speakers should use **facial expressions** to communicate and build rapport with the audience. Your face should reflect and reinforce the meanings of your words. An expressionless face suggests that the speaker is afraid or indifferent.

Establishing a relationship with your audience, maintaining its interest in your topic, and developing your credibility are important objectives for a successful professional presentation. In order to accomplish these goals, you must be well prepared and you must control your anxiety about speaking. Hopefully, preparation can help you to reduce speech apprehension. These two issues are discussed in the sections that follow.

What nonverbal behaviors do you exhibit during oral presentations that may indicate to your audience that you are nervous? What can you do to eliminate or control these behaviors?

Preparing for Your Presentation

Preparing for your presentation involves two basic steps: 1) gathering and organizing your material; and 2) practicing your delivery.

One of the best ways to reduce anxiety and to enhance your credibility is to increase your confidence by becoming an expert in the subject you are to discuss. Consequently, it is very important that you have thoroughly researched your topic and looked at it from all angles. This latter aspect is important, because your audience may be able to detect if you have a one-sided or superficial understanding of the topic, which would undermine your credibility. You may also be faced with questions from your audience, some of which may be objections to your idea, and you must be able to answer these questions with reasonable, quality information in order to maintain your credibility and persuasiveness.

Extemporaneously

Extemporaneous public speaking is delivered spontaneously, rather than being read or memorized in advance.

After you have gathered all the relevant information on your subject and internalized it, you should practice delivering your presentation. Typically, business presentations are expected to be delivered **extemporaneously.** That means that you should be well prepared for your presentation but should deliver your material spontaneously. In other words, you should not read your material or memorize it, although you may want to memorize some important parts of your speech, such as quotations, figures, or examples. If you read your presentation, you will lose your audience's interest because you will probably have difficulty maintaining eye contact with it, and your voice will tend to be monotone in delivery.

In addition, if you memorize your speech, you increase the risk of heightening your anxiety and losing credibility, because if you forget a passage, you probably will need to stop and repeat your presentation quietly to yourself to find the place in your memorized script at which to resume speaking. These long pauses can be a distraction to your audience and can increase your own discomfort, affecting the overall quality and credibility of your speech. Memorized speeches also tend to lack spontaneity, which affects your ability to maintain your audience's interest. Your goal should be to appear and sound like an expert in your subject, one who can speak about it in an informative, well-organized, yet spontaneous manner.

This means that you should use notes sparingly and judiciously. If you can deliver your presentation without notes, your credibility and ability to relate to the audience will be enhanced. However, if you find that you need to use notes, guidelines exist for their proper use.

- **Use only 3-by-5-inch notecards.** Small notecards are less obtrusive and distracting for your audience. If you use 8½-by-11-inch sheets of paper, you may become nervous and unintentionally wave them as you gesture. You don't want to look like a sailor on a flight deck, guiding a plane through its landing, signal flags waving.

- **Put only an outline or keywords on your notes.** If you write out your entire presentation on the cards, you will have a greater tendency to read from them.

- **When you look at your notes, stop speaking.** The proper way to reference your notes is to stop speaking, glance down at your cards, then look up and begin speaking again. In most cases, you should not speak unless you are looking at your audience.

You might find it helpful to practice your presentation before a small audience of family or friends, or in front of a mirror. Either way, you can receive feedback about how you look and sound, and you can adjust your delivery and nonverbal communication to better support the message that you wish to send. Practice can also help you reduce your anxiety about speaking, since it may help you feel more confident. Techniques to reduce speech apprehension are discussed in the following section.

Reducing Presentation Anxiety

As mentioned above, one of the best ways to reduce presentation anxiety is to prepare thoroughly and practice sufficiently for an oral presentation. By doing so, you should increase your confidence about your knowledge of your topic, what you need to accomplish and how, as well as your ability to communicate your message successfully.

Feeling some anxiety when faced with an oral presentation situation is not unusual or necessarily bad. Generally, we perform better if we feel a small amount of anxiety. However, you should keep your anxiety at a manageable level, one that does not affect your ability to perform. Techniques to reduce anxiety include visualization and breathing techniques. Visualizing yourself giving a successful presentation can help you to achieve those results. Taking deep, slow, regular breaths—during which you visualize yourself drawing your breath down into and expanding your stomach rather than your chest—can also help to calm yourself. This technique triggers a natural relaxation response. You might try both these techniques to find which works better for you.

Another technique is to ask yourself whether your fears are reasonable. For example, we may believe that if we make one mistake, our audience will judge us harshly. But this is typically not the case; most audiences want us to succeed. By realizing that your audience is probably on your side, you may be able to reduce some of your fears and perform more confidently.

Handling Question-and-Answer Sessions

Question-and-answer (Q&A) sessions are a common part of business presentations and typically take place at the end of a presentation. How you handle question-and-answer sessions can impact your ability to maintain credibility and goodwill as well as achieve your larger communication purposes. Because of their importance in achieving your communication goals, question-and-answer sessions also deserve adequate preparation and strategy formulation. These issues are addressed in the following sections.

Preparing for Q&A How well you have prepared for your presentation and have anticipated your audience's questions can help you to enhance your credibility as well as to achieve your message purposes. The steps for preparing for a question-and-answer session are provided below.

Prepare for questions by listing every fact or opinion you can think of that challenges your position.

1. Divide potential questions into three categories: the known, the knowable, and the notable.

   - The known list contains questions to which you know the answers. Depending on how well you know the particulars, you may want to write down the answers and practice them out loud.

   - The knowable list contains questions to which you may not know the answers. Do the research, find the answers, and practice them.

   - The notable list contains the questions that require a strategy. These are the broad questions that do not have simple answers or which may jeopardize the success of the presentation without planning. Your strategy for answering these questions should validate the overall purpose and message of your presentation.

2. Treat each objection seriously and try to think of a way to deal with it.

3. If you are talking about a controversial issue, you may want to save one point for the question period, rather than making it during the presentation.

4. Speakers who have visuals prepared to answer questions seem especially well prepared and thus enhance their credibility and professionalism.

During the Q&A   During the question-and-answer session, you should follow some basic rules. Remember, you are in control of the question-and-answer period, so you should state the rules for the process, if appropriate. For example, near the beginning of your presentation, you might ask the audience to hold its questions until the end of the presentation. At the beginning of the question-and-answer session, you might state a time limit, number of questions per person, and identify who—if this has been a team presentation—will answer the audience's questions.

During the Q&A, you should keep the discussion focused on the topic or issue at hand. Most important, you do not want to lose your temper, appear confused, or become emotional. Your objective is to appear well-prepared, confident, objective, reasonable, and calm. If you become agitated or confused, or the session becomes a free-for-all, you have lost control of the situation and probably damaged your credibility and perhaps jeopardized your ability to achieve your other communication purposes. The basic rules for question-and-answer sessions are listed below.

- Don't nod your head to indicate that you understand a question as it is asked, since it may be interpreted as a sign of agreement.

- Look directly at the questioner.

- When you answer the question, expand your focus to take in the entire group.

- If the audience may not have heard the question or if you want more time to think, repeat the question before you answer it.

- Ask for clarification if you don't understand the question.

- If a question starts to take your talk into a new direction, offer to discuss that issue at a later date.

- Link your answers to the points you made in your presentation.

- Keep the purpose of your presentation in mind and select information that advances your goals.

- Sometimes someone will ask a question that is designed to state his or her opinion. Respond to the question if you want, or say, "I'm not sure what you are asking" or "That's a clear statement of your position. Any other questions?"

- If someone asks a question that you have explained in your presentation, answer it rather than embarrass him or her.

- Look for a point of agreement in your answers. An example is provided below.

   Audience member: Your ideas about this new business proposal sound farfetched to me. I think that we need to solidify our regional market before we try to expand abroad.

Speaker: You have a good point—our regional sales have traditionally been the backbone of this company. But we need to expand so that we can avoid slumps if the regional economy takes a downturn.

■ If you don't know the answer to a question, say so. You can tell the asker that you will get back to him or her with the answer. You might also ask if someone else in the room knows the answer; if they don't, then your "ignorance" is vindicated. This strategy can also present a risk; don't do it if you think you will lose control of the questioning period. You can also ask your group members if one of them knows the answer if you are presenting as a team.

■ At the end of the Q&A, take the opportunity to summarize your position one more time. Take advantage of having the floor to repeat your message briefly and forcefully.

Dealing with Hostile Questions   On some occasions, you may be faced with audience members who do not like you, your company, your product or service, or your proposed idea. Sometimes, these audience members may have such strong feelings that they are unable or unwilling to control them. Do not stoop to their level. Your goal in these situations is to enhance yourself and your position by remaining confident, objective, reasonable, and calm. In these cases, the hostile audience members may do much to undermine their own credibility without your help or comment. However, if you are faced with hostile questions, there are some strategies for dealing with them.

■ If a question is hostile or biased, rephrase it before you answer it: "You're asking whether . . ." or suggest an alternative question: "I think there are problems with both positions you describe. It seems to me that a third solution . . ." By rephrasing or reframing the question, you are attempting to remove the hostile or biased perspective from the situation.

■ Be fair to a hostile questioner, perhaps by indicating the need to disagree, and then agree on a statement of that disagreement.

■ Most important, if someone asks a hostile question, do not respond in kind. You might even try to respond with a compliment as long as it isn't insincere: "That's a very important question. Thank you for asking it."

To handle question-and-answer sessions effectively, you must anticipate your audience's questions and prepare answers that advance the overall purposes of your message. You must strategize ways to maintain control of the session and to remain calm, confident, and reasonable.

EMPLOYMENT INTERVIEWS

During an employment interview, the interviewer is typically attempting to discover whether the interviewee is a good match with the company culture in terms of attitude, values, and motivation as well as attempting to ensure that the interviewee has the skills, knowledge, and experience needed for the position. An interview is a competitive situation in which the interviewee must show that he or she is a better match and has the best skills compared to other applicants.

This section will cover what an applicant should do to prepare for an employment interview and what he or she should do during the interview itself.

Preparing for Employment Interviews

Many of the issues of concern for effectively handling presentations and question-and-answer periods—as well as the techniques for preparing for both those situations—are similar to those for employment interviews. In both, you have a communication purpose or purposes to achieve; often these are to persuade, to convey goodwill, and to establish your credibility. In the case of an employment interview, it is to persuade your audience that you are the best person for the job by informing the interviewer that you have the skills, experience, knowledge, and personal characteristics for which the organization is looking. You are also attempting to convey goodwill by establishing the beginnings of a relationship with the interviewer and to show that you are a professional, honest, likeable, competent, motivated, and responsible person and potential employee.

In addition, in both presentations and question-and-answer sessions, as well as in job interviews, you must prepare by conducting research, strategizing, and practicing your message or answers in order to help ensure your ability to achieve your communication purposes and to meet your audience's needs. To prepare for a job interview, you should:

1. Research the organization. The most important information you must gather is related to the job for which you are applying. What skills, experience, and knowledge is the organization looking for? What personal characteristics does the job require or the company seek in applicants? This information is critical because it will help you to identify the key messages you must succeed in conveying to the interviewer. The best resource for this information can often be the advertisement for the job itself. Typically, the job posting includes all the qualifications and skills for which the company is looking.

   Of course, you should also gather other information about the company, such as the industry in which the organization is involved, the company's history, its products and services, its financial situation, its future directions and growth potential, and its corporate culture. You will need this information to show how your skills, experience, knowledge, and personal characteristics are useful to the organization. Your secondary purpose is to show the interviewer that you want the job enough to spend time learning more about the organization. Showing that you are knowledgeable about the company also can indicate that you possess other personal characteristics, such as thoroughness, preparedness, initiative, and professionalism. Demonstrating these characteristics can help set you apart from other applicants, who may be less well prepared.

Gathering this information can also help you to determine whether you are a good fit for the organization and its culture. The theory of person-organization fit essentially says that people leave jobs that are not compatible with their personalities (Robbins, 2001, p. 103). So it is important to know yourself and your preferences regarding the kind of environment in which you will work, and find out whether prospective employers offer that type of environment.

In addition to the organizational culture, you should also ask questions about your direct supervisor and perhaps the company's general management philosophy. According to employment consultant Gary Moore (2004), "it's easy to underestimate the influence individuals you'll interact with on a daily basis will have on your accomplishment or failure" (p. E1). Moore recommends that you ask the following questions to determine the organizational culture and management philosophy of a company:

- How does the manager deal with problems in the workplace?

- Does the employee group work well together as a team?

- Are there internal candidates for the position? (If not, it may be indicative that the job, or the boss, really isn't a desirable one, according to Moore.)

- Why do the employees like to work for the company?

- What is the average length of employment for employees? (If the average is less than one year or more than five, this may be a clue to the attractiveness of working at this organization.)

2. Identify your skills, experience, knowledge, and personal characteristics that match those for which the company is looking. For example, if you are applying for a position that has a lot of customer contact, the hiring organization is probably interested in your people skills. These might include patience, desire to help others, and the ability to put others at ease. If you are applying for a job in which you produce data that is used by others, the organization might be interested in your analytical skills. In this case, you might talk about your accuracy, attention to detail, and systematic or organized approach to completing tasks. Table 7-2 below lists personality types and personal characteristics that are generally congruent with or attractive for particular occupations (Holland, 1985).

Table 7-2. *Holland's typology of personality and congruent occupations.*

HOLLAND'S TYPOLOGY OF PERSONALITY AND CONGRUENT OCCUPATIONS

Type	Personality Characteristics	Congruent Occupation
Realistic: Prefers physical activities that require skill.	Shy, genuine, persistent, stable, conforming, practical	Mechanic, drill press operator, assembly line worker, farmer
Investigative: Prefers activities that involve thinking, organizing, and understanding.	Analytical, original, curious, independent	Biologist, economist, news reporter, mathematician

Continued on next page.

TABLE 7-2. *Continued*

Social: Prefers activities that involve helping and developing others.	Sociable, understanding, cooperative, friendly	Social worker, teacher, clinical psychologist, counselor
Conventional: Prefers rule-regulated, orderly, and unambiguous activities.	Unimaginative, conforming, efficient, practical, inflexible	Accountant, bank teller, corporate manager, file clerk
Enterprising: Prefers verbal activities in which there are opportunities to influence others and attain power.	Self-confident, ambitious, energetic, domineering	Lawyer, real estate agent, public relations specialist, small business manager
Artistic: Prefers ambiguous and unsystematic activities that allow creative expression.	Imaginative, disorderly, idealistic, emotional, impractical	Painter, musician, writer, interior decorator

3. Obtain lists of the various types of questions an interviewer might ask you. (Refer to Table 7-3 below for a list of behavioral interview questions.)

4. Practice answering the interview questions you have gathered. Your answers should, whenever possible, highlight the skills, experience, knowledge, and/or personal characteristics that you know the company is seeking (see step 2 on the previous page). Your goal is to show that you are a perfect fit for the job and the organization.

Because hiring can be a costly undertaking for organizations, some have begun to practice interview techniques designed to better identify how an individual will actually perform on the job. One such technique is called a *behavioral interview,* which is intended to identify an individual's attitude toward and abilities in planning, communicating, problem solving, leadership, teamwork, goal setting, and decision making, among others. (Please see Table 7-3 below for a list of sample behavioral interview questions.)

TABLE 7-3. *Behavioral interview questions by skill.*

BEHAVIORAL INTERVIEW QUESTIONS BY SKILL

To answer behavioral interview questions effectively, you should first identify the skill the interviewer is asking you about; provide a brief, yet relevant example in which you exercised that skill; describe your actions in the situation; and end by stating the results of that action. Listed below are some typical behavioral interview questions by skill.

Adaptability

- Tell me about a situation when you had to be tolerant of an opinion that was different from your own.

- Tell me about a time when you had to adjust to changes over which you had no control.

Communication

- Tell me about a time when you were able to use persuasion to convince someone to see things your way.

- Tell me about a time when you dealt with an irate customer.

Continued on next page.

TABLE 7-3. *Continued*

Goal Setting

- Describe a goal you set for yourself and how you reached it.

- Tell me about a goal that you set and did not reach.

Problem Solving

- Tell me about a situation where you had to solve a difficult problem.

- Tell me about a time when you had to analyze information and provide a recommendation.

Teamwork

- Tell me about a time when you worked on a team and a member was not doing his or her share.

- Tell me about a time when you on a team in which the members did not get along.

Time Management

- Describe a situation in which you had to do a number of things at the same time.

- Tell me about a time when you were unable to complete a project on time.

5. Prepare questions to ask the interviewer about the job and the company. (Some of these questions were addressed in number 2 on page 192.)

Performing the Employment Interview

As in other business communication situations, your primary purposes in a job interview are to 1) convey goodwill by showing your enthusiasm and general likeability; 2) establish credibility as a professional; and 3) persuade the interviewer that you are the best person for the job by providing quality evidence of your skills, experience, knowledge, and personal characteristics.

In other words, you must immediately make a good impression on the interviewer and then show that you are a doer and that you know how to be a valuable contributor to the organization. Making a good first impression is critical, since research shows that most interviewers make up their minds about an applicant in the initial 30 seconds of an interview.

To achieve these purposes, you should do the following during the interview:

1. Dress professionally to help you establish your credibility. This means that in most cases, you should dress conservatively: wear a suit; avoid excessive jewelry, makeup, perfume, or cologne; and wear conservative shoes and a conservative hairstyle.

2. Arrive on time; be friendly to the receptionist; and bring a notepad, pen, and extra copies of your résumé.

3. Greet the interviewer with a smile and a firm handshake.

4. Sit forward in your chair to indicate interest, show enthusiasm for the interview and job, maintain eye contact, and be clear and specific in your answers and questions.

During employment interviews, it is important to dress professionally, to be friendly and enthusiastic, and to show interest in order to establish credibility and goodwill.

5. At the close of the interview, you should bring up any positive points about yourself that you may not have been able to address during the interview. Depending upon the situation, you might ask for feedback from the interviewer regarding your suitability for the position. If the interviewer has not provided this information, you should ask what the next steps in the hiring process are, when you might receive a response, or what you need to do to follow up. If you are really interested in the job, you might ask for it.

After the interview, if you are interested in the position, you should write the interviewer a thank-you note, expressing your interest in the position and covering any points you were unable to make in the interview. This is one last opportunity for you to distinguish yourself from other applicants, who often do not follow through with this last step. Handwritten notes often make the best impression, since they are personal. However, if you have been communicating with the interviewee via e-mail, this channel has become more acceptable as a means of expressing appreciation.

Responsible Communication

Those little lies on people's résumés tend to grow during important job interviews, say researchers at the University of Massachusetts at Amherst. "Basically, the more stringent the job requirements, the more candidates lie about their qualifications," says Brent Weiss, a psychology graduate student and coauthor of a study presented at a meeting of the Society for Personality and Social Psychology (Pirisi, 2003).

Weiss's study examined how often people lied in job interviews and how personality influences the propensity to fib. Thirty-eight college students applied for and were granted interviews for tutorial jobs that didn't exist (Pirisi, 2003). The interview focused on their math or verbal skills. After researchers came clean about the study, they asked students to review their videotaped interviews and identify what they had lied about. Overall, 84 percent admitted to lying at some point (Pirisi, 2003). People told straight-out lies, such as, "I'm very good at math," when they had no facility with arithmetic whatsoever (Pirisi, 2003).

Other studies indicate the rate of lying on résumés or in job interviews at 20 to 44 percent (Lying, n.d.). That includes lies about degrees, past jobs, and responsibilities.

"A lot of HR managers are recognizing that lying is pervasive," said Westaff Vice President and Director of Human Resources Joe Coute. "For too many candidates, the desire to get ahead at all costs is more important than honesty. Because of that, interviewers can find themselves focusing on what might be wrong with what someone's saying rather than what might be right. They figure that if a candidate will lie during the interview, then they are going to lie once they're in the door" (Lying, n.d.).

Questions for Thought

1. **What are the dangers of lying during a job interview?**

2. **Is omitting information during an interview a form of lying?**

EFFECTIVE LISTENING

While you may be asked to communicate orally in a professional workplace setting, you will more likely be on the receiving end of such messages. In fact, in the business world, people, both those with and without management responsibilities, spend most of their time listening. Businesspeople spend nearly 33 percent of their time listening, about 26 percent of their time speaking, and nearly 19 percent of their time reading (Weinrach & Swanda, 1975). Although we spend most of our time in communication situations involved in listening, the skill often receives little attention. A survey conducted by a corporate training and development firm indicated that 80 percent of the corporate executives who responded rated listening as the most important skill in the workforce. However, nearly 30 percent of those same executives said that listening was the communication skill most lacking in their employees (Salopek, 1999). According to Madelyn Burley-Allen (2001), only 35 percent of us are efficient listeners. The lack of effective listening can often lead to missed opportunities, misunderstanding, conflict, or poor decision making.

Conversely, the ability to listen effectively can have a big impact on your ability to communicate well with others. Effective listening can help us build relationships, be more productive, and determine whether others are being deceptive.

Listening does not mean the same thing as hearing. Hearing is the sensory ability to receive sound. Hearing takes no effort or energy on your part. You receive and hear sounds constantly. However, listening is a more active, engaged process. According to the International Listening Association, listening is "the active process of receiving, constructing meaning from, and responding to spoken and/or nonverbal messages. It involves the ability to retain information, as well as to react empathically and/or appreciatively to spoken and/or nonverbal messages." Listening requires energy and effort, while hearing is automatic and passive.

Listening Styles

There are three levels of listening, and it is beneficial to distinguish between them and identify which type of listener you are.

Level one is referred to as a good listener. A level one listener exhibits all the qualities of being involved in conversations, including taking the other person's interests into consideration and staying focused on the speaker (Burley-Allen, 2001). A level one listener keeps an open mind and is always eager to hear what the other person has to say. A level one listener is respectful of the other person's feelings and is not quick to pass judgment.

Level two listeners hear the words being spoken but do not have full understanding of what the words mean (Burley-Allen, 2001). Many times listening involves recognizing nonverbal forms of communication. A level two listener focuses on the words being said, but might not pay attention to the facial expressions, hand gestures, or tone of voice. They do not give much effort to understanding the speaker's intent, and this oversight can lead to conflicts and misunderstandings.

A level three listener does not acknowledge the speaker at all. While another person is speaking, the level three listener spends time thinking about something else (Burley-Allen, 2001). The level three listener's thoughts are centered on himself or herself, and he or she may only appear to be listening. The problem that arises with this level of listening is the amount of confusion it can create. While the speaker is talking, the listener is daydreaming about something else and may have possibly missed an important piece of information. This leads to making unhealthy life decisions and poor judgment, and creates barriers to effective communication.

According to Burley-Allen (2001), only about 20 percent of the people in the work force are at a level one. The rest of the 80 percent go back and forth between levels two and three, and only sometimes are at level one. In Table 7.4 below, you will find a short quiz intended to help you identify the quality of your listening skills.

TABLE 7-4. *Are you a good listener?*

ARE YOU A GOOD LISTENER?

Take this short quiz, using the following rating scale: A "3" means you are very strong in this area; a "2" that you try to perform the stated behavior; and a "1" that you are not sure how often you perform the behavior.

1. I am aware that to listen effectively I must listen with a purpose.

2. I have trained myself to listen at least twice as much as I speak.

3. I listen for understanding rather that evaluation.

4. I recognize the importance of my nonverbal signals to the speaker.

5. I am aware of the words, phrases, or behaviors that are likely to make me defensive.

6. I wait until the speaker has finished before responding.

7. I have often heard a person say to me, "Thank you for listening."

8. I concentrate on what the speaker is saying, even though other things could distract me.

9. I am able to exercise emotional control when listening even if I disagree with the message.

10. I realize that listening powerfully may be the key to my success.

If you scored 12 or less, you probably need a listening program. If you scored 13 to 20, you are an average listener. If you rated higher than 20, you are an excellent listener.

Source: Effective listening skills. *Women in Business.* March/April 1994, Vol. 46 Issue 2: 28–32.

Listening Types

Listening is classified into four main types: active, empathic, critical listening, and listening for enjoyment. Listening for enjoyment is typically not an activity in which we engage in the workplace, so it will not be discussed here.

Active listening

Active listening is listening with a purpose.

However, the other three types of listening are relevant to and useful in the workplace. **Active listening** is "listening with a purpose" (Barker, 1971). Active listening is a key part of successful interpersonal or face-to-face communication. It involves four steps:

1. Listen carefully by using all available senses, including observation.

2. Paraphrase what is heard both mentally and verbally. This step is intended to help you remember the information and to accomplish step 3. Paraphrasing involves such statements as "If I hear you correctly, you are saying . . ."

3. Check your understanding to ensure accuracy. To check understanding, you might follow your paraphrased statement by asking, "Is that right?"

4. Provide feedback.

Feedback consists of the listener's verbal and nonverbal responses to the speaker and his or her message. Feedback can be either positive or negative. Positive feedback consists of the listener's verbal and nonverbal responses that are intended to affirm the speaker and his or her message. Negative feedback consists of the listener's verbal and nonverbal responses that are intended to disaffirm the speaker and his or her message. In productive communication situations, negative feedback should not be used to disaffirm the speaker or typically to discredit the message, since this may negatively affect your relationship and your ability to communicate effectively in the future. However, you should feel free to say "no" to the speaker or to disagree with his or her message. Disagreeing is generally more effective if you can provide good reasons for doing so.

Empathic listening

Empathic listening is active listening with the goal of understanding the speaker.

Empathic listening is a form of active listening with the goal of understanding the other person. To listen empathetically, you must be fully engaged in the conversation at the moment and empathize with the person who is speaking. Empathy is the ability to perceive another person's worldview as if it were your own. Empathic listening is useful in the workplace if you find yourself in a situation in which it is appropriate to be supportive of colleagues and team members or if you are a supervisor, dealing with an employee with a problem. Empathic listening is useful in establishing and maintaining relationships with others by showing that you care about them and their concerns. Empathetic messages include such statements as "I understand why you feel that way" and "I can see how you might interpret my actions as you did."

Critical listening

Critical listening is a form of active listening that is used to evaluate the accuracy, meaningfulness, and usefulness of a message.

Critical listening is used to evaluate the accuracy, meaningfulness, and usefulness of a message. In the workplace, critical listening is particularly important in any decision-making process. Critical listening can help you to determine whether information is sound, relevant to the issue, and adequate. It can also help you to determine whether the speaker is pursuing a hidden or personal agenda or the intentions of the group. It can also help you to determine whether the person is objective and forthright. All this information is necessary and may affect your ability to reach a sound business decision.

Your skills as a critical listener are dependent upon your abilities as a critical thinker. *Critical thinking* is necessary to analyze a communication situation—your purposes, your audiences, and the situational factors that affect the way you communicate—and based upon that analysis, to create an effective communication strategy for that situation. Conversely, critical thinking is also used to analyze a speaker, the situation, and the speaker's ideas to make critical judgments about the message being presented. This last issue, message analysis, requires two steps: 1) evaluating the process by which information or knowledge was discovered; and 2) evaluating specific elements of message content. In other words, you should evaluate whether the information contained in the message is accurate and unbiased and that the speaker has drawn logical conclusions from the information. The common errors in reasoning were discussed in Chapter 6: Content.

critical **thinking**

Are you skilled at practicing active listening? Empathic listening? Critical listening? If not, what steps might you take to become a more effective listener? How might improving your listening skills provide you opportunities in the workplace?

Verbal Strategies for Effective Listening

One way to indicate to the person with whom you are communicating that you are actively engaged in the listening process is to use effective verbal communication techniques, such as those listed below.

■ **Ask questions.** Asking questions shows that you are interested in what the speaker has to say and enables you to gather more information, which is necessary for clear understanding.

■ **Show interest and support.** You can do this by encouraging the speaker to continue or by encouraging him or her to share ideas.

■ **Use descriptive, nonevaluative responses when paraphrasing or responding.** An example of such a statement would be: "Your information comes from a think tank that has openly expressed its partisan affinities. I am not sure that the data gives us a complete picture of the situation." Compare that to the following response: "You give us biased and therefore one-sided information, since its source clearly has a political agenda." The second response contains language that has negative connotations—"biased," "one-sided," "political"—which can put the speaker on the defensive or make him or her feel attacked. Use of such language can also be interpreted as a subtle form of name-calling, since it implies that the speaker is biased, one-sided, and political in his or her intentions.

■ **Identify areas of agreement or common interests.** An example of such a statement is: "I believe we both are interested in pursuing decisions that will enable the department to meet its objectives." Such statements are intended to reduce the perception that you and the speaker are far apart in your bigger concerns or experiences.

■ **Respond with affirming statements.** Making such statements as "I understand," "I know," and "yes," indicates support for the speaker and his or her ideas or feelings, as well as empathy.

■ **Avoid silence.** Silence can be interpreted in a variety of negative ways, such as a sign of a lack of interest, inattentiveness, or disapproval.

■ **Don't dominate a conversation or cut the other person off.** If you wish to indicate that you are interested in the speaker's ideas or feelings, you should allow that person to express himself or herself fully. If you are perceived as someone who dominates a conversation or cuts people off, others will typically begin to avoid conversing with you.

■ **Restate and paraphrase the speaker's message as well as the intent**. This activity shows that you are listening and are concerned about interpreting the speaker's message accurately. It may be appropriate in certain situations to openly express your interpretation of the speaker's intentions. An example might be: "As I understand it, you are telling me this information so that it can be used to make a decision about the pending policy change. Is that correct?"

In Table 7-5 below, active listening responses are compared to those that block communication.

TABLE 7-5. *Active listening vs. blocking responses.*

ACTIVE LISTENING VS. BLOCKING RESPONSES

■ **Active response: Paraphrasing content**

"You're saying that you don't have time to finish the report by Friday."

Blocking response: Ordering, threatening

"I don't care how you do it. Just get the report on my desk by Friday."

■ **Active response: Mirroring feelings**

"It sounds like the department's problems really bother you."

Blocking response: Preaching, criticizing

"You should know better than to air the department's problems in a general meeting."

■ **Active response: Stating one's feelings**

"I'm frustrated that the job isn't completed yet, and I'm worried about getting it done on time."

Blocking response: Interrogating

"Why didn't you tell me that you didn't understand the instructions?"

■ **Active response: Asking for information or clarification**

"What parts of the problem seem most difficult to solve?"

Continued on next page.

TABLE 7-5. *Continued*

Blocking response: Minimizing the problem

"You think that's bad? You should see what I have to do this week."

- **Active response: Offering to help solve the problem together**

"Is there anything I could do that would help?"

Blocking response: Advising

"Why don't you try listing everything you have to do and seeing which items are most important?"

Source: The five responses that block communication are based on a list of 12 in Thomas Gordon's and Judith Gordon Sands's *P.E.T. in Action* (New York: Wyden, 1976), 117–118.

Nonverbal Strategies for Effective Listening

As has been expressed earlier, your nonverbal communication is as important, if not more so, than your oral statements in interpersonal communication situations. Therefore, providing appropriate nonverbal communication is also useful in indicating that you are actively listening to others. These nonverbal communication behaviors are listed below.

- **Use movements and gestures to show understanding and responsiveness.** You can nod your head to show approval or understanding, or shake your head in disbelief.

- **Lean forward.** Leaning toward a speaker shows interest. This technique is also useful in job interview situations, since it expresses your interest in the speaker and the position for which you have applied.

- **Establish an open body position.** Crossing your arms or legs sends a subtle message that you are not completely comfortable with the speaker or his or her ideas, or that you are not receptive to them. This principle is also true in oral presentations. You should maintain an open body position while delivering speeches or presentations to indicate your confidence and receptiveness to the audience.

- **Use an alert but relaxed posture.** In other words, do not look too relaxed or too stiff. Being too relaxed may indicate that you don't take the speaker or situation seriously. Being too stiff may show that you are uncomfortable or rigid in your thinking.

- **Use direct body orientation.** You should directly face the speaker or your audience rather than regarding it from an angle. An angled position may be interpreted as sign that you are attempting to move away from the speaker. It also may inhibit your ability to observe the nonverbal communication of the speaker.

- **Use facial expressions that indicate involvement**. You can raise your eyebrows to express interest and smile to show encouragement.

- **Maintain direct eye contact.** Failing to maintain direct eye contact may be interpreted as showing deceptiveness, a lack of interest, or a lack of confidence.

- Subtle yet powerful messages can be communicated through our use of verbal, vocal, and nonverbal elements in both our written and oral messages. They can help us to achieve our communication purposes of establishing and maintaining a relationship with our audience, as well as our credibility.

- The style of written business messages should be correct yet easy to read. This goal can be achieved by using short sentences, plain English, and short paragraphs. Business messages should typically be friendly and positive in tone. In the worse case, they should be neutral in tone so as not to negatively affect your relationship with your reader.

- In oral presentations, your voice can be used to engage your audience, emphasize key points, and indicate your confidence and professionalism. Loudness, articulation, rate of delivery, pitch, and the use of pauses can help to enhance oral presentations.

- Nonverbal communication conveys more information than the spoken word. Our use of space and time, our bodily movement and appearance, our clothing, and use of touch all convey information about ourselves and our relationships with others. Likewise, nonverbal communication—eye contact, posture, and facial expressions—can be used to convey confidence and work to create a positive relationship with your audience during oral presentations.

- Proper preparation for oral presentations can also help us to achieve a confident, professional persona. To achieve this goal, you must also control speech apprehension. Experimenting with different techniques to reduce this anxiety—such as visualization and breathing exercises—can help you identify the ones that work best for you.

- Just as preparation is crucial to successful oral presentations, so it is to question-and-answer sessions and employment interviews. As with all business communication, in these situations, you should find out as much about your audience as possible so that you can anticipate its concerns and formulate answers to its questions that can help you to achieve your goals.

- While it is important to understand and be able to practice the skills associated with effective oral communication, it may be more important in ensuring communication success to improve our ability to listen and engage with the oral communication of others.

  Three types of listening exist: Active, empathic, and critical. Active listening is "listening with a purpose" and is a key part of successful interpersonal or face-to-face communication. Empathic listening is a form of active listening with the goal of understanding the other person. Empathy is the ability to perceive another person's worldview as if it were your own. Critical listening is used to evaluate the accuracy, meaningfulness, and usefulness of a message. In the workplace, critical listening is particularly important in any decision-making process.

Key Terms

Active listening, 198
Articulate, 179

Chronemics, 182
Critical listening, 198

FEDERAL BUREAU OF INVESTIGATION
NEW YORK FIELD OFFICE

DISCUSSION QUESTIONS

1. What are some examples of how physical appearance sends messages in your world?

2. With what artifacts do you surround yourself? What do they mean to you?

3. What is the worst possible thing that could happen to you during a speech? What strategies might you use to reduce this fear?

4. Which is more important in an oral presentation, delivery style or content?

5. What are some of the barriers to effective listening that you commonly encounter? What are some strategies for overcoming each of these barriers?

APPLICATIONS

1. Rewrite the following letter, paying particular attention to tone.

Justin Yates, Manager
Yates Family Restaurant
356 Copper Road
Butte, Montana 84001

Dear Mr. Yates:

Your restaurant has the worst service and food of any place I have ever eaten. How you can call yourself a restaurateur is beyond me!

Last Sunday, I took my family to your restaurant for my oldest son's birthday. Even though it was clearly a special occasion for our family, we had to wait in the cold entryway of your restaurant for over 20 minutes until a table large enough for our party was available. When we were seated and received our food, it was lukewarm and the waiter got two of the orders wrong. I have never seen such incompetence. The very least your employee could have done was to give us our meals for free, but he said that was against company policy. (He did give us free desserts.)

This was a very important occasion for our family, and it was ruined by your restaurant and your employees. I demand that you provide us some recompense. How do you expect to remain in business when you treat customers with such callousness?

Sincerely,

Roberta Miles

2. Read the letter provided in application number one above. Act as if you are Justin Yates and write a letter in response to Ms. Miles's concerns.

3. Choose a specific country, such as Argentina, Germany, India, or Thailand. Research the culture

and write a brief summary of the nonverbal communication behaviors of which a person doing business in that country should be aware.

4. Find and observe a speaker. Analyze the speaker's vocal delivery and nonverbal communication. How did these elements contribute to or detract from the speaker's credibility and goodwill?

5. Prepare written answers to all the behavioral interview questions listed in Table 7.3, which can be found on page 193 of this chapter.

 INFOTRAC ACTIVITIES

1. Using InfoTrac College Edition, type the words "nonverbal communication" in the keyword search engine. Select the eight related topics and read about eye contact, flirting, hugging, and other related practices.

2. Using InfoTrac College Edition, type the words "employment interviews" in the keyword search engine. Visit some of the Web sites that are found to learn more about the different types of questions that might be asked in employment interviews.

Case Analysis

Tone and appropriate content are just as important when drafting e-mail messages as when producing other forms of written communication. Language that is obscene, racist, sexist, discriminatory, menacing, harassing, threatening, or in any way hostile or offensive can negatively effect an organization's business relationships, damage its reputation, trigger a lawsuit, or be used as evidence in litigation or an investigation.

In one high-profile case in 1995, Chevron Corporation was ordered to pay female employees $2.2 million to settle a sexual harassment lawsuit stemming from inappropriate jokes e-mailed internally by male employees. Among other gems, the offending jokes included one entitled "Twenty-Five Reasons Why Beer Is Better than Women" (Flynn, 2004).

In another case, a former employee of Microsoft sued the company for sexual discrimination, alleging that she was denied a promotion because she was female. Admitted into evidence were offensive e-mails from the woman's male supervisor.

In one of the e-mails, the supervisor referred to himself as "president of the amateur gynecology club," while in another he called a female employee the "Spandex queen" (Flynn, 2004). Other e-mail messages from the supervisor contained a sexual innuendo referring to male genitalia, a parody of a play entitled "A Girl's Guide to Condoms," and a news story on Finland's proposal to initiate a sex holiday (Flynn, 2004).

While the court recognized that the e-mail was "not directly connected to Microsoft's promotion and termination decisions," the court nonetheless admitted the e-mail into evidence (Flynn, 2004). By allowing the jury to hear evidence related to the supervisor's general office conduct, including his use of e-mail, the court permitted the jury to infer, if it wished, that the supervisor's attitudes toward women influenced his decision not to promote the former employee.

But sending e-mail messages containing sexual content is not the only transgression employees can make. A $70 million lawsuit was filed by Morgan Stanley employees against their employer, claiming that racist jokes on the company's electronic mail system created a hostile work environment (Schulman, 1998).

Discussion

1. What do you think about sending jokes via e-mail in the workplace? What are the risks?

2. Is it ever appropriate to discuss rumors or make negative comments in e-mail messages in the workplace? Again, what are the risks?

3. What other kinds of language should never be used in e-mails in a professional environment?

4. Should organizations act to restrain the sending and receiving of negative e-mail messages? If so, how?

GLOBAL MEDIA VENTURES, INC.: HIRING INTERNS

Lana Lindler works in the human resources department of GMV's film division. Every spring, she is deluged with applications from hundreds—sometimes thousands—of college students hoping to get an internship.

Lindler receives applications in response to GMV's postings to career center Web sites on select university campuses, as well as unsolicited employment packages mailed from all over the country.

Lindler and her colleagues use a multi-step process to identify qualified students. First, they scan the employment messages to check for obvious errors in formatting, grammar, and spelling. Once those containing errors have been eliminated, the staff skims the letters and résumés again, looking for the qualifications that have been advertised for each position. Those packages that do not clearly discuss these qualifications are then eliminated.

Lindler and her staff spend seconds on each package during these first two steps. Finally, those applicants who appear to be qualified receive a more in-depth reading of their employment packages, and those that seem best qualified are scheduled for interviews.

discussion...

1. Were you aware of the process that many organizations use to screen applicants' employment packages? Were you aware of the importance of following conventional formats and providing neat, correct, and well-organized messages and résumés?

2. What can you do to ensure that your employment package makes it through a similar screening process?

Consider and incorporate the elements of visual impression into your written messages. These include:

- **Overall appearance of the message.**

- **Its format.**

- **Font selection.**

- **Use of headings.**

- **Use of lists.**

Design and use PowerPoint slides in oral presentations.

Choose and use graphics, such as graphs, tables, diagrams, and drawings, in written messages as well as PowerPoint slides.

In the professional world, visual impression is important to consider for both written documents as well as visual aids for presentations. For written documents, visual impression can often help or hinder how your audience receives and responds to the information presented. The design and layout of text, the use of space, and the addition of graphics all combine to convey an impression to your audience. Therefore, visual aspects of professional messages can affect your ability to convey information clearly to establish and maintain your image as a credible, professional communicator.

VISUAL IMPRESSION IN WRITTEN MESSAGES

There are several aspects of visual impression to consider when designing a written message. These include the following:

- Overall appearance of the message.

- Its format.

- Use of space.

- Font selection.

- Use of headings.

- Use of lists.

- Use of graphics.

These will be explained in more detail below, except for the last item, use of graphics, which receives a separate discussion at the end of this chapter, since its considerations are appropriate for both written messages as well as oral presentations.

Overall Appearance

The *overall appearance* of a message refers to the immediate response of your audience to its general appearance. This has to do with audience expectations about professional documents as well as the psychological effect of the visual appearance of your document. The appeal of your document may be enhanced through your use of space, formatting, fonts, heading, and layout. It may "invite" your audience to continue to read simply by the way it is laid out on the page or, on the opposite side, discourage your audience from doing so. Your document should indicate that you took some care in creating it, since this aspect may affect your credibility and relationship with your audience. If a document is sloppy in appearance, for example, it may show that you have little regard for your reader or that you are a sloppy person who puts little time into the details of a message.

critical **thinking**

Have you received messages that were sloppy in appearance or did not follow the formatting convention for that particular type of message? What was your response? Did it affect your perception of the sender? If so, how?

Format

The *format* of the document should use the conventions of business writing. Most business audiences know what a memo should look like, just as they know the conventional format for a letter. Reports also have conventional formats with which most business audiences are familiar. If you do not follow these formats, you indicate to your reader that you are not familiar with those conventions and thus are undereducated in this regard or are not a professional, since you aren't aware of professional expectations and practices. This perception, of course, can affect your credibility.

The proper format to use depends upon your audience and purpose. If you are writing a hard-copy message to an audience that is *internal* to your organization, you should use a memo format. If you are writing a hard-copy message to an audience that is *external* to your organization you should use a letter format. E-mail messages to both internal and external audiences use a combination of features from both letters and memos. Similarly, reports and proposals can be prepared for both internal and external audiences. These formats are typically used to deliver longer, more complex messages than those conveyed in a memo, letter, or e-mail message. Another common business format is that of the résumé. Examples of each of these common business formats are provided in the sections that follow.

Memo Format   Much of the difficulty of properly formatting business messages has been eliminated by word-processing and other types of software that provide document templates. An example of a memo format is provided in Figure 8-1 below.

FIGURE 8-1. *Example of a memo format.*

Memorandum

To:	All employees
From:	Jane Doe, HR supervisor
Date:	May 15, 2006
Subject:	Memorial Day holiday observance

As you may know, the Memorial Day holiday falls on Monday, May 29 this year. That means that we will be closing our offices on Monday, May 29 to honor the holiday. Our offices will reopen on Tuesday, May 30.

We in the Human Resources department wish you all a happy and safe Memorial Day holiday.

A memorandum is an internal message that is characterized by its header, as shown in the example above. An important feature of the header is the Subject line. The Subject line should contain a specific, informative phrase intended to capture your audience's attention.

Like most business messages, memos are typically single-spaced, with double spaces between paragraphs. Typically, memos are not signed by the sender. However, if you wish to personalize a memo, signing your initials by your name is a common practice.

Common Letter Formats   You may choose from several types of letter formats. The two most common are the block and the modified block format. An example of a block format for a letter is provided in Figure 8-2 on the next page.

As you can see in Figure 8.2, in a block format letter, all text is left justified or lined up with the left margin. This format is probably the most commonly used because the left justification makes it easier and faster to create.

An example of the second common type of letter format, modified block, is provided in Figure 8-3 on the next page.

In the modified block format letter in Figure 8.3, you will notice that the address of the sender, the date, and the signature block are aligned on the right side of the page.

Salestek, Inc.
128 Main Street
Middletown, IA 73220

December 3, 2006

Melanie Smith
ABC Products Co.
346 Center Avenue
Berg, PA 23009

Dear Ms. Smith:

Your order of November 20, 2006 has been received and processed by our company. You should·be receiving the shipment in five to seven business days.

Your business is appreciated, so please let us know how we might continue to provide you the best service possible. If you have any questions about the products you receive, please call me toll free at 1-800-644-9900.

Sincerely,

Todd Jones
Shipping Manager

FIGURE 8-2. *Example of a block format letter.*

Salestek, Inc.
128 Main Street
Middletown, IA 73220

December 3, 2006

Melanie Smith
ABC Products Co.
346 Center Avenue
Berg, PA 23009

Dear Ms. Smith:

Your order of November 20, 2006 has been received and processed by our company. You should be receiving the shipment in five to seven business days.

Your business is appreciated, so please let us know how we might continue to provide you the best service possible. If you have any questions about the products you receive, please call me toll free at 1-800-644-9900.

Sincerely,

Todd Jones
Shipping Manager

FIGURE 8-3. *Example of a modified block format letter.*

E-mail Format Formatting e-mail messages is fairly simple, since the computer program you are using prompts you for the elements of the header. These elements are similar to those used in a memo: To, From, and Subject. Typically, the program you are using will automatically insert the information for the sender (yourself), while you need to type in the receiver's e-mail address and the Subject line. As in a memo, you should insert a specific, informative phrase intended to capture your audience's attention.

An e-mail message also incorporates elements from a letter format. Both letters and e-mail messages, for example, typically include a salutation at the beginning and a signature at the end. Most e-mail programs enable you to create a signature file that will automatically be added to the end of each message when it is sent. A signature file includes the name, title, organization, and contact information of the sender.

Finally, it is important for an e-mail message to be as grammatically correct as any other type of written message and to use correct punctuation and spelling, since errors can negatively affect the clarity of the message as well as the credibility of the sender. You should avoid using all capital letters when writing e-mail messages, because it can appear as if you are shouting at the receiver. The use of all capital letters in an e-mail can thus negatively affect the tone of the message.

Attention to tone is particularly important in e-mail messages, since they can be written so quickly and sent. You should never write an e-mail message when you are experiencing negative emotions, such as frustration, impatience, or anger, since the emotions will undoubtedly come through in your message and may negatively affect your credibility and relationship with your audience.

Components of Reports and Proposals Reports and proposals can be either informal or formal in design, style, and content. Informal reports and proposals typically use memo formats. The components that are often included in a formal report are listed below.

- Title page.

- Table of contents.

- Executive summary.

- Introduction.

- Background.

- Discussion of the problem.

- Conclusions.

- Recommendations.

- Appendices, if appropriate.

Proposals are sales documents that are intended to recommend changes or purchases within a company, or to show how your organization can meet the needs of another, if intended for an external audience. A formal proposal may include the following components:

- Proposed idea and purpose, or what is often called the "project description."

- Scope, or what you propose to do.

- Methods or procedures to be used.

- Materials and equipment needed.

- Qualifications of personnel who will be working on the project.

- Follow-up and/or evaluation of the project.

- Budget or costs of the project.

- Summary of proposal.

- Appendices, if appropriate.

Formats for formal reports and proposals not only include conventional topic coverage but also follow the rules for the use of fonts, headings, lists, and space, which are discussed later in this chapter and also are applicable to letters, memos, and other types of written business messages.

Résumé Formats Another conventional format used in business situations is the résumé. The contents of a résumé should be narrowly targeted to show that you are well qualified for a particular position. Information is typically provided in three areas: work experience, education, and leadership or organization membership. Under each of these categories, information is typically provided in the form of bullet lists. Using complete sentences and paragraphs should be avoided in a résumé, since they require your reader to spend more time retrieving the information he or she is looking for.

Several formats for résumés exist, but the most common and often most favored is the chronological résumé, in which you present your qualifications chronologically. In other words, your most recent experiences should appear at the top of each category, followed in descending order by those that are your least recent in time. An example of a chronological résumé is provided in Figure 8-4 on the next page.

An element that you might consider adding to a chronological résumé is an "Objective" statement at its beginning. Experts disagree about the inclusion of an Objective statement. Some say it is a necessary element, while others say that the Objective statement often adds little to a résumé. All agree that excellent Objective statements are difficult to write. An excellent Objective statement should identify the unique contributions that you can make to a particular employer.

Increasingly, résumés are being submitted electronically to Web job banks. Résumés submitted to job banks are reviewed by a search engine that is

FIGURE 8-4. *Example of a chronological résumé format.*

Joan Donne
348 Elm Street
Middletown, MO 73301
203-667-3211

Work Experience

May 2004 to present	Staff Accountant, EST International Jonestown, MO • Prepared accounting reports for wholesale importer ($1 million annual sales). • Handled budgeting, billing, and credit-processing functions. • Audited financial transactions with suppliers in three Asian countries.
May 2003/ Aug. 2003	Accounting Intern, Outerwear Sports St. Louis, MO • Assisted in billing and credit-processing functions of retail business ($500,000 annual sales). • Assisted in launching an online computer system to automate all accounting functions.
Education	Bachelor's degree, Accounting, University of Missouri, 2000–2004 Dean's List 2001, 2002, 2003

Leadership Experience

• Scholarship Chair of Kappa Phi Fraternity.
• Vice President of University of Missouri Student Accounting Club.
• Volunteer for Habitant for Humanity.

---

programmed to search for keywords that correspond to the qualifications for which the employer is looking. For this reason, it is important to list the qualifications for the job in the Objective statement of an electronically submitted résumé. Of course, it is important that you do in fact have these qualifications, since eventually a human being will read your résumé carefully and discover whether you are indeed qualified for the job.

Use of Space

Use of *space* on the page involves decisions about various design elements, including the width of the margins, the space between paragraphs, and the use of lists, headings, and graphics. Using space appropriately can make a document more pleasing and inviting to read. Use of space can have subtle effects upon the reader and can also send messages about you as the writer.

Typically, the margin width of business documents is one inch at the top, sides, and bottom of the page. Margins should not be too wide, since that sends the message that you are attempting to make your document look longer or more complete. They should not be too narrow, since that sends the message that you need to edit your document to make it fit the space provided, and that you may have failed to do so.

The conventional spacing of business documents, regardless of the format, is single spacing within paragraphs and double spacing between paragraphs.

Because of this visual cue—a blank space between paragraphs—indenting the beginning of each paragraph is not necessary. Use of too much space between paragraphs can also make your document look as if it is not substantial in content or that you are stretching your information to make it look more substantial than it is.

Paragraphs in business documents should be seven to eight lines in length. Creating paragraphs that are shorter in length is called *chunking*. Chunking has a psychological effect on the reader that makes a document look easier to skim; provides more white space, which makes it more pleasing in appearance; and makes a document look easier to read overall. Readers may be discouraged from reading a document that contains one large paragraph or a few large paragraphs, because the document looks too difficult to skim or too time-consuming to read.

Font Choice

Font choice can affect the readability of a document as well as subtly set a tone for the document. There are two types of font: serif and sans serif. Examples of serif type include Times New Roman, Courier, Helvetica, and Bookman. Examples of sans serif type are Arial, Univers, and Verdana. Serif is typically used for large blocks of text, because it provides more information for the eye and is thus considered easier to read. However, serif type also gives a document a more conservative visual impression. It can therefore be used as a design element to create a particular image for your company.

Sans serif type, because of its cleaner appearance, gives a document a more modern look. If you wish your documents to look more modern, yet still be highly readable for your audiences, you might use sans serif type for headings and other design elements and serif for large blocks of text.

Another consideration when selecting a font is its size. Typically, a 12-point font size for written messages is considered large enough to be easily read by most audiences.

Use of Headings

The use of design features, such as *headings* and lists, is both a graphic technique and a writing strategy, since you, as the writer, decide whether and how to use them and what form they will take. The use of headings is considered a graphic technique, since it is one way to incorporate additional white space into a document and to add visual interest. Headings also are cueing devices that let your audience know what to expect in terms of content and organization. They are therefore very useful as a skimming device. Headings should not, however, take the place of accurate topic sentences, since people read differently: some people read headings, and some people skip them and read the first sentence of each paragraph.

Headings also indicate the relationship between ideas. For less complex documents, such as memos, most headings indicate an equal or parallel relationship between ideas. However, for more complex documents, such as reports and proposals, information can be arranged in a hierarchy. In other words, some elements of the information provided in the document are more important than others, encompass others, and come before or after others. An outline is an example of a hierarchy of information. Figure 8-5 below illustrates the hierarchical arrangement of heading levels.

I. First-level heading
   A. Second-level heading
      1. Third-level heading
      2. Third-level heading
         a. Fourth-level heading
         b. Fourth-level heading
   B. Second-level heading
      1. Third-level heading
      2. Third-level heading
         a. Fourth-level heading
         b. Fourth-level heading
II. First-level heading
   A. Second-level heading
      1. Third-level heading
      2. Third-level heading
         a. Fourth-level heading
         b. Fourth-level heading
   B. Second-level heading
      1. Third-level heading
      2. Third-level heading

FIGURE 8-5. *The hierarchical arrangement of heading levels.*

What this means in terms of heading use is that in more complex documents, you must design headings that show your reader the hierarchical ordering of information. Typically, ideas of a higher order in the hierarchy are indicated by a heading that is of larger size than those headings that indicate information that is lower in order.

The most important considerations for headings are that you use a consistent style and format and that you place them strategically to position your points to their best advantage, and for your audience's benefit. When choosing a heading design, you can consider the use of three font characteristics: appearance, size, and placing. Font appearance refers to whether the font is italicized, bolded, underlined, or capitalized. As with font type, the appearance of the font you choose to use can affect the impression of your document. For example, the use of italicized or all-capital-letter headings tends to make a document feel more traditional or conservative, while the use of upper- and lowercase letters makes a document appear more modern.

A common way to distinguish heading levels is to use a different font size. As explained above, higher-order headings typically use a larger font size, while those of a lower order use a smaller size font.

Placement refers to where the heading is placed on the page. Typically, headings are left-justified, centered, or indented, depending upon the feel you wish to create and the order of the heading. Centered headings, like the use of serif type, tend to give a document a more conservative feel than those that are left-justified.

When deciding upon a heading design, you should limit the number of devices you use to no more than three. More than three may detract from the professional image you wish to convey by making your design look amateurish and chaotic.

Headings should be informative; in other words, they should contain sufficient information to be meaningful. One word headings are called "labels" and tend to be less informative than short phrases used as headings. On the other hand, you should avoid overly long headings that begin to read like a topic sentence. In that case, you may have inadvertently provided two topic sentences for the section you are referencing—one your actual topic sentence and the other your heading—creating a redundancy problem.

Use of Lists

Lists are a useful device for providing more white space in a document and to make it easier to skim. Two types of lists exist: number and bullet lists, and they have differing purposes. *Number lists* are used for information that is to be used sequentially as in a series of steps for instructions. *Bullet lists* are used to identify separate items that are equal and related or parallel in importance. For example, bullet lists are often useful devices for forecasting the contents of a message as in the case below.

EXAMPLE OF A BULLET LIST FOR FORECASTING

This memo will show you the advantages of adopting a flex-time policy for employees. More specifically, it will explain:

- Why a policy change is needed.

- How the policy change will benefit employees and the company.

- How to implement the policy change.

You should resist the temptation to overuse or misuse bullet lists. Inexperienced business writers often make the mistake of believing that they can use bullet lists to provide all the information in a message. This belief arises from an understanding that business messages should be concise; however, it ignores the corresponding importance of clarity. If your entire message is made up of bulleted phrases, for example, those phrases will not convey complete meaning but merely fragments of information that your reader must attempt to interpret, elaborate on, and connect. Oftentimes, such messages take on the appearance and content of an outline rather than a well-written and well-reasoned message.

Whenever you place the burden of interpretation on your reader, you risk two outcomes: 1) your reader will not wish to take on that burden, so he or she will stop reading in frustration; or 2) your reader will interpret your meaning incorrectly.

Furthermore, if you are attempting to persuade, a list format typically will not help you achieve that goal, since it will probably not contain the evidence that is necessary to achieve your purpose.

To reiterate, lists are typically used as forecasting devices, not to deliver the main content of your message.

Lists should be grammatically parallel in structure, which means that each item in the list should begin with the same kind of word. For example, in the sample list on page 216, each list item begins with an adverb. In business writing, it is useful to consider using a verb as the beginning word of a list, since it implies action. Such a strategy should be used when creating lists in résumés, since your intent is to subtly indicate to your audience, the prospective employer, that you are action- and achievement-oriented. A list of common action words used at the beginning of lists in résumés is provided in Table 8-1 below.

TABLE 8-1. *List of action words for use in résumés and lists.*

LIST OF ACTION WORDS FOR USE IN RÉSUMÉS AND LISTS

achieved	coordinated	expedited	maintained	prioritized	researched
accomplished	created	facilitated	managed	processed	retrieved
administered	decided	formed	mediated	produced	reviewed
advised	demonstrated	formulated	monitored	programmed	revised
aided	determined	generated	motivated	promoted	scheduled
allocated	developed	guided	negotiated	provided	screened
analyzed	devised	handled	operated	purchased	selected
balanced	diagnosed	hired	organized	recommended	served
budgeted	directed	improved	oversaw	recorded	sold
calculated	distributed	increased	performed	recruited	started
coached	earned	initiated	planned	reduced	supervised
communicated	enlisted	interviewed	predicted	reorganized	taught
compared	established	inventoried	prepared	repaired	trained
compiled	estimated	led	presented	reported	verified

VISUAL IMPRESSION IN ORAL PRESENTATIONS

Visual aids are also useful in oral presentations to help you more clearly communicate your message, as well as to make your message more interesting. Various types of visual aids exist, including white boards, transparencies, flip charts, and handouts. But the most common type of visual aid used in business presentations is slide presentation software, such as PowerPoint.

Much has been written about the uses and misuses of slide presentation software. The biggest mistake that presenters make is believing that all their information should be delivered using the software. A visual aid is just that: an aid that should be used to enhance and emphasize the main points of your oral presentation. If the text and content of your message are delivered in large-text format, there is really no reason for you to be in the room. Such a presentation could be made by automating the slide software to deliver the text of your presentation for your audience to read, or you might simply send your audience a written report or proposal to read at its convenience.

Presentation software, like other visual aids, should be used for two primary purposes: 1) to indicate the main ideas you will cover or the structure of your presentation; and 2) to convey information that is more easily understood visually.

Organizing PowerPoint Presentations

Just as in a written message, your PowerPoint presentation should include slides for each of the three main parts of a message: the introduction, body, and conclusion. The introduction should include two slides:

- Opening title slide. This slide contains the title of your presentation and the name(s) of the presenter(s) and the organization he or she represents.

- Overview slide. This slide lists the main topics you will cover in your presentation.

Examples of a title and overview slide are provided in Figures 8-6 and 8-7 on the next page.

For the body of your presentation, you should include at least one slide for each of the main points of your presentation. In addition, you should include slides that convey the information that is best communicated visually in the form of tables, charts, graphs, and diagrams. The creation of these visual elements is discussed in more detail in the section, "Use of Graphics," on page 222.

The conclusion of your presentation should include two slides:

- The conclusion slide. This slide should summarize your main points or, in the case of a persuasive presentation, sell those points.

- Ending title slide. Ending with the slide you began with provides closure for your audience, since it indicates you have come full circle. Additionally, this

FIGURE 8-6. *Example of a title slide.*

**Dexus Computer Systems:
Solutions for Business**

Presented by Joseph Williams
Sales Manager

FIGURE 8-7. *Example of an overview or agenda slide.*

Today's Agenda

- **Features of the Dexus Computer System.**

- **Ease of use of the Dexus Computer System.**

- **Financial benefits of using the Dexus Computer System.**

slide acts as a subtle sales message, much like giving your audience your business card, which contains yours and your company's names. It is a preferable backdrop to a question-and-answer session than a slide, containing the single word "Questions" or the phrase "Thank you," since it enhances name recognition.

Designing PowerPoint Presentations

When designing presentation aids, it is important to ensure that all their elements are *visible* from all parts of the room. Presentation aids should *emphasize* the main points of your speech. Visuals should therefore be simple, and each visual should make only one point.

communication IN YOUR WORLD

Despite PowerPoint's unequivocal popularity with business users, not everyone is a fan. One of the Internet's inventors, Vint Cerf, gets laughs from audiences by quipping, "Power corrupts and PowerPoint corrupts absolutely." Cerf, now an MCI executive and chairman of the Internet's key oversight body, doesn't shun Power-Point completely, but said avoiding it "actually improves communication because people have to listen rather than being distracted by fancy Power-Point charts."

Perhaps the most vocal PowerPoint hater is Edward R. Tufte, a Yale University professor and author of the graphic design book, *Envisioning Information*. Tufte believes that Power-Point's emphasis on format over content commercializes and trivializes subjects. In a *Wired* magazine editorial in September 2003 entitled "Power-Point Is Evil," Tufte compared Power-Point presentations to a school play: "very loud, very slow, and very simple."

Such disagreements have spawned a series of PowerPoint parodies, the first being credited to Peter Norvig, 46, engineering director at Google Inc., who, in 1999, published an online slide show of Abraham Lincoln's Gettysburg Address. The spoof, which by Norvig's estimate has been viewed by at least 500,000 people, includes bullet points such as "unfinished work (great tasks)," "new birth of freedom," and "government not perish."

A similar spoof was undertaken by a more high-profile artist, David Byrne, lead singer of the pop group Talking Heads. But after spending several hours designing a mock slide show, Byrne became intrigued. He decided to experiment with PowerPoint as an artistic medium and ponder whether it shapes how we talk and think. In his book and DVD compilation, *Envisioning Emotional Epistemological Information,* Byrne twists PowerPoint from a marketing tool into a multimedia canvas, pontificating that the software's charts, graphs, bullet points, and arrows have changed communication styles.

"I just got carried away and started making stuff," Byrne said. "It communicates within certain limited parameters really well and very easily. The genius of it is that it was designed for any idiot to use. I learned it in a few hours, and that's the idea." Byrne's 96-page compilation, which debuted in September, 2003 for $80, can best be described as a coffee table book for nerds. The book includes mostly lucid musings on how PowerPoint has ushered in "the end of reason," with pictures of bar charts gone hideously astray, fields of curved arrows that point at nothing, disturbing close-ups of wax hands and eyebrows, and a photo of Dolly the cloned sheep enclosed by punctuation brackets.

But by fixating on PowerPoint, Byrne—idolized by millions as a rock star for intellectuals—has heated up the debate. Norvig, who recently ordered a copy of Byrne's compilation for himself, said Byrne is wading in treacherous waters. "People are asking whether, ultimately, PowerPoint makes us all stupid, or does it help us streamline our thoughts?" said Norvig, who first saw Talking Heads in the late 1970s. "My belief is that PowerPoint doesn't kill meetings. People kill meetings. But using Power-Point is like having a loaded AK-47 on the table: you can do very bad things with it."

Discussion

1. **Have you seen PowerPoint misused? Do you agree with Tufte's and Norvig's opinions?**

2. **Based on this discussion, how should PowerPoint best be used?**

Adapted from "Does PowerPoint Make Us Stupid" (2003, Dec. 30). Retrieved April 1, 2005, from http://www.cnn.com/2003/TECH/ptech/12/30/byrne.powerpoint.ap/

The basic rules for creating PowerPoint slide presentations are listed below.

- The colors chosen for the slide background and the text should be of high contrast: light on dark or dark on light.

- The font size of the text should be large enough to be read from the back of the room (generally 28 point or larger).

- Slide text should be limited to informative phrases (bullet list format). Text should not be presented in sentence or paragraph form.

- Bullet lists should be grammatically parallel in structure and, whenever possible, begin with or contain a verb so that list items are more informative. In other words, you should avoid bullet list items that contain only one word, since one word often does not convey much information and is more like a placeholder.

- Each slide should contain no more than five to six bullet points.

- Use of clip art should generally be avoided, since much of it is not clearly related to the topic or is cartoonish in character. In other words, much clip art creates an unprofessional impression. Some even consider the use of PowerPoint templates unprofessional, since they have been so overused.

The best design element you can use on a PowerPoint slide is your company logo. This adds interest and name recognition to your slides.

Remember that a PowerPoint presentation should not deliver all the details of your oral presentation. It is a *visual aid.* Therefore, it is best used to remind your audience of the main points you will cover (like a map) and to illustrate information best conveyed in visual form, such as charts, tables, and diagrams. This latter issue is discussed in the section on the next page, "Use of Graphics."

critical **thinking**

Whether you are a traditional student or a workplace professional, you have probably viewed numerous PowerPoint presentations. What is the most common mistake you observe in the PowerPoint presentations you have seen? Do you believe that PowerPoint is often misused or overused? Why?

Using PowerPoint Slides

Presentation aids should be skillfully *integrated* into the presentation. That means that a visual should not be displayed until you are ready for it and it should be removed after discussing it. The use of visual aids should be *practiced* so that their use does not distract from your presentation or adversely affect your credibility by making you look unprepared.

Remember, your presentation slides are for use by your audience. Although many presenters often use them as notecards, you should avoid reading from

During formal presentations, business audiences often expect information about numbers, statistics, and trends to be presented in a visual form, such as a graph, a table, or a diagram.

them or use them in such a way that your attention is drawn away from your audience.

USE OF GRAPHICS

The power of conveying information visually has been recognized for hundreds of years. In 1801, the father of modern graphics, William Playfair, claimed, "As much information may be obtained in five minutes [from a graph] as would require whole days to imprint on the memory" if it were communicated in a series of figures. Using graphics appropriately provides a number of benefits:

- Information is more easily understood than the use of words alone.

- Use of visuals helps to make the information conveyed more memorable.

- Use of visuals enhances your professionalism and credibility.

However, as with all forms of information, graphic information can be misused. When using graphics to convey information, you should ensure that your data is valid, reliable, and drawn from a representative sample, if appropriate.

The most common forms of visual aids used in both written and oral presentations are the graph, table, and diagram or drawing.

Graphs

Graph

A graph is a visual element used to compare the values of several items.

Graphs, sometimes called charts, are used to compare the value of several items: the amount of advertising money spent on different media, the annual profit of a company over time, and so on. Two common types of graphs are the bar graph and the pie graph. Examples of each are provided in the figures below and on the next page.

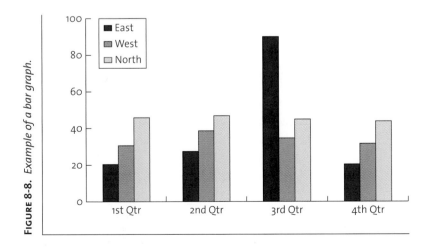

FIGURE 8-8. *Example of a bar graph.*

The bar graph is typically used to emphasize comparisons or contrasts between two or more items.

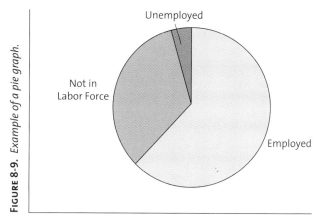

FIGURE 8-9. *Example of a pie graph.*

Source: U.S. Department of Labor.

A pie graph is often used to indicate the distribution of something or the relative size of the parts of a whole.

Tables

Table

A table is a visual element used to present data in words, numbers, or both, in columns and rows.

1. **Tables** are useful for emphasizing key facts and figures. They are especially effective for listing steps, highlighting features, or comparing related facts. A table presents data in words, numbers, or both, in columns and rows. An example of a table comparing the benefits of large and small companies is provided below.

FIGURE 8-10. *Example of a table.*

COMPARISON OF COMPANY BENEFITS BY SIZE

Type of Benefit	Companies with Fewer than 100 Employees	100 or more Employees
Paid vacation	88%	96%
Paid holidays	82	92
Medical insurance	71	83
Life insurance	64	94
Paid sick leave	53	67
Dental care	33	60

Source: U.S. Bureau of Labor Statistics.

Tables easily convey large amounts of numerical data and often are the only way to show several variables for a number of items.

There are myriad ways to misuse statistics. Some misuses are intentional while others are not. Even some scientists have been known to fool themselves accidentally with statistics, due to lack of knowledge of probability and lack of standardization of their tests. Common methods of misusing statistics are listed below.

Misuse of statistics by being selective or discarding data. In marketing terms all you have to do to promote a product is to find one study with a certainty level of 95 percent that is favorable to the product. There may be 19 other studies with unfavorable results, but these studies are simply ignored. Similarly, a study might indicate that a product is inferior in all aspects except for one very narrow range, in which it is considered superior. When the statistics are used from the narrow range and the rest is not used, this is called discarding data and is lying by omission.

Choosing the question to get a certain answer. You can easily influence the answer to a survey question by asking the query differently. You can also precede the question by 10 other questions that make the respondent aware of 10 issues that seem unfavorable to your cause or candidate. Or, you can omit the third-party view from the questionnaire; this will make many would-be, third-position supporters take the side you favor.

Biased samples. If you conduct a survey of homelessness by calling participants' home phone numbers, you will find a homeless rate near zero. That's because homeless people don't have home phones! For samples to be unbiased they must be representative of the general population. For that reason, studies that are conducted using college students are not representative of the general population; they are representative of college students.

The truncated graph or one-dimensional drawing. Sometimes graphs can be misleading. This can occur when the bottom portion of a graph is cut off, which can make a trend look more significant than it is because of the change in proportion. Likewise, you might use a drawing to indicate

Diagrams and Drawings

Diagram

A diagram is a two-dimensional drawing that shows the important parts of objects.

Diagrams are two-dimensional drawings that show the important parts of objects.

Diagrams are useful for conveying information about size, shape, and structure. Types of diagrams include drawings, maps, and floor plans. An example of a diagram is provided below.

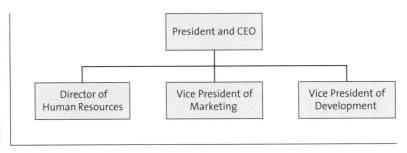

Figure 8-11. *Example of a diagram: organizational chart.*

double the proportion of a comparable object; however, the drawing might be twice as tall but four times as large in total volume. Therefore, the drawing looks twice as large as you intended.

The well-chosen average. Most measures follow the distribution of the bell curve. However, not all things follow this distribution, one of them being income (Huff, 2005). For example, most incomes may fall under $35,000, but if you add in the comparatively small number of people with incomes over $1 million, the average will raise disproportionately. Therefore, when an income average is given in the form of a mean, nearly everybody makes less than that (Huff, 2005).

Statistical error. Many measures are useful within a certain range of statistical error. For example, the Revised Stanford-Binet IQ test has a statistical error range of 3 percent (Huff, 2005). What that means is that a child who measures 97 may not be less intelligent than one who measures 100 on the test, since the preciseness of the test may vary by 3 percent. Ignoring this range of reliability can significantly affect the intelligibility of the results of some surveys with outcomes of little variability.

False causality. The interrelation of cause and effect can also be obscured by statistics. Throughout the ages, many erroneous assumptions of cause and effect have occurred. For example, leaches were believed to cure sick people, when it was often unknown what actually caused the recovery. Similarly, the people of Hebrides once believed that body lice produced good health. It didn't occur to them that the inverse might be true: body lice preferred healthy people (Huff, 2005).

Questions for Thought

1. **Have you heard of incidences in which statistics were misused to make a false or misleading argument? Can you identify advertisements that misuse statistics?**

2. **What are some steps you might take to avoid the misuse of statistical information?**

An organizational chart is a form of block diagram that indicates lines of authority and responsibility in an organization.

A guide for selecting the appropriate graphic is provided in Table 8-2 below.

TABLE 8-2. *Selecting the right graphic.*

SELECTING THE RIGHT GRAPHIC

- To present detailed, exact values, use a table.
- To illustrate trends over time, use a line graph or a bar graph.
- To show frequency or distribution, use a pie graph or segmented bar graph.
- To compare one item with another, use a bar graph.
- To compare one part with the whole, use a pie graph.
- To show correlations use a bar graph, a line graph, or a scatter graph.
- To show geographic relationships, use a map.
- To illustrate a process or a procedure, use a flow chart or a diagram.

critical **thinking**

What type of information would best be illustrated through the use of a bar graph? A pie graph? A table? A diagram or drawing? Why?

Integrating Graphics into Text

Once you have identified the need for a graphic, selected the appropriate graphic, and created it, you need to give some consideration to integrating it into your text if you are using it in a written message. Those considerations include:

- Placing the graphic in an appropriate location. For ease of use by your reader, a graphic should be placed directly after the related point in the text.

- Labeling the graphic. Every graphic should have a brief, clear, and informative label.

- Introducing the graphic in the text. You should refer to the graphic in the text before it appears.

- Explaining the graphic in the text. You should explain in the text what your readers should learn from the graphic.

- Visual impression may be more important in business messages than other types because of the importance of establishing credibility in professional situations. For this reason, care should be taken to ensure that written business messages as well as presentation visuals are professional in appearance and use.

- When creating a written message, you should consider several visual elements, including:

  □ The overall appearance of the message.

  □ Conventions regarding formatting.

  □ Use of space.

  □ Font selection.

  □ Use of headings.

  □ Use of lists.

  □ Use of graphics.

- When designing visual aids for an oral presentation, it is important to remember that visual aids are important for providing a clear structure of the presentation to the audience, as well as presenting information that is best conveyed visually. Some information is more easily and quickly understood when it is presented visually. Visuals also make information more vivid and thus more memorable. Finally, much of the information that is presented to business audiences and that is expected by them is best presented in visual form. Therefore, presenting information about numbers, trends, and comparisons using a graphic better meets a business audience's needs and expectations.

- When creating PowerPoint slides, the colors chosen for the background of the slide and the text should be of high contrast. The font size of the text should be large enough to be read from the back of the room in which the presentation will take place. The amount of information presented on each slide should be limited to five to six bulleted items or one graphic. Finally, clip art should be used judiciously.

- In both written and oral messages, information can be presented in graphic form. Common types of graphics include the bar graph, the pie graph, tables, and diagrams and drawings. Each type of graphic is designed to present particular kinds of information, so it is important to choose the correct graphic to achieve your communication purposes.

KEY TERMS

Diagram, 224
Graph, 222
Table, 223

DISCUSSION QUESTIONS

1. When creating written business messages, why is it important to know and to use their conventions of formatting?

2. What are the primary reasons for using visuals, such as PowerPoint slides, in oral presentations?

3. What are the common mistakes that should be avoided when designing PowerPoint slides?

4. What kind of information is best conveyed in a graph or chart? A table? A diagram or drawing?

5. What are the ethical challenges of presenting statistical information in graphic form?

APPLICATIONS

1. Using the Internet, locate job descriptions of the type of position for which you will be applying when you graduate. Review these descriptions to create a composite of the skills or characteristics organizations are seeking for this particular position, then identify those that you can best provide. Create a résumé, using the format provided in this chapter, that emphasizes your ability to meet these needs.

2. Using one of the letter forms discussed in this chapter, write an application letter to accompany your résumé. Use the organizational techniques described in Chapter 5 and the persuasive techniques discussed in this chapter to clearly demonstrate that you are well qualified for the position.

3. Plan and create a PowerPoint slide show to accompany an oral presentation on the following topic: business trends for the industry or field in which you intend to gain employment upon graduation.

4. Create a graph, table, and diagram or drawing that you could use as a visual aid in the oral presentation described in application 2.

5. Using a memo format, write an informal report for the presentation you created in application 2. Properly incorporate the graph, table, and diagram or drawing you created for application 3 into your informal report.

 INFOTRAC ACTIVITIES

1. Using InfoTrac College Edition, type the word "PowerPoint" in the keyword search engine. Visit some of the Web sites to learn more about using PowerPoint effectively in business presentations.

2. Using InfoTrac College Edition, type the words "electronic résumés" in the keyword search engine. Visit some of the Web sites to learn more about the ins and outs of submitting résumés electronically.

Case Analysis

With the increase in legal Web sites devoted to the digital downloading of music, the recording industry is expected to experience a shift in the way that product is distributed in the next five years.

Global sales of recorded music were flat in 2004, with the total music industry worth $33 billion. Music enthusiasts in Great Britain bought more CDs than those in any other country (Sherwin, 2005). Each Briton bought on average of 3.2 CDs per person per year, compared with the 2.8 bought by American fans, the International Federation of the Phonographic Industry reported (Sherwin, 2005). France (2.1), Germany (2.2) and Japan (2.0) also trailed Great Britain (Sherwin, 2005).

Informa Media's "Music on the Internet" report says that online sales of CDs and music DVDs, individual digital downloads, and subscriptions to monthly services, such as Napster, made up 6.3 percent of all music sales worldwide in 2004 (Informa predicts global sales, 2005). It predicted this figure will almost triple to 17.1 percent by 2010. Of this overall 17.1 percent market share, digital sales—downloads and subscriptions—will represent 8.8 percent, the report claims (Informa predicts global sales, 2005). The rest will be made up of physical formats bought online.

Of online music sales, physical media made up 85 percent in 2004 (Informa predicts global sales, 2005). However, paid-for downloaded tracks increased tenfold to more than 200 million in the four major digital music markets (America, Britain, France, and Germany) (Sherwin, 2005). The trend has continued in 2005, with digital sales in the first two months more than double that of the same period in 2004 (Sherwin, 2005).

Consumers in North America will buy the most music over the Internet. The region is estimated to contribute 42.4 percent of total online sales in 2010 (Informa predicts global sales, 2005). Europe will make up just over a third of all online sales (37.6 percent), while Asia Pacific will bring in 18 percent (Informa predicts global sales, 2005).

Discussion

1. Identify three possible messages that could be derived from analyzing the numbers in the passage above.

2. Create the type of graphic that should be used to communicate each of your messages.

References

Alsop, R.J. (2004). Corporate reputation: Anything but superficial—the deep but fragile nature of corporate reputation. *Journal of Business Strategy, 25* (6), 21–30.

Arenofsky, J. (2001). Control your anger before it controls you! *Current Health 1, 24* (7), 6–12.

Arkin, R.M. & Burger, J.M. (1980). Effects of unit relation tendencies on interpersonal attraction. *Social Psychology Quarterly, 43*, 380–391.

Avery, C.M. (2001). *Teamwork is an individual skill: Getting your work done when sharing responsibility.* San Francisco: Berrett-Koehler.

Baird. J.S. (1980). Current trends in college cheating. *Psychology in the School, 17*, 512–522.

Barker, L.L. (1971). *Listening behavior.* Englewood Cliffs, NJ: Prentice-Hall.

Barnlund, D.C. (1970). A transactional model of communication. In K.K. Sereno and C.D. Mortensen (Eds.), *Foundations of communication theory* (pp. 98–101). NY: Harper and Row.

Barnlund, D.C. (1986). Toward a meaning-centered philosophy of communication. In J. Stewart (Ed.), *Bridges not walls: A book about interpersonal communication* (pp. 36–42). NY: Newbury Award Records.

Baumgardner, A.H. & Levy, P.E. (1988). Role of self-esteem in perceptions of ability and effort: Illogic or insight? *Personality and Social Psychology Bulletin, 14*, 429–438.

Blake, R. & Mouton, J. (1964). *The managerial grid.* Houston: Gulf Publishing.

Bond, M.H. & Shiu, W.Y. (1997). The relationship between a group's personality resources and the two dimensions of its group process. *Small Group Research, 28*, 194–217.

Bonney, M.E. (1947). Popular and unpopular children: A sociometric study. *Sociometry Monographs,* No. 99, A80.

Bonta, B.D. (1997). Cooperation and competition in peaceful societies. *Pyschological Bulletin, 121*, 299–320.

Booher, D. (2002). Leading your first meeting? An overview of the basics can help. *Essential Assistant, 15* (9), 12.

Boon, S.D. & Lomore, C.D. (2002). Admirer-celebrity relationships among young adults: Explaining perceptions of celebrity influence on identity. *Human Communication Research, 27* (3), 432–465.

Bornstein, R.F. (1992). The dependent personality: Developmental, social, and clinical perspectives. *Psychological Bulletin, 112*, 3–23.

Bowie, N.E. (2004). Why conflict of interest and abuse of information asymmetry are keys to lack of integrity and what should be done about it. In G.E. Brenkert (Ed.), *Corporate integrity and accountability* (pp. 59–71). Thousand Oaks, CA: Sage Publications.

Boyd, M. (1995, April). Four ways to more efficient, effective meetings. *Incentive, 169* (4), 69.

Brickner, M.A., Harkins, S.G., & Ostrom, T.M. (1986). Effects of personal involvement: Thought-provoking implications for social loafing. *Journal of Personality and Social Psychology, 51*, 763–770.

Brody, J.E. (1994, March 21). Notions of beauty transcends culture, new study suggests. *The New York Times,* A14.

Browne, M.N. & Keeley, S.T. (1981). *Asking the right questions.* Englewood Cliffs, NJ: Prentice-Hall.

Buhler, P. (1991). Managing in the 90's. *Supervision, 52*, 18.

Buie, E. (2001, March 29). Concern as research reveals that juggling finances, studies, and part-time jobs proves more of a danger than wild lifestyle; Overworked students find ill health on curriculum. *The Herald* (Glasgow, UK), 3.

Burgoon, J.K, Johnson, M.L., & Koch, P.T. (1998). The nature and measurement of interpersonal dominance. *Communication Monographs, 65*, 308–335.

Burgoon, J.K. & Saine, T. (1978). *The unspoken dialogue: An introduction to nonverbal communication.* Boston: Houghton Mifflin.

Burley-Allen, M. (2001). Listen up. *HR Magazine, 46* (11), 115–119.

Chatman, J.A. & Jehn, K.A. (1994). Assessing the relationship between industry characteristics and organizational culture: How different can you be? *Academy of Management Journal, 37*, 522–553.

Cheney, G. & Vibbert, S. (1987). Corporate discourse: Public Relations and issues management. *Quarterly Journal of Speech, 69*, 143–158.

Cialdini, R. (1993). *Influence: The new psychology of modern persuasion.* Glenview, IL: Scott, Foresman.

Clark, K.B. (1971). The pathos of power. *American Psychologist, 26,* 1047–1057.

Clark, R., (1998). Meetings: Valuable but misunderstood. *Cornell Hotel & Restaurant Administration Quarterly, 39* (4), 12.

Coie, J.D., Dodge, K.A., & Kupersmidt, J.B. (1990). Peer group behavior and social status. In S.R. Asher & J.D. Coie (Eds.), *Peer rejection in childhood* (pp. 17–59). New York: Cambridge University Press.

Conger, J. (1998). The necessary art of persuasion. *Harvard Business Review, 76,* 84–95.

Conrad, C. (1985). Chrysanthemums and swords: A reading of contemporary organizational communication theory and research. *Southern Speech Communication Journal, 50,* 189–200.

Conrad, C. (1990). Nostalgia and the nineties. Paper presented at the conference on Organizational Communication in the 1990s: A research agenda, Tempe, Arizona.

Cooling explosive encounters (1997, July). *Successful Meetings, 46* (8), 44–46.

Corcoran, E. (2004, May 10) Unoutsourcing: Dell moves product support back to U.S. *Forbes, 173* (10), 50.

Crainer, S. & Dearlove, D. (2004). Making yourself understood. *Across the Board, 41,* (3) 23–27.

Crown, D.F., & Spiller, M. S. (1998). Learning from the literature on college cheating: A review of empirical research. *Journal of Business Ethics, 17,* 683–700.

Davidson, J. (1996). The shortcomings of the information age. *Vital Speeches, 62,* 495–503.

Davis, J.H., Kameda, T., & Stasson, M. (1992). Group risk taking: Selected topics. In J.F. Yates (Ed.), *Risk-taking behavior* (pp. 63–199). Chichester: Wiley.

Dealing with emotions in the workplace (2002, November). *USA Today Magazine Online.* Retrieved December 13, 2003, from http://www.findarticles.com/cf_dls/m1272/2690_131/94384310/p1/article.jhtml.

Derber, Charles (1996). *The wilding of America: How greed and violence are eroding our nation's character.* New York, NY: Worth Publishing.

DeVito, J. (1989). *The interpersonal communication book.* New York: Harper and Row.

DeVito, J.A. (1986). *The communication handbook: A dictionary.* NY: Harper and Row.

Di Salvo, V.S., Nikkel, E., & Monroe, C. (1989). Theory and practice: A field investigation and identification of group members' perceptions of problems facing natural work groups. *Small Group Behavior, 20,* 551–567.

Donovan, M.A. (2002). E-mail exposes the literacy gap *Workforce, 81* (12), 15.

Dorsett, L. (2001, Jan.) A week in a digital collaboration space: Fast electronic work groups. *Training & Development.* Retrieved February 20, 2005, from http://www.findarticles.com/p/articles/mi_m4467/is_1_55/ai_69414464/.

Douty, H.I. (1963). Influence of clothing on perception of persons. *Journal of Home Economics, 55,* 197–202.

Dryer, D.C. & Horowitz, L.M. (1997). When do opposites attract? Interpersonal complementarity versus similarity. *Journal of Personality and Social Psychology, 72,* 592–603.

Dutton, J. & Dukerich, J. (1991). Keeping an eye on the mirror: Image and identity in organizational adaptation. *Academy of Management Journal, 34,* 517–554.

Effective listening skills. *Women in Business, 46* (2), 28–32.

Eisenberg, E.M. (1984). Ambiguity as strategy in organizational communication. *Communication Monographs, 51,* 227–242.

Eisenberg, E.M. & Goodall, Jr., H.L. (1993). *Organizational communication: Balancing creativity and constraint.* New York: St. Martin's Press.

Elizabeth, J. & Hayes, C. (1995). Manager's meeting 9 A.M. sharp. *Black Enterprise, 25* (8), 58.

Ethridge, M., (2004, January 12). Workplace expert offers advice on conducting meetings. *Akron Beacon Journal, via Ohio Knight Ridder/Tribune Business News,* NA.

Evered, R. & Tannebaum, R. (1992). A dialog on dialog. *Journal of Management Inquiry, 1,* 43–55.

Festinger, L. (1954). A theory of social comparison processes. *Human Relations, 7,* 117–140.

Festinger, L. (1957). *A theory of cognitive dissonance.* Stanford, CA: Stanford University Press.

Fisher, A. (1998). The high cost of living and not writing well. *Fortune, 138* (11), 244.

Fisher, J.D., Rytting, M., & Heslin, R. (1976). Hands touching hands: Affective and evaluative effects of interpersonal touch. *Sociometry, 3,* 416–421.

Fisher, S. (1975). Body decoration and camouflage. In L.M. Gurel & M.S. Beeson (Eds.), *Dimensions of dress and adornment: A book of readings.* Dubuque, IA: Kendall/Hunt.

Flynn, N. (2004). *Instant messaging rules.* New York, NY: American Management Association. Retrieved March 26, 2005, from http://www.amanet.org/books/catalog/0814472532_ch.htm.

Frank, R., Gilovich, T., & Regan, D. (1993) Does studying economics inhibit cooperation? *Journal of Economic Perspectives, 7,* 159–171.

Franken, R.E. & Brown, D.J. (1995). Why do people like competition? The motivation for winning, putting forth effort, improving one's performance, performing well, being instrumental, and expressing forceful/aggressive behavior. *Personality and Individual Differences, 19*, 175–184.

Franken, R.E. & Prpich, W. (1996). Dislike of competition and the need to win: Self-image concerns, performance concerns, and the distraction of attention. *Journal of Social Behavior and Personality, 11*, 695–712.

French, J.R.P. Jr. (1941). The disruption and cohesion of groups. *Journal of Abnormal and Social Psychology, 36*, 361–377.

French, J.R.P. & Raven, B. (1959). The bases of social power. In D. Cartwright (Ed.), *Studies in social power.* Ann Arbor, MI: Institute for Social Research.

Friedman, M. (1996). Facilitating productive meetings. *Training & Development, 50* (10), 11.

Friedman, W. (2004, September 6). A bilingual quandary: Young viewers elusive, but English-language nets make strides. *TelevisionWeek, 23* (36), 34.

Frost, P., Moore, L.,.Louis, M. Lundberg, C., & Martin, J. (1991). *Reframing organizational culture.* Newbury Park, CA: Sage Publications.

Fry, D.P. & Bjorkqvist, K. (Eds.). (1997). *Cultural variations in conflict resolution: Alternatives to violence.* Mahwah, NJ: Erlbaum.

Fry, R. (1999). We've got to start meeting like this: How to reach for results in every team meeting. *Successories, Inc.,* 6.

Gardner, H. & Krechevsky, M. (1993). *Multiple intelligences. The theory in practice.* New York: Basic Books.

Gerard, H.B. & Orive, R. (1987). The dynamics of opinion formation. *Advances in Experimental Social Psychology, 20*, 171 202.

Gibb, J. (1961). Defensive communication. *Journal of Communication, 11*, 141–148.

Gibson, J. Hodgetts, R. (1986). *Organizational communication: A managerial approach.* New York: Academic Press.

Gilbert, M.B. (1988). Listening in school: I know you can hear me—but are you listening? *Journal of the International Listening Association, 2*, 121–132.

Gilchrist, J.C. (1952). The formation of social groups under conditions of success and failure. *Journal of Abnormal and Social Psychology, 47*, 174–187.

Goethals, G.R. & Zanna, M.P. (1979). The role of social comparison in choice shifts. *Journal of Personality and Social Psychology, 37*, 1469–1476.

Gogoi, P. (2005, February 2). How far from sugar is Splenda? *BusinessWeek Online.* Retrieved March 15, 2005, from http://www.businessweek.com/ technology/ content/feb2005/tc2005022_7832_ tc024.htm.

Gold, J. (2005, February 18). New Jersey claims Blockbusters' new late fee policy violates state's consumer laws. *The Associated Press.* Lexis-Nexus Academic. Retrieved Feb. 22, 2005, from http://web.lexis-nexis.com.

Gould, S.J. (1981). *The mismeasure of man.* New York: W.W. Norton.

Gray, J., Jr. (1993). *The winning image.* New York: AMACOM.

Gudykunst, W. (1991). *Bridging differences: Effective intergroup communication.* Newbury Park, CA: Sage.

Gully, S.M., Devine, D.J., & Whitney, D.J. (1995). A meta-analysis of cohesion and performance: Effects of levels of analysis and task interdependence. *Small Group Research, 26*, 497–520.

Hall, E.T. (1966).*The hidden dimension.* New York: Doubleday.

Harkins, S.G. & Jackson, J.M. (1985). The role of evaluation in eliminating social loafing. *Personality and Social Psychology Bulletin, 11*, 457–465.

Harkins, S.G. & Szymanski, K. (1987). Social loafing and facilitation: New wine in old bottles. *Review of Personality and Social Psychology, 9*, 167–188.

Harkins, S.G. & Szymanski, K. (1988). Social loafing and self-evaluation with an objective standard. *Journal of Experimental Social Psychology, 24*, 354–365.

Haslett, B., Geis, F.L., & Carter, M.R. (1992). *The organizational woman: Power and paradox.* Norwood, NJ: Ablex Publishing.

Haythorn, W., Couch, A.S., Haefner, D., Langham, P., & Carter, L.F. (1956). The effects of varying combinations of authoritarian and equalitarian leaders and followers. *Journal of Abnormal and Social Psychology, 53*, 210–219.

Heider, F. (1958). *The psychology of interpersonal relations.* New York: Wiley.

Henley, N. (1973–1974). Power, sex, and nonverbal communication. *Berkeley Journal of Sociology, 18*, 10–11.

Henricks, S.H., Kelley, E.A., & Eicher, J.B. (1968). Senior girls' appearance and social acceptance. *Journal of Home Economics, 60*, 167–172.

Hensley, W. (1992). Why does the best looking person in the room always seem to be surrounded by admirers? *Psychological Reports, 70*, 457–469.

Hinsz, V.B. (1995). Goal setting by groups performing an additive task: A comparison with individual goal setting. *Journal of Applied Social Psychology, 25*, 965–990.

Hirokawa, R. & Rost, K (1992). Effective group decision making in organizations. *Management Communication Quarterly, 5,* 267–388.

Hocker, J. & Wilmot, W.W. (1995). *Interpersonal conflict* (4th ed.). Dubuque, IA: W. C. Brown.

Hofstede, G. (1980). *Culture's consequences: International differences in work-related values.* Beverly Hills, CA: Sage.

Holland, J.L. (1985). *Making vocational choices: A theory of vocational personalities and work environments* (2nd ed.). Englewood Cliffs, NJ: Prentice Hall.

Houle, C.O. (1989). *Governing boards: Their nature and nurture.* San Francisco: Jossey-Bass.

Huff, D. (2005). How to lie with statistics. In K.J. Harty (Ed.), *Strategies for business and technical writing* (pp. 347–354.) New York, NY: Pearson Education.

Hui, C.H. & Triandis, H.C. (1986). Individualism-collectivism: A study of cross-cultural research. *Journal of Cross-cultural Psychology, 17,* 225–48.

Hunt, M. (1982). *The universe within: A new science explores the human mind.* New York: Simon and Schuster.

If it weren't for donuts, I wouldn't even bother. (1995). *Business Meeting Planning, 18* (2), 7.

Ifert, D.E. & Roloff, M.E. (1997). Overcoming expressed obstacles to compliance: The role of sensitivity to the expressions of others and ability to modify self-presentation. *Communication Quarterly, 45,* 55–67.

Infante, D., Trebling, J., Sheperd, P., & Seeds, D. (1984). The relationship of argumentativeness to verbal aggression. *Southern Speech Communication Journal, 50,* 67–77.

Informa predicts global online music sales to triple by 2010 (2005, February, 24). *New Media Age* (London), 11.

Insko, C.A. & Schopler, J. (1972). *Experimental social psychology.* New York: Academic Press.

International Listening Association (1995). An ILA definition of listening. *ILA Listening Post, 53,* 1.

Iverson, M.A. (1964). Personality impressions of punitive stimulus persons of differential status. *Journal of Abnormal and Social Psychology, 68,* 617–626.

Jablin, F.M. (2001). Organizational entry, assimilation, and disengagement/exit. *The new handbook of organizational communication* (pp. 732–818). Thousand Oaks, CA: Sage Publications.

Jackson, J.M. & Latane, B. (1981). All alone in front of all those people: Stage fright as a function of number and type of co-performances and audience. *Journal of Personality and Social Psychology, 40,* 73–85.

Janus, I. (1983). *Groupthink: Psychological studies of policy decisions and fiascos.* Boston: Houghton Mifflin.

Jay, A. (1999). How to run a meeting. In *Harvard Business Review on effective communication* (pp. 25–58). Waterton, MA: Harvard Business School Press Books.

Jesdanun, A. (2005, March 20). Beware of blog: Firings over work-related content on personal web sites prompt calls for better company policies. *Daily Breeze,* C1 and C6.

Jourard, S.M. (1968). *Disclosing man to himself.* Princeton, NJ: Van Nostrand.

Jourard, S.M. & Rubin, J.E. (1968). Self-disclosure and touching: A study of two modes of interpersonal encounter and their inter-relation. *Journal of Humanistic Psychology, 8,* 39–48.

Kanter, R.M. (1989). The new managerial work. *Harvard Business Review, 67,* 85–92.

Kaplan, R.M. (1978). Is beauty talent? Sex interaction in the attractiveness Halo Effect. *Sex Roles, 4,* 195–204.

Kelley, H.H. (1997). Expanding the analysis of social orientations by reference to the sequential-temporal structures of situations. *European Journal of Social Psychology, 27,* 373–404.

Kelley, H.H. & Thibaut, J.W. (1978) *Interpersonal relations: A theory of interdependence.* New York: Wiley.

Kerckhoff, A.C. & Davis, K.E. (1962). Value consensus and need complementarity in mate selection. *American Sociological Review, 27,* 295–303.

Keys, B. & Case, T. (1990). How to become an influential manager. *Academy of Management Executive, 4,* 38–50.

Kilmann, R. & Thomas, K. (1977). Developing a force-choice measure of conflict-handling behavior: The "MODE" instrument. *Educational and Psychological Measurement, 37,* 309–325.

King, T. & Bannon, E. (2002). At what cost? The price that working students pay for a college education. The State Public Interest Research Groups' (PIRG) Higher Education Project.

Knapp, M.L. & Hall, J.A. (1992). *Nonverbal communication in human interaction,* (3rd ed.). Fort Worth: Harcourt Brace Jovanovich.

Kraepels, R.H. & Davis, B.D. (2003). Designation of "communication skills" in position listings. *Business Communication Quarterly, 66* (2), 90.

Laughlin, P.R. & Earley, P.C. (1982). Social combination models, persuasive arguments theory, social comparison theory, and choice shift. *Journal of Personality and Social Psychology, 42,* 273–280.

Lehman, C.M. & Dufrene, D. (2002). *Business communication* (13th ed.). Mason, OH: South-Western.

Lencioni, P.M. (2002). *The five dysfunctions of a team.* San Francisco: Jossey-Bass.

Lerner, M. (1992, May 14). Looters living out the cynical American ethos. *Los Angeles Times,* B7.

Levinger, G., Senn, D.J., & Jorgensen, B.W. (1970). Progress toward permanence in courtship: A test of the Kerckhoff-Davis hypothesis. *Sociometry, 33,* 427–433.

Lying: How can you protect your company? (n.d.) *Your Workplace, Monthly Newsletter of Westaff* XXXVI. Retrieved March 25, 2005, from http://www.westaff.com/yourworkplace/ywissue37_full.html.

Maassen, G.H., Akkermans, W., & Van der Linden, J.L. (1996). Two-dimensional sociometric status determination with rating scales. *Small Group Research, 27,* 56–78.

Manley, W. (2001). Mightier than the pen. *American Libraries, 32* (9), 124.

McCabe, D. L. & Trevino, L. K. (1993). Academic dishonesty: Honor codes and other contextual influences. *Journal of Higher Education, 64* (5), 522–538.

McClintock, C.G., Messick, D.M., Kuhlman, D.M., & Campos, F.T. (1973). Motivational bases of choice in three-choice decomposed games. *Journal of Experimental Psychology, 9,* 572–590.

McCune, J.C. (n.d.) Managing emotions in the workplace. Retrieved September 15, 2004, from bankrate.com/brm/news/biz/tcb/20020927a.asp?prodtype=biz.

McGrath, J.E. (1984). Small group research, that once and future field: An interpretation of the past with an eye to the future. *Group Dynamics: Theory, Research, and Practice, 1,* 7–27.

McNamara, C. (1999). Basic guide to conducting effective meetings. Retrieved March 18, 2004, from http://www.mapnp.org/library/misc/mtgmgmnt.htm.

McVey, J. W. (1997, August). Pressure is on to educate workers. *Business Journal Serving Southern Tier, 11*(16), 17.

Mehrabian, A. (1971). *Silent messages.* Belmont, CA: Wadsworth.

Messmer, M. (2002). Conducting effective meetings. *National Public Accountant, 47* (6), 15.

Meyer, J.P. & Pepper, S. (1977). Need compatibility and marital adjustment in young married couples. *Journal of Personality and Social Psychology, 35,* 331–342.

Miller, G.R., Boster, F.J., Roloff, M.E., & Seibold, D. (1977). Compliance-gaining message strategies: A typology and some findings concerning effects of situational differences. *Communication Monographs, 44,* 37–51.

Mintzberg, H. (1975). The manager's job: Folklore and fact. *Harvard Business Review, 68,* 163–177.

Mitchell, T. & Scott, W. (1990). America's problems and needed reforms: Confronting the ethic of personal advantage. *The Executive, 4,* 23–35.

Moerke, A. (2004). Business writing brush-up. *Sales and Marketing Management, 156* (5), 63.

Molloy, J.T. (1996). *New woman's dress for success.* New York: Warner.

Moore, G. (2004, August 29). Investigation during job search allows you to select wisely. *The Daily Breeze,* E1.

Moreland, R.L. & Levine, J.M. (1982). Socialization in small groups: Temporal changes in individual-group relations. *Advances in Experimental Social Psychology, 15,* 137–192.

Moreland, R.L. & Levine, J.M. (1987). Group dynamics over time: Development and socialization in small groups. In J. McGrath (Ed.), *The sociology of psychology of time.* Beverly Hills, CA: Sage.

Moreland, R.L., Levine, J.M., & Wingert, M.L. (1996). Creating the ideal group: Composition effects at work. In E. Witte & J. Davis (Eds.), *Understanding group behavior: Small group processes and interpersonal relations* (Vol. 2), (pp. 11–35). Mahwah, NJ: Erlbaum.

Morrill, C. (1995). *The executive way.* Chicago: University of Chicago Press.

Mount, M.K., Barrick, M.P., & Strauss, J.P. (1994). Validity of observer ratings of the Big Five Personality Factors, *Journal of Applied Psychology, 79,* 272–281.

MSNBC (2005, February 20). Blockbuster's "no more late fees" under fire. *MSNBC News.* Retrieved February 22, 2005, from www.msnbc.msn.com/id/6994178/.

Mullen, B. & Copper, C. (1994). The relation between group cohesiveness and performance: An integration. *British Journal of Social Psychology, 27,* 333–356.

Mutari, E. & Lakew, M. (2003) Class conflict: Tuition hikes leave college students in debt and torn between paid work and coursework. (Special Section on Education). *Dollars & Sense,* Jan.–Feb., 18–22.

Myers, A.E. (1962). Team competition, success, and the adjustment of group members. *Journal of Abnormal and Social Psychology, 65,* 325–332.

Myers, D.G. (1978). The polarizing effects of social comparison. *Journal of Experimental Social Psychology, 14,* 554–563.

Myers, D.G. & Lamm, H. (1975). The polarizing effect of group discussion. *American Scientist, 63,* 297–303.

Myers, D.G. & Lamm, H. (1976). The group polarization phenomenon. *Psychological Bulletin, 83,* 602–627.

Nelson, B. (2002). Plan for spontaneity. *Corporate Meetings & Incentives, 21* (9), 46–47.

Newcomb, A.E., Bukowski, W.M., & Pattee, L. (1993). Children's peer relations: A meta-analytic review of popular, rejected, neglected, controversial, and average sociometric status. *Psychological Bulletin, 113,* 99–128.

O'Reilly, III, C.A., Chatman, J. & Caldwell, D.F. (1993). People and organizational culture: A profile comparison approach to assessing person-organization fit. *Academy of Management Journal, 34,* 487–516.

Ohbuchi, K., Chiba, S., & Fukushima, O. (1996). Mitigation of interpersonal conflicts: Politeness and time pressure. *Personality and Social Psychology Bulletin, 22,* 1035–1042.

Okabe, R. (1982). Cultural assumptions of east and west: Japan and the United States. In B. Gudykunst (Ed.), *International communication theory* (pp. 212–244). Newbury Park, CA: Sage Publications.

Olsen, L.A. & Huckin, T.N. (1991). *Technical writing and professional communication* (2nd ed.). New York: McGraw-Hill.

Opatow, S. (1990). Moral exclusion and injustice: An introduction. *Journal of Social Issues, 46,* 1–20.

Orbe, M.P. (1996). Laying the foundation for co-cultural communication theory: An inductive approach to studying "nondominant" communication strategies and the factors that influence them. *Communication Studies, 47,* 157–176.

Orive, R. (1988a). Group consensus, action immediacy, and opinion confidence. *Personality and Social Psychology Bulletin, 14,* 573–577.

Orive, R. (1988b). Social projection and social comparison of opinions. *Journal of Personality and Social Psychology, 54,* 943–964.

Pagano, B., Pagano, E., & Lundin, S. (2003). *The transparency edge: How credibility can make you or break you in business.* New York, NY: McGraw-Hill.

Pearson, J.C., Nelson, P.E., Titsworth, S., & Harter, L. (2003). *Human communication.* New York: McGraw-Hill.

Pepitone, A. & Reichling, G. (1955). Group cohesiveness and the expression of hostility. *Human Relations, 8,* 327–337.

Peters, T. & Waterman, R (1982). *In search of excellence.* New York: Harper and Row.

Pirisi, A. (2003). Lying in job interviews. *Psychology Today* (May-June). Retrieved March 25, 2005, from http://cms.psychologytoday.com/articles/pto-20030711-000001.html.

Playfair, W. (1801). *The commercial and political atlas* (3rd ed.). London: J. Wallis.

Polzer, J.T., Kramer, R.M., & Neale, M.A. (1997). Positive illusions about oneself and one's group. *Small Group Research, 28,* 243–266.

Pop Quiz (2003, March) *Corporate Meetings and Incentive, 22* (3), 41.

Postman, N. (1976). *Crazy talk, stupid talk.* New York: Dell.

Postman, N. (1981, January 19). Interview. *U.S. World & News Report,* 43.

Price, H.T. (2004). Writing well in business. *Business & Economic Review, 50* (3), 13.

Pruitt, D.G. & Ruben, J.Z. (1986). *Social conflict: Escalation, stalemate, and settlement.* New York: Random House.

Rank, H. (1982). *The pitch.* Park Fork South, IL: The Counter Propaganda Press.

Redding, W.C. (1991). Unethical messages in the organizational context. Paper presented at the Annenberg Convention of the ICA, Chicago, IL.

Robbins, S.P. (2001). *Organizational behavior* (9th ed.). Upper Saddle River, NJ: Prentice Hall.

Rogers, P.S. & Rymer, J. (1996). Analytical writing assessment diagnostic program. *Graduate Management Admission Council.*

Rohlen, T. (1973). "Spiritual education" in a Japanese bank. *American Anthropologist, 75,* 1542–1562.

Rosenbaum, M.E. (1986). The repulsion hypothesis: On the nondevelopment of relationships. *Personality and Social Psychology, 51,* 1156–1166.

Rosenberg, M. (2003). What's making you angry? Retrieved December 1, 2003, from PsychNET® © 2003 American Psychological Association.

Rothwell, J.D. (1998). *In mixed company: Small group communication* (3rd ed.). Fort Worth, TX: Harcourt Brace College Publishers.

Rotter, J.B. (1966). Generalized expectancies for internal versus external control of reinforcement. *Psychological Monographs, 80* (1), 1–28.

Saeki, M. & O'Keefe, B. (1994). Refusals and rejections: Designing messages to serve multiple goals. *Human Communication Research, 21,* 67–102.

Salopek, J. (1999). Is anyone listening? Listening skills in the corporate setting. *Training and Development, 53,* 58–59.

Saltzman, J. (2004, September). All the news that fits our views. *USA Today (Magazine),* 133: 2712, 55.

Samovar, L. & Porter, R. (1995). *Communication between cultures.* Belmont, CA: Wadsworth.

Sanders, G.S. & Baron, R.S. (1977). Is social comparison irrelevant for producing choice shifts? *Journal of Experimental Social Psychology, 13,* 303–314.

Schachter, S. (1951). Deviation, rejection, and communication. *Journal of Abnormal and Social Psychology, 46*, 190–207.

Schilling, G.A. (2000) Oh, no.......not another meeting! *AFP Exchange, 20* (3), 28.

Schoda, Y., Mischel, W. & Peake, P.K. (1990). Predicting adolescent cognitive and self-regulatory competencies from preschool delay of gratification. *Developmental Psychology, 26*, 978–986.

Schulman, M. (1998). Little Brother is watching you. Retrieved February 11, 2005, from http://www.scu.edu/ethics/publications/iie/v9n2/brother.html.

Schutz, W.C. (1958). *FIRO: A three-dimensional theory of interpersonal behavior*. New York: Rinehart.

Shaw, M.E. (1964). Communication networks. *Advances in Experimental Social Psychology, 1*, 111–147.

Shaw, M.E. (1981). *Group dynamics: The psychology of small group behavior* (3rd ed.). New York: McGraw-Hill.

Shaw, M.E. & Shaw, L.M. (1962). Some effects of sociometric grouping upon learning in a second grade classroom. *Journal of Social Psychology, 57*, 453–458.

Shedletsky, L.J. (1989). The mind at work. In L.J. Shedletsky (Ed.), *Meaning and mind: An intrapersonal approach to human communication*. ERIC and The Speech Communication Association.

Sherwin, A. (2005, March, 23). Britons top world chart of CD buyers. *The Times* (London, UK), Final 1st Ed., 29.

Snyder, M. (1979). Self-monitoring processes. In L. Berkowitz (Ed.), *Advances in experiemental social psychology*. New York: Academic Press.

Souther, J.W. (1985). What to report. *IEEE Transactions on Professional Communication, 28* (3), 6.

Spencer, D (1986). Employee voice and employee retention. *Academy of Management Journal, 29*, 488–502.

Stasser, G. (1992). Pooling of unshared information during group discussions. In S. Worchel, W. Wood, & J.A. Simpson (Eds.) *Group process and productivity* (pp. 48–67). Newbury Park, CA: Sage.

Stasser, G., Taylor, L.A., & Hanna, C. (1989). Information sampling in structured and unstructured discussions of three- and six-person groups. *Journal of Personality and Social Psychology, 57*, 67–78.

Steers, R.M. & Porter, L.W. (1991). *Motivation and work behavior* (4th ed.). New York: McGraw-Hill.

Swap, W.C. & Rubin, J.Z. (1983). Measurement of interpersonal orientation. *Journal of Personality and Social Psychology, 44*, 208–219.

Szalay, L. B. (1981). Intercultural communication—A process model. *International journal for intercultural research*, *5* (2), 135–147.

Szymanski, K. & Harkins, S.G. (1987). Social loafing and self-evaluation with a social standard. *Journal of Personality and Social Psychology, 53*, 891–897.

Taylor, L.C. & Compton, N.H. (1968). Personality correlates of dress conformity. *Journal of Home Economics, 60*, 653–656.

Thebaut, J.W. & Kelley, H.H. (1959). *The social psychology of groups.* New York: Wiley.

Tjosvold, D. (1995). Cooperation theory, constructive controversy, and effectiveness: Learning from crisis. In R.A. Guzzo, E. Salas, & Associates, *Team effectiveness and decision making in organizations* (pp. 79–112). San Francisco: Jossey-Bass.

Triandis, H. (1990). Cross-cultural studies of individualism and collectivism. In J. Berman (Ed.), *Cross-cultural perspectives*, (pp. 41–133). Lincoln, NE: University of Nebraska Press.

Tuckman, B.W. (1965). Developmental sequences in small groups. *Psychological Bulletin, 63*, 384–399.

Tuckman, B.W. & Jensen, M.A.C. (1977). Stages of small group development revisited. *Group and Organizational Studies, 2*, 419–427.

Tyler, K. (2003) Toning up communications: business writing courses can help employees and managers learn to clearly express organizational messages. *HR Magazine 48* (3), 87.

Tziner, A. & Eden, D. (1985). Effects of crew composition on crew performance: Does the whole equal the sum of its parts? *Journal of Applied Psychology, 70*, 85–93.

University of Buffalo (2004, March 22). Emotional intelligence key to winning on "The Apprentice." *AScribe Health News Service*, NA.

Van Lange, P.A.M., De Bruin, E.M.N., Otten, W., & Joireman, J.A. (1997). Development of prosocial, individualistic, and competitive orientations: Theory and preliminary evidence. *Journal of Personality and Social Psychology, 37*, 858–864.

Wall, V.D., Jr. & Nolan, L.L. (1987). Small group conflict: A look at equity, satisfaction, and styles of conflict management. *Small Group Behavior, 18*, 188–211.

Wang, Q. (2000). Cultural effects on adults earliest childhood recollection and self-description: Implications for the relation between memory and self. *Journal of Personality and Social Psychology, 81*(2), 220–233.

Watson, J. (n.d.). Writing: expanding your sphere of influence through better business communications. Retrieved April 27, 2004, from http:// jwatsonassociates.com/Articles.

Weick, K (1979). *The social psychology of organizing* (2nd ed.). Reading, MA: Addison-Wesley.

Weinrauch, J. & Swanda, J. (1975). Examining the significance of listening: An exploratory study of contemporary management. *Journal of Business Communication, 13*, 25–32.

Weldon, E. & Weingart, L.R. (1993). Group goals and group performance. *British Journal of Social Psychology, 32*, 307–334.

Wessel, H. (2003, February 12). Speaking their piece: Feedback from workers plays a major role in the vitality of a company. *Orlando Sentinel*, G1.

Widgery, R.N. (1974). Sex of receiver and physical attractiveness of source as determinants of initial credibility perception. *Western Speech, 38*, 13–17.

Wiggins, J.A., Wiggins, B.B., & Vander Zanden J. (1993). *Social psychology.* (4th ed.). New York: McGraw-Hill.

Williams, K.D., Harkins, S., & Latane, B. (1981). Identifiability as a deterrent to social loafing: Two cheering experiments. *Journal of Personality and Social Psychology, 40*, 303–311.

Wilson, S.R. (1998). Introduction to the special issue on seeking and resisting compliance: The vitality of compliance-gaining research, *Communication Studies, 49*, 273–275.

Wittenbaum, G.M. & Stasser, G. (1996). Management of information in small groups. In J.L. Nye & A.M. Brower (Eds.), *What's social about social cognition? Research on socially shared cognitions in small groups* (pp. 3–28). Thousand Oaks, CA: Sage.

Wood, J.T. (1997). *Communication theories in action.* Belmont, CA: Wadsworth.

Write on! Tips for effective communication (1993). *HR Focus, 70* (8), S4.

Wurman, R. (1989). *Information anxiety.* New York: Doubleday.

Yates, D. (1985, May 9). Many students admit cheating. *Western Front*, NA.

Zuber, J.A., Crott, J.W., & Werner, J. (1992). Choice shift and group polarization: An analysis of the status of arguments and social decision schemes. *Journal of Personality and Social Psychology, 62*, 50–61.

Glossary

A

Active listening Listening with a purpose.

Aggressiveness A series of behaviors and characteristics including hurtful expressiveness, self-promotion, attempting to control others, and argumentativeness.

AIDA approach A popular model for organizing persuasive messages. AIDA is the acronym for attention, interest, desire, and action.

Analysis In a message, the ability to identify the message's main topic and break it down into its component parts.

Anticipatory socialization The process we use to develop our expectations and beliefs about how people communicate in various formal and informal work situations.

Appropriate feedback Honest, reflecting the communicator's true understanding and judgment, and is appropriate for the subject, audience, and occasion or context.

Articulate To pronounce all words clearly and fluently.

Assertiveness Self-enhancing communication that takes into account not only the communicator's needs, but those of others as well.

Audience-centered A method of communication that takes into account the needs, concerns, and expectations of the audience.

Avoidance The strategy of knowingly avoiding engagement with those in the dominant group.

C

Call to action A conclusion to a persuasive message that is intended to convince the reader to fully consider the writer's or speaker's proposal and, ideally, to commit to a decision or to take the next step.

Chronemics The study of how people organize and use time.

Claim; Evidence A claim is often general or abstract; on the other hand, evidence is more specific.

Coherence The logical flow of ideas throughout a paragraph.

Collectivist cultures One in which cooperation is encouraged, rather than competition, and in which individual goals are sacrificed for the good of the group.

Common ground The interests, goals, and/or commonalities of belief that the communicator shares with the audience.

Comparison level for alternatives The lowest level of outcomes a member will accept in light of available alternative opportunities.

Comparison level The standard by which individuals evaluate the desirability of group membership and which is based upon our past experiences in groups.

Competitors People who view group disagreements as win-lose situations and find satisfaction in forcing their views on others.

Compliance-gaining Attempts a communicator makes to influence another person to do something that the other person might otherwise not do.

Compliance-resisting The refusal to comply with another person's attempts at influence.

Confirmation bias A tendency to distort information that contradicts the beliefs and attitudes we currently hold.

Cooperators Value accommodative interpersonal strategies.

Correlation A consistent relationship between two or more variables.

Critical listening A form of active listening that is used to evaluate the accuracy, meaningfulness, and usefulness of a message.

D

Defensive Climate is one in which individuals feel threatened.

Demographics The statistical data about a particular population, including its age, income, education level, and so on.

Diagram A two-dimensional drawing that shows the important parts of objects.

Dialogic model of communication Takes other people's points of view into account, acknowledging that the speaker and the listener may have different perspectives.

Disfluencies Such speaking errors as stammers, stutters, double starts, and excessive use of "filler" words such as "um" and "uh."

Emotional intelligence The assortment of noncognitive skills that influence our ability to cope with the pressures and demands of the environment.

Empathic listening Active listening with the goal of understanding the speaker.

Ethnocentrism The belief that one's own cultural background is correct, and that other cultures are somehow inferior.

Ethos Information that provides credibility to ourselves or to our position.

Extemporaneously Public speaking is delivered spontaneously, rather than being read or memorized in advance.

Fallacy The deceptive appearance of a false or mistaken idea, an often plausible argument that uses a false or invalid reference.

False dichotomy A dichotomy that is not jointly exhaustive (i.e., there are other alternatives), or that is not mutually exclusive (i.e., the alternatives overlap). A false dichotomy may be the product of either/or thinking.

Forecasting Those that tell the audience what the reader or speaker will cover next.

Free-riding Describes the phenomenon of group members working less hard on collective tasks than when they are working for themselves.

Fundamental attribution error The tendency of group members to misperceive others and to assume that personal rather than situational factors cause other members' behavior.

G

Goodwill In the business communication context, the ability to create and maintain positive relationships with others.

Graph A visual element used to compare the values of several items.

Groupthink The pressure on individuals in a group to conform to the extent that critical analysis and discussion are avoided or abandoned.

H

Haptics The study of touch and its relation to communication.

High self-monitors People who are acutely aware of their impression management efforts.

I

Impression management The attempt to control the impression of ourselves that we present to others in any communication situation.

Indirect opening That does not explain the specific proposal you are addressing.

Individualist cultures One with an "I" focus, and in which competition is encouraged, rather than cooperation, and in which individual achievement is highly valued.

Individualists Care only about their own outcomes.

Inferences A conclusion about the unknown based upon the known.

Influence The power to affect the thoughts or actions of others.

Informational influence Information the group provides to members that they can use to make decisions and form opinions.

Interchange compatibility Exists when the members of a group have similar expectations about the group's intimacy, control, and inclusiveness.

Intercultural communication The exchange of information among people of different cultural backgrounds.

Interpersonal dominance The relational, behavioral, and interactional state reflecting the achievement—by means of communication—of control or influence over another person.

Interpersonal influence Occurs when the group uses verbal and nonverbal influence tactics to induce change.

Interpersonal intelligence The ability to understand others.

Intimate distance Extends no farther than about 18 inches, is used to communicate affection, give comfort, and protect. Intimate distance is more common in private than in public.

Intrapersonal communication Encompasses our communication with ourselves, including memories, experiences, feelings, ideas, and attitudes.

Intrapersonal intelligence The ability to form an accurate model of oneself and to use this model effectively.

Kinesics The study of posture, movement, gestures, and facial expressions.

L

Locus of control The degree of control we believe we have over our lives.

Logos Information such as facts or statistics.

Low self-monitors People who have little awareness about how others perceive them, and little knowledge about how to interact appropriately with others.

N

Norm of reciprocity Suggests that any behavior tends to result in that same behavior in return.

Normative influence Occurs when group members tailor their actions to fit the group's standards and conventions.

O

Organizational culture The system of shared meanings and practices within an organization that distinguish it from other organizations.

Originator compatibility Exists when people who wish to act on their needs for control, inclusion, and affection join in groups with people who wish to accept these expressions of control, inclusion, and affection.

Oversampling The tendency for groups to spend too much of their discussion time examining shared information.

Pathos An emotional appeal, an attempt to win over the audience by appealing to its emotions, often by telling a story or evoking a picture with which the audience can empathize.

Perceptual mindsets Our cognitive and psychological predispositions to see the world in a certain way.

Personal distance The distance used by people in the United States for conversation and non-intimate exchanges. It ranges from about 18 to 48 inches.

Personal space The distance between ourselves and others with which we feel comfortable.

Pitch The sound quality of the speaker's voice, ranging from low and deep to high and squeaky.

Plurality The concept that recognizes that there are multiple different interpretations of any situation, and that no one communicator can control all these interpretations.

Process losses Reductions in performance effectiveness caused by faulty group processes.

Proxemics The study of human space, and revolves around the concepts of territoriality and personal space.

Public distance Used for public speaking, exceeds 12 feet.

R

Rate of delivery The speed at which one speaks.

Reasoned skepticism The process of searching actively for meaning, analyzing and synthesizing information, and judging the worth of that information.

Relevance of supportive information The quality of the evidence or information provided and how appropriate it is for supporting and explaining the topic or subtopic.

S

Self-awareness An honest understanding of oneself, including strengths and weaknesses, values, attitudes, and beliefs.

Self-centered A communication that fails to take into account the needs, concerns, or interests of its audience.

Self-esteem How we like and value ourselves, and how we feel about ourselves.

Self-fulfilling prophecy The idea that we see ourselves in ways that are consistent with how others see us.

Social distance Ranges from 4 to 8 feet and is the distance used for professional communication.

Social loafing Describes the phenomenon of people working less hard as group members than as individuals.

Somatotype A combination of a person's height, weight, and muscularity.

Stereotypes A generalized perception about a certain nationality or group of people.

Strategic alignment Making oral messages consistent with the nonverbal messages the speaker is sending.

Style The level of formality in written communications.

Sufficient information The quantity of the information, or whether the writer or speaker has provided enough supporting evidence.

Supportive climate One in which individuals do not feel threatened.

Table A visual element used to present data in words, numbers, or both, in columns and rows.

Territoriality A person's need to establish and maintain certain spaces as one's own.

Tone The implied attitude of the communicator toward his or her audience.

Transition Elements that assist the audience in moving from one topic to another through words and phrases that link the ideas the writer or speaker is developing.

Vocal variety The varying use of the vocal aspects of volume, rate, and pitch.

Volume The relative sound level of speech; it must be loud enough to be heard, but not so loud as to be overwhelming.

Index